GAZA, 1917
First Battle 26 March & Second Battle 19 April

Martin Glen

Published by Martin Glen
Publishing partner: Paragon Publishing, Rothersthorpe
First published 2018
© Martin Glen 2018

The rights of Martin Glen to be identified as the author of this work have been asserted by him accordance with the Copyright, Designs and patents Act of 1988.

All rights reserved; no part of this publication may be reproduced, stored in a retrieval system, or transmitted in any form or by any means, electronic, mechanical, photocopying, recording or otherwise without consent of the publisher or a licence permitting copying in the UK issued by the Copyright Licensing Agency Ltd.
www.cla.co.uk

ISBN 978-1-78222-560-7

Book design, layout and production management by into Print
www.intoprint.net
44(0)1604 832149

**Dedicated to the memory of Captain Harry Keppel Chester
and all those who served in the Palestine Campaign.**

CONTENTS

Part One
FIRST BATTLE 26 & 27 MARCH 6

Part Two
SECOND BATTLE 17 TO 19 APRIL 98

Appendices
ORDERS OF BATTLE 192
CASUALTY CRITERIA 203
CASUALTY TOTAL CHARTS FOR THE FIRST & SECOND BATTLES 204
GALLANTRY AWARDS FOR THE FIRST & SECOND BATTLES 213
BIBLIOGRAPHY 241
APPEALS FOR INFORMATION 243
APPRECIATION 244
CONVENTIONS & ABBREVIATIONS 247

First Battle of Gaza

Introduction 6
Prologue 8

Map of Desert Column operations on 26 March 9
Map of Eastern Force operations on 26 March 10

The Mounted Troops Screen Operations from 25 March 1917 11
2nd Light Horse Brigade 11
5th and 6th Mounted Brigades 19
3rd Light Horse Brigade 21
New Zealand Mounted Rifles Brigade 24

The Attack from Sheikh Abbas 26/27 March 1917 28
158th Infantry Brigade 38
Narrative: Captain Walker's account 40
160th Infantry Brigade 41
Artillery Action 48
159th Infantry Brigade 53
Narrative: Account by officers of the 5th Welsh Regiment 62
161st Infantry Brigade 63
Narrative: Account by officers of the Essex Regiment 73
Epilogue 75

Photographs 77
5th Essex 1915 77
7th Essex officers 1915 78
Ali el Muntar 79
Broken ground south-east of Gaza 79
Ali el Muntar from Mansura Ridge 80
Gaza from Ali el Muntar 81
Captain HK Chester 82
Private TH Davies 83
Private A Hawkins 84
Sergeant R Price 85
Farrier Corporal SG Tucker 86

Appendix 1
Order of Battle for 26 March 88

First Battle of Gaza

Introduction

BY 1917 THE WAR WAS in its fourth year, with the now-infamous Somme campaign still fresh in the public mind, but the mud and mind-numbing despair of Passchendaele yet to come. Until now, the objectives of the British forces in the East had been to protect the Suez Canal and the defence of Egypt against Turkish attack, but in December 1916 the War Office began to regard the capture of Jerusalem, with the consequent defeat of Turkey, a worthwhile aim.

Since early 1916, moves into the Sinai Desert had been undertaken with the remit of preventing a Turkish advance across the waterless peninsula. The Battle of Romani at the end of July had been a resounding victory, similar tactics being employed on December 23 at Magdhaba to the same effect, el Arish having been occupied without opposition on the 22 December. The limiting factor then became the progress of the railway and construction of the water pipeline, both of equal importance for the operations in the desert. As this was pushed further across the wastes of Sinai, the Turkish troops were withdrawn, first from Khan Yunis and then from Shellal, the result being a strong garrison force in the town of Gaza. Until now the advance of the British forces had been along the coast in order to avoid moving parallel to the Turkish lines, and so it was decided that a swift attack on Gaza was necessary before the town could be evacuated deeper into the hostile countryside.

Lieutenant-General Sir Archibald Murray, Commander in Chief of the Egyptian Expeditionary Force, had long stated he required five divisions plus mounted troops for the successful occupation of el Arish and operations towards Rafah; a further division would be needed to progress to Beersheba. Not only were these requests denied, in January 1917 the 42nd Division was withdrawn to France to leave three divisions at full strength for operations at the beginning of March.

The First Battle of Gaza took place on the 26 March 1917. Two distinct forces were employed, namely the Eastern Force and Desert Column. The Desert Column was composed of mounted troops of Australia, New Zealand and the Yeomanry Regiments of Britain. Its role was to encircle Gaza from the east and north thereby creating a screen. This would both prevent reinforcement of the town from known strong-points to the east, as well as prevent wholesale withdrawal from the town.

The main assault on the town was carried out by the Eastern Force, using two divisions, the third being in reserve. In contrast to advances of a few hundred yards on the Western Front, the men of the Territorial Forces attacked across an open plain several thousand yards deep. By sunset, at the end of a long and trying day, and after having been heavily engaged by the entrenched Turks, the battle was all but won, enemy evacuation of Gaza by the remaining troops taking place. However, the order to retire was given and the all-but victorious troops carried out the incomprehensible order with bewilderment. Further action on the 27 March was unsuccessful in restoring the gains of the previous day and a general retirement was ordered.

The First Battle of Gaza became, briefly, another byword for incompetent general-ship. The view that the retirement at the point of victory was a disgrace prevailed, although hardly reported in the national press, no explanations were given. Many factors however contributed to the decision and these will be highlighted.

However, it is not the intention of the author to pass judgement on the events of 1917. The aim has always been to tell the story of the forgotten men who fought in the largely unknown campaign for many years without home-leave; many left their families in 1915 and did not return. Men from East Anglian hamlets and villages, the Welsh Valleys and the South Downs. The Scotsmen from the Lowlands and the horsemen from the Home Counties. The incomparable Light Horsemen from Australia and the Mounted Riflemen from New Zealand. The sacrifice of those who died and the lifelong suffering of the survivors has been the motivation, and it is to their memory and honour that this story is told.

Narrative format.

The format describes the actions of each Brigade in detail, with maps to indicate the movements of each Battalion; where information has been available, or the action so intense and fractured, this has been detailed down to Company and Platoon level. Personal accounts and quotations have been used to try and gain some small insight into the feelings of the men themselves. The end of each Brigade's chapter is an account of some of the casualties sustained. To repeat information noted elsewhere in the book, the fact that officers are sometimes described in more detail than other ranks in no way reflects any bias. Simply, at the time of World War One, officer deaths were often reported in more detail. Where other ranks such as Privates and Sergeants have been illustrated in some depth, this has been due to relatives having provided the extra details for records such as the Commonwealth War Graves Registers or local newspapers. Lastly, the inclusion of photographs of some of the soldiers who took part, and several who were killed, is due to the incredible generosity of their relatives who responded to the author's many requests for information

Orders of Battle are at two levels.

DIVISIONAL Orders give an overview of the large units such as Corps and Divisions, with a list of Battalions. Support Troops such as Artillery, Medical units and Yeomanry are also included.

BRIGADE Orders show the Battalions in more detail, with Commanding Officers where known.

Gallantry Awards

Gallantry awards were issued, for the most part, after the battles had finished. Awards were officially announced in the London Gazette and higher awards such as the Military Cross generally included a citation. The lower awards of the Military Medal rarely had a citation, and where these are shown they have been obtained from Regimental Histories, War Diaries or newspapers. Accordingly, it has not always been possible to determine if an award was for the First Battle or Second Battle, hence the different lists.

Prologue

Getting out of bed was more a battle of mind against body these days. The body railed against moving from its comfortable position, knowing however that once the transition was completed, the day would be tolerable. Not since the long-gone days of Gallipoli and the Sinai Desert was the mind likely to oversleep. Too much going on then to ever sleep once the first hint of dawn appeared, be it sunshine or a dull-aching gloom, a pattern that had set itself on his long life. Slowly turning the pages of his newspaper while the kettle did its work, the word leapt out at him.

Gaza! The appeal for information stirred memories which he had thought were his alone. No-one had cared then about his war, a distant affair only he and his long-gone chums had understood. He'd seen his pals, the ones who'd returned at any rate, slowly pass away until he could well have been the last. The last to know of the desert marches, the constant thirst, the men he'd left to die as he was urged forward. The last to know of the family he'd missed for four years, the sickness that took as many as the bullets, the agonies of the wounded. The last to know of the pride only they could share.

Now maybe, just maybe . . . . .

26 March 1917
Desert Column

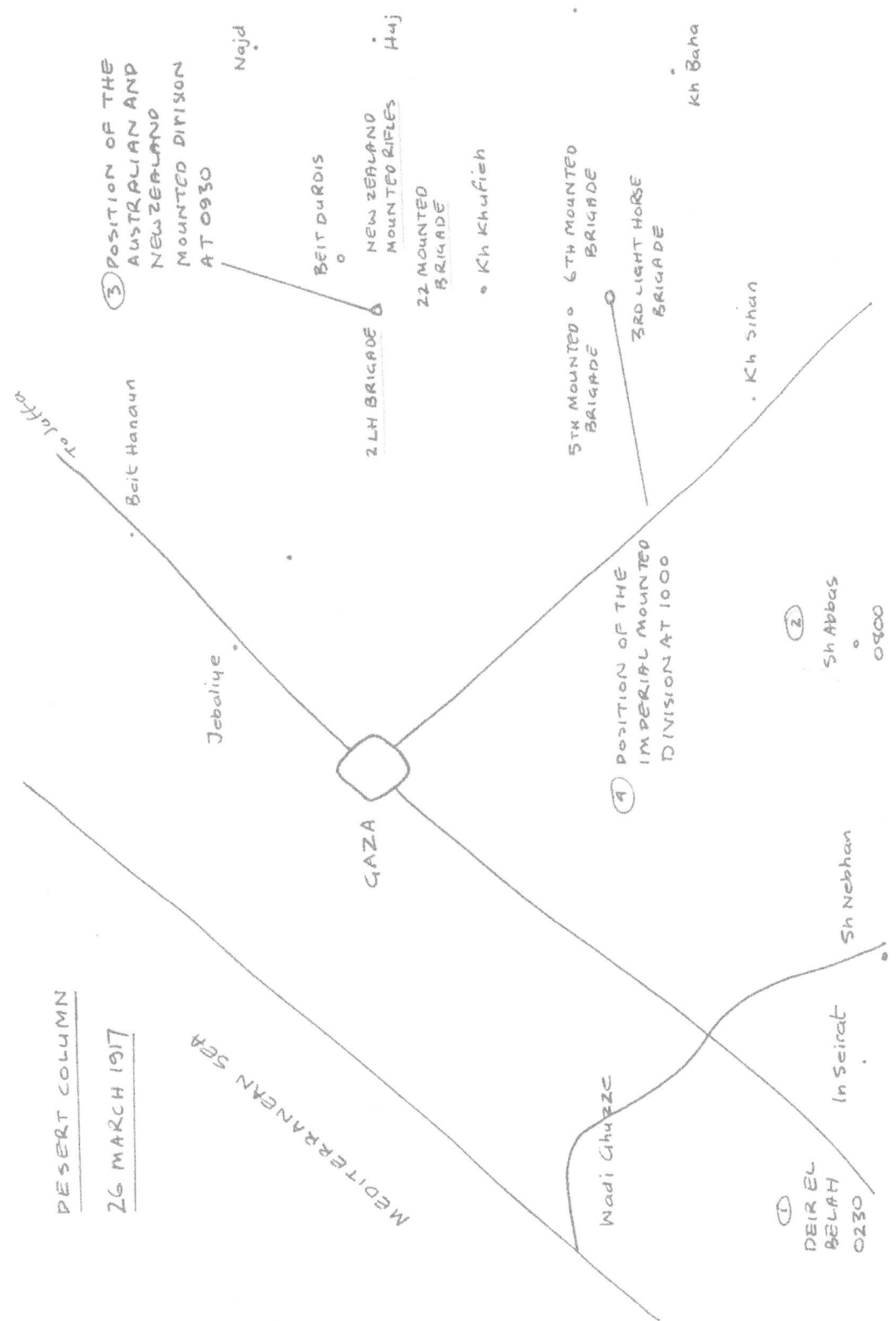

EASTERN FORCE
26 MARCH 1917

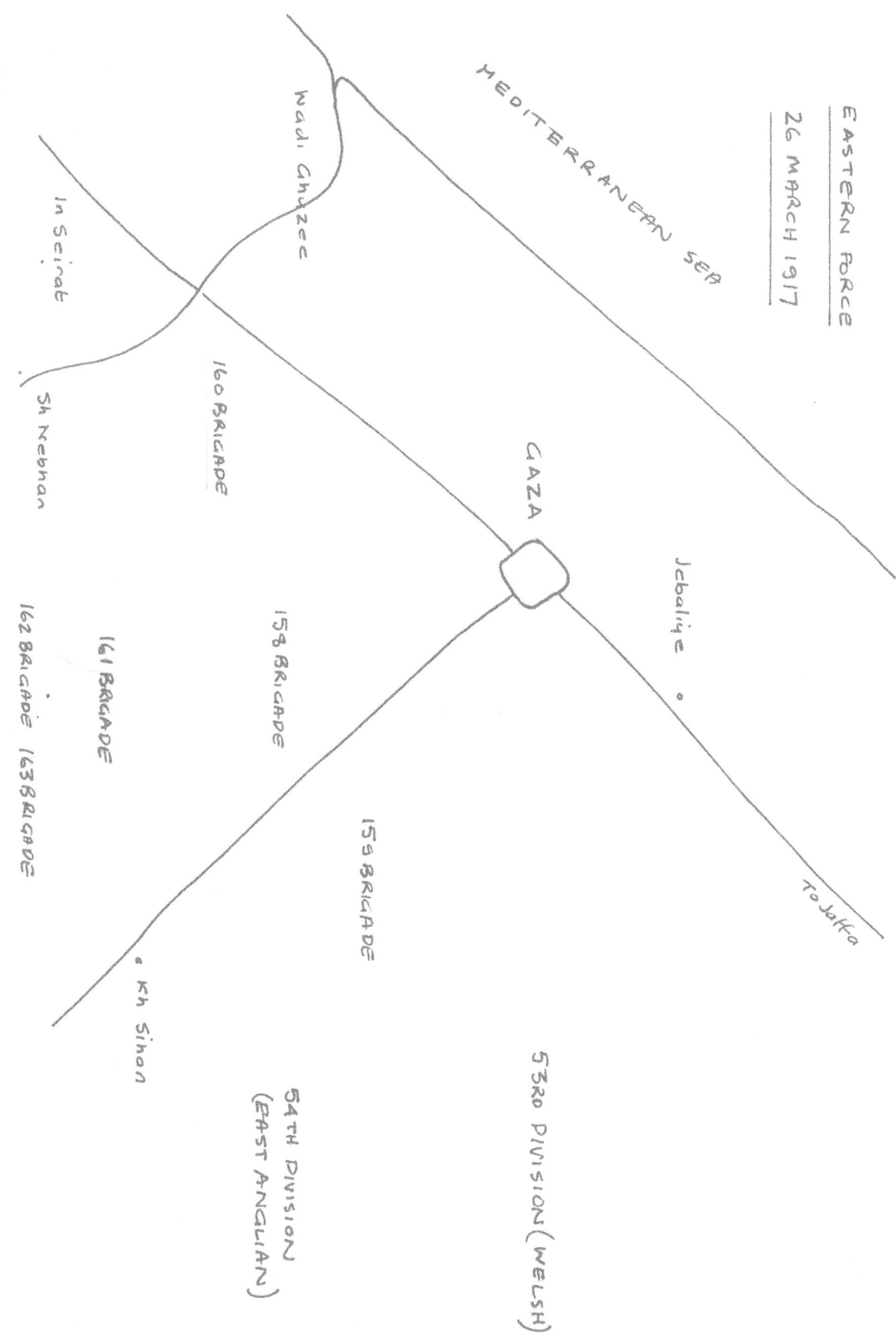

The 2nd Light Horse Brigade

THE AUSTRALIAN AND NEW ZEALAND Mounted Division was one of two mounted divisions which would establish a screen to the east and north of Gaza, observing enemy movements and engaging them where possible. Commanded by Major-General H CHAUVEL it was to form the extreme right flank of the screen, and would operate mainly to the north and north-east of Gaza. With such a large force to be deployed, the preparatory marches had necessarily started many days previously. The following quote from a captain with the 5/Suffolk Regiment, 54th Division describes the changing countryside as well as the initial stages of the advance on the 26 March.

On the 20th March, the Brigade left El Arish, marching about seven miles to El Burj. From now on we marched only at night. The country began to show signs of cultivation, thin patches of oats being occasionally visible from the road.

The following day we reached Sheikh Zowaid through country steadily improving, and showing, in addition to more green, banks of brilliant red poppies. On the 24th March, we arrived about 1pm at Rafa, the boundary post between Sinai and Palestine, and the scene of the smart capture on January 9th of a body of 2,000 Turks, with guns and machine guns. The scene of the engagement was marked by the remains of the trenches. The police post, a small dismal looking building, now housing half a dozen prisoners, contained the remains of one of our abandoned aeroplanes, and not far from it were the boundary pillars, marking the beginning of the Turkish Empire. The ground itself was commonplace enough, but the knowledge that we were about to step again on Turkish territory fired our imagination. Here we had at last arrived ready to try another tussle with the Turk, and meet him on his own ground. A greater contrast to the Gallipoli Peninsula could not be imagined. The ground around Rafa was brilliant green, and the country, as far as the eye could reach to the north and north-east, stretched away in gently rolling downs, with groups of trees here and there.

Before dawn on the 25th we moved forward, arriving by 7am in the gardens of peach and almond, surrounding Khan Yunis. We were hoping to surprise the Turk, and so we lay concealed during the day, while two enemy aeroplanes came over. The sand was out of sight; and it seemed as if the "Land of Promise" had been reached at last. All that hot Sunday we lay in the shadow of the trees, many attended a service which the Padre held; and then just as it was getting dusk we moved on again by devious routes and with many halts to In Seirat, where the Battalion bivouacked at 1am. No matches or fires could be lit lest the Turk should know of our arrival. Everyone was thoroughly tired, and as orders for an early move were given, we all tried to snatch some sleep. At 4am, yawning, cold, hungry, but filled with something of the glamour the Crusaders must have felt, we fell in; but as the Mounted Infantry who were to precede us were delayed by a heavy fog, we stood by for two hours while they crossed the Wadi Ghuzze.

When this fine Division had crossed we pressed on, the Battalion being advance guard to the Brigade. The day was a glorious one; our objective-the ridge known as Sheikh Abbas-stood out clear and well-defined. The Anzac Mounted Division could be seen riding ahead, examining every building, making good every ridge, and finally reaching the skyline of Sheikh Abbas itself. Meanwhile, the Battalion, its eyes fixed on the two highest points, was pressing on knee-deep through fields of barley, heavy with dew. The many-coloured spring flowers shone like gems among the barley, and the green and golden carpet stretching as far as the eye could reach made a wonderful picture. It was morning never to be forgotten.

History of the 1/5th Suffolk Regiment.
Captain Fair and Captain Wolton. Pages 55-56.

AUSTRALIAN & NEW ZEALAND MOUNTED DIVISION
2ND LIGHT HORSE BRIGADE
26 MARCH 1917

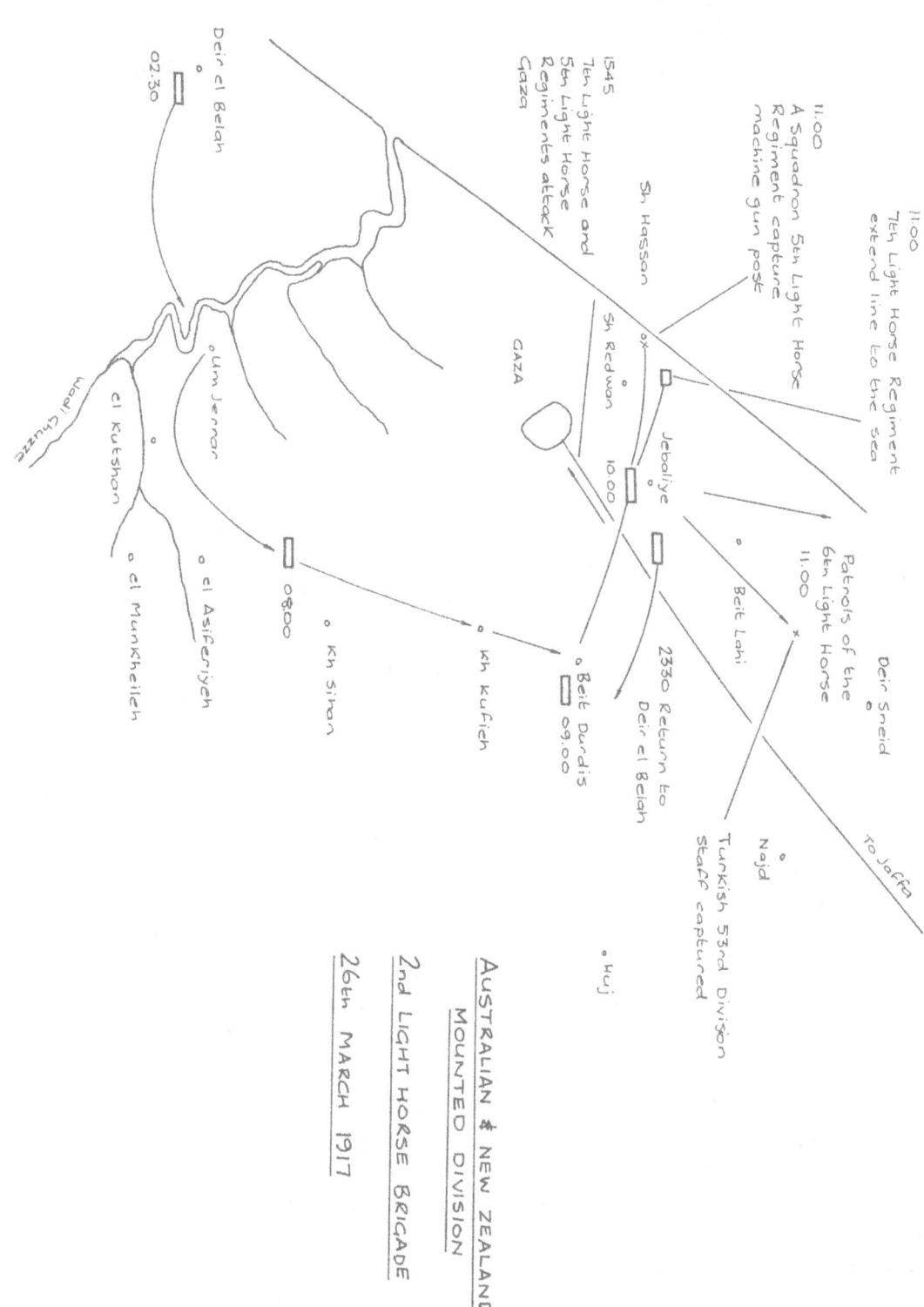

2nd Light Horse Brigade
5TH LIGHT HORSE REGIMENT
26 MARCH 1917

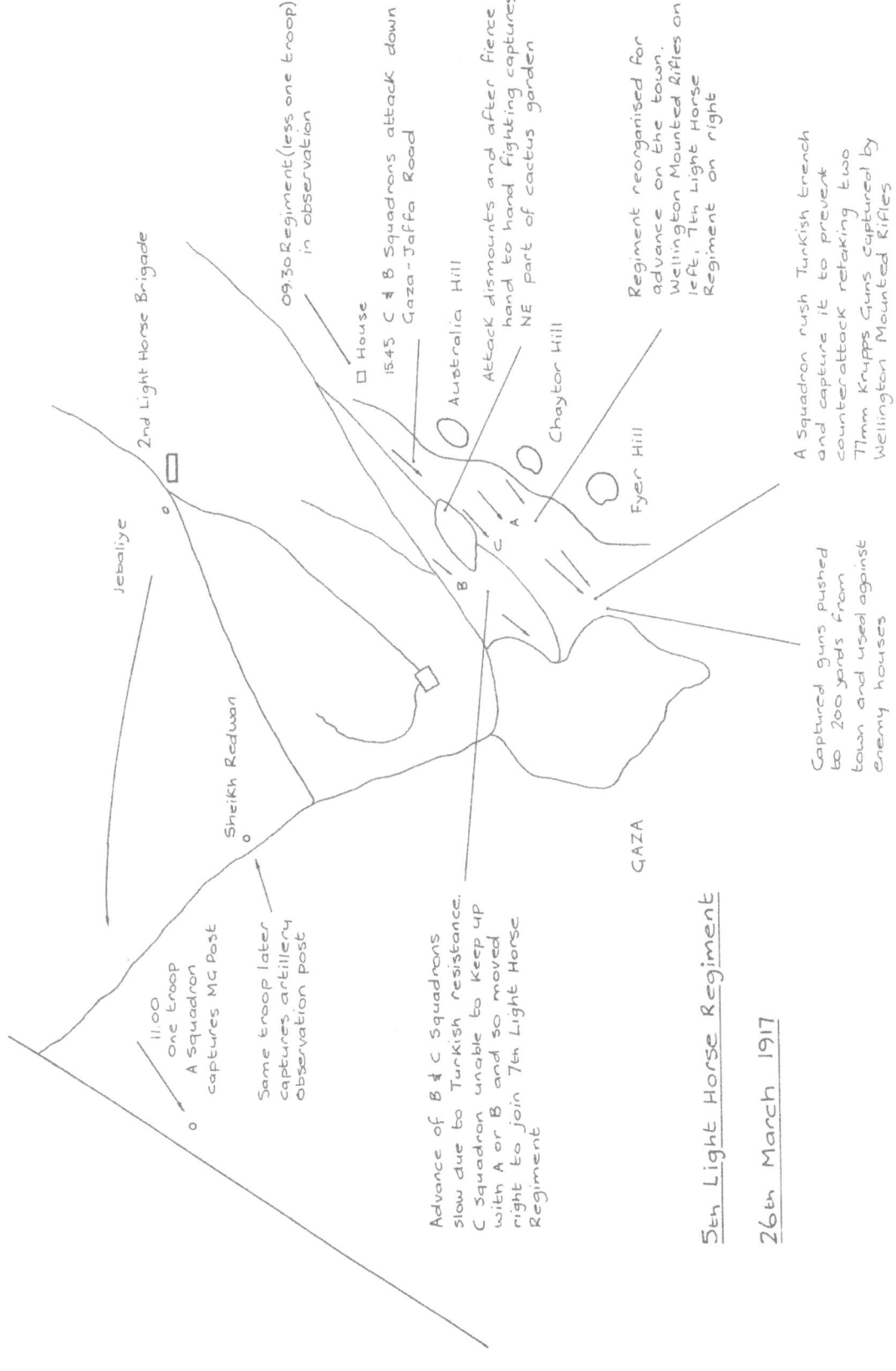

At 02.30 on the 26 March the 2nd Light Horse Brigade led the division from its bivouac at Deir el Belah. Passing the sleeping infantry of the 54th Division at In Seirat, the column rode along the track to the Wadi Ghuzze, four miles to the east. There was some confusion at this stage as no place of assembly had been set, and various lines of troops crossed and re-crossed each other on the way. Crossing by means of a prepared earth ramp, the line of the Wadi Sharta was taken, skirting to the south of high ground on the way to Sheikh Abbas. The heavy fog which had risen with the dawn made progress slow but Sheikh Abbas was taken against slight opposition at 08.00, only about twenty minutes behind schedule.

Another hour's ride brought the brigade within sight of Beit Durdis, five miles further on. Enemy snipers firing on the advance were outflanked by B Squadron, 5th Light Horse Regiment who also captured several wagons and prisoners. Beit Durdis was entered and the brigade halted to reorganise and rest until the arrival of the remainder of the division. Divisional Headquarters was established and the brigade moved out north-west to continue the encirclement of Gaza. Moving across the open plain, several more wadis were encountered before the ground rose to form the last natural obstacle to the troop. Ahead of them stood the northern-most end of the ridge, which ran from north-east to south-west, its summit about a hundred feet above the plain. On its far side it dropped away sharply, giving an uninterrupted view of Gaza in the foreground with the Mediterranean Sea beyond.

Gaza lies in a shallow fertile valley, which is about two miles wide, and runs parallel with the sea between a belt of coastal sand-hills and an extensive table-land. The belt of dunes is almost two miles wide. The table-land rises gradually, and in the distance can be seen the blue Judean hills. On its coastal and southern sides, this table-land is fringed by ridges of Mansura and Sheikh Abbas. On the side overlooking Gaza there rises up the great rock of Ali el Muntar, 272 feet in height, just south-east of the city, the gates of which are said to have been carried up this hill by Samson. It is a commanding height overtopping everything within several miles to the south. This is the key position. From Muntar there runs southward, for nearly five miles, the ridges of El Sire, terminating at the Wadi Ghuzze. Parallel to it, from the southern edge of the table-land, two other ridges run down to this great wadi, the centre one of the three being called El Burjaliye after a small garden. These ridges are separated by a labyrinthine tangle of nullahs, from ten to twenty feet deep, which twist and turn in every direction. The Wadi Ghuzze is a deep, wide nullahs, running generally from east to west, and joined by innumerable other nullahs. South of this great wadi rises more high ground, fringed immediately to the south-east by the ridge of In Seirat.

Gaza is the usual white-walled Eastern town, with red roofs and minarets showing here and there. It is embosomed in palms trees, and all around it is a belt, to the southward almost three miles deep, of small fields and gardens, each surrounded by high cactus hedges. Theses cactus hedges grow out of mud banks, and are from six to twelve feet high, and about a yard or more deep. They form natural barbed entanglements, and give perfect cover from view. Shrapnel does little more than pierce their leaves. Direct Hits from H.E. will blow holes in them, and, after much labour, gaps can be cut in them with hedging tools and sickles, but such expedients could have little effect, since they ran for miles. The Turks made use of these hedges by digging their machine-gun emplacements, fire trenches, and snipers' posts below them. Tanks alone can cope with them effectively.

The 52nd Division 1914-1918. Page 309.
Lieutenant Colonel RR Thompson MC

Two squadrons of the 5/LHR remained at this position to cover the Gaza-Jaffa Road as the rest of the brigade continued to advance, entering the village of Jebaliye at 10.00. Extending the line to the sea, the 7/LHR completed the encirclement of Gaza at 11.00.

With the division being responsible for the north and north-east sides of the town, as soon as each village or landmark was taken, patrols were pushed out to observe enemy movements towards Gaza. Two squadrons of the 6/Light Horse Regiment heading towards Deir Sneid, surprised and captured the commander and staff of the Turkish 53rd Division, who were quite oblivious of the situation as they were in full dress uniform complete with medals! Other patrols were sent to the north, and the result of these observations was to show that Gaza was totally isolated, with no immediate prospect of relief.

As the screen was completed, tentative patrols were sent towards the town now only about two miles away. One troop of A Squadron, 5/LHR surrounded and captured a Turkish Machine Gun post near Sheikh Hasan on the coast and an observation point was established. A division of Turkish infantry about five-hundred strong was seen leaving Gaza and heading north at about 12.30. Rifle and machine-gun fire was opened up on them, which inflicted many casualties and drive the survivors back into Gaza.

The left flank of the brigade was prolonged at 14.30 with the arrival of the New Zealand Mounted Rifles Brigade on the ridge above the Gaza-Jaffa Road.

A pause to consider the positions held and the overall situation may now be in order. Gaza was totally surrounded by infantry to the south and mounted troops to the east and north, the latter having met with very little opposition. Enemy reinforcements were expected but none were reported from any of the outposts which fanned out from the encircling troops. At 15.40 a combined attack by the three brigades of the division was ordered in an attempt to assist the infantry attack from the south which had suffered heavy casualties and was now held up.

The country held by the brigade was dominated by the hundred-foot-high ridge; the village of Jebaliye was at the northern-most end. It then formed a series of hills before it reached Ali el Muntar and eventually tapered down to the Wadi Ghuzze.

"...open sand ridges run close to and parallel with the beach. Between the sand ridges and the Jebaliye-Ali el Muntar Ridge there is a valley running to the rear of Gaza town. The SE side of this valley consists of an olive grove; the NW side consists of small allotments fenced with cactus and in which are numerous small villages."
5th Light Horse Regiment War Diary PRO WO95/4359

The 2/LH Brigade was to attack between the sea and the Gaza-Jebaliye Road, being supported on their left by the New Zealand Mounted Rifle Brigade. On the right of the line was the 7/Light Horse Regiment who advanced through the sand dunes along the coast, meeting the single troop of the 5/LHR at their observation post on the way. In the centre of the brigade line was the village of Sheikh Redwan against which the 6/LHR moved.

The 5/Light Horse Regiment was also to co-operate with the NZMR Brigade and advance through the olive grove. C Squadron led the attack, closely followed by B Squadron with the remainder of A Squadron in reserve. With bayonets fixed they galloped down the Gaza-Jaffa Road but were soon forced to dismount as a heavy fire was opened from the olive grove and villages to their right. With the assistance of the 2nd Australian Machine Gun Squadron the enemy was engaged in small numbers amongst the olive trees and labyrinthine cactus hedges, overcoming all opposition and killing or capturing many Turks.

"This work was done at very short range, openings had to be cut through the cactus hedges to get at the enemy, as soon as our men got to close quarters the Turks surrendered. Lieutenant Waite's troop kept to their horses, jumped the hedges and got amongst them still mounted, Lieutenant Waite using his revolver until shot in three places, and some of the troopers firing from their horses."
5/Light Horse Regiment War Diary PRO WO 95/4359

After capturing the north-east end of the cactus plantation, the 5/LHR halted to reorganise before the advance on Gaza. A Squadron on the left flank, in touch with the Wellington Mounted Rifles, were able to advance rapidly across the open ground. An enemy trench about two-hundred yards from the guns was rushed by A Squadron, assisted by about twenty New Zealanders. Of the two hundred Turks in the trench, over seventy were killed where they stood, many more were wounded and thirty-two were taken prisoner. When very close to the town, the Commanding Officer WMR asked for assistance to remove two captured guns, a Turkish counter-attack being expected.

While this section of line was being assaulted, Major BOLLINGBROKE took the two troops of A Squadron from their position on the coast and raided Sheikh Redwan. A Turkish artillery observation post was captured, but the party was forced to retire under a heavy enemy machine-gun fire. The advance of the right flank was much slower as the Turks put up a stubborn resistance amongst the cactus hedging. C Squadron in the centre of the regiment's line had the slowest advance of all and they eventually moved off to the right to join the 7/LHR.

IMPERIAL MOUNTED DIVISION
5TH AND 6TH MOUNTED BRIGADES
OPERATIONS TO 16.30 ON 26 MARCH 1917

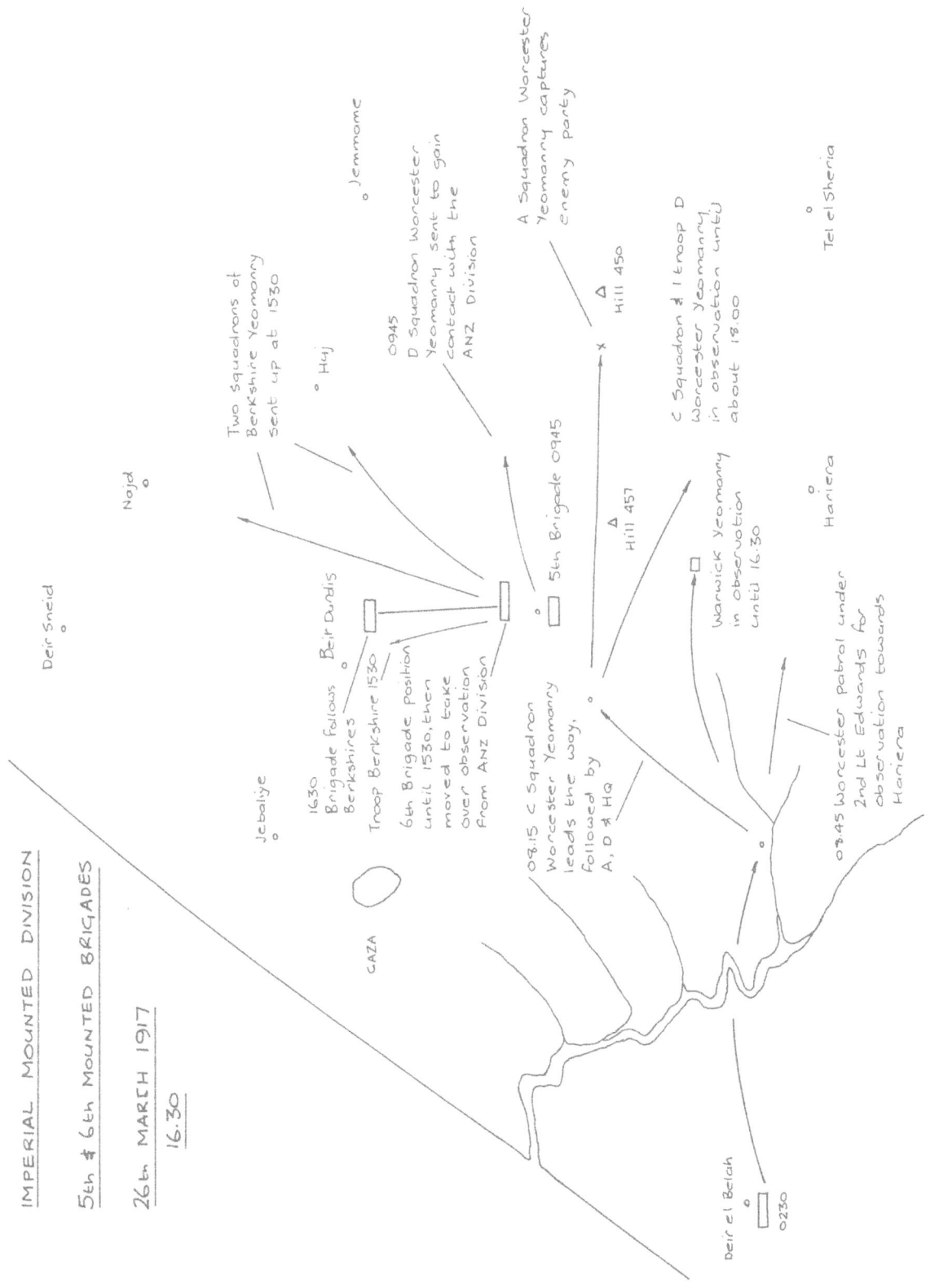

IMPERIAL MOUNTED DIVISION
5TH AND 6TH MOUNTED BRIGADES
OPERATIONS AFTER 16.30 ON 26 MARCH 1917

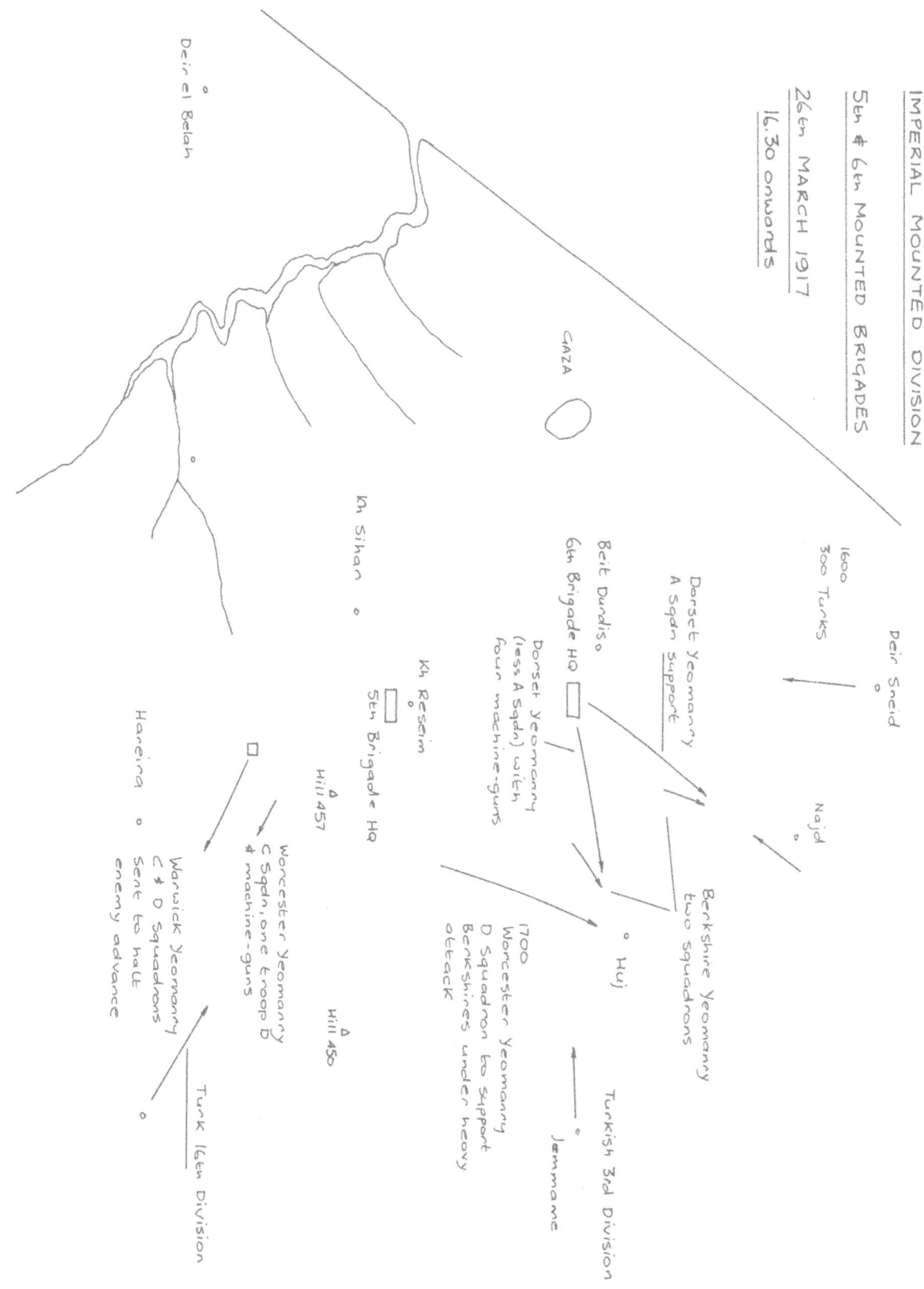

The 5th & 6th Mounted Brigades.

THE 5TH MOUNTED BRIGADE LED the Imperial Mounted Division from its bivouac at Deir el Belah at 02.30 on 26 March. Only two yeomanry regiments were present as the Gloucestershire Yeomanry had been detached for operations with Colonel MONEY's column on the left flank. With the Worcestershire Yeomanry leading, closely followed by the Warwickshire Yeomanry and support troops, the brigade crossed the Wadi Ghuzze and arrived at el Khutshan at 07.45. In accordance with the division's objective of preventing troops from Tel el Sheria and Hariera reinforcing Gaza, a patrol of six men under 2nd Lieutenant JW EDWARDS, Worcester Yeomanry, left for observation towards Hareira. At 08.15 C Squadron of the Worcester Yeomanry left as advance guard for Khirbet Sihan and after reporting the "all clear" was joined by the remainder of the regiment. The Warwick Yeomanry, following closely behind, arrived at Kh Sihan soon after, having sent out a small patrol under Lieutenant JOYNSON to the south.

As soon as Brigade Headquarters had been established at Kh Sihan, three squadrons of the Worcestershire Yeomanry were despatched eastwards. At 09.45, A Squadron under Major St J.O.B. fFRENCH BLAKE headed due east past Hill 457 and on towards Hill 450 where they surprised and captured an enemy camp near the Wadi Khirkity.

"Total 57 prisoners AAA Two pack mules which are bringing in all captured documents AAA Remainder of camp including tents and large disinfector and kits of German Officers destroyed AAA Three German Officers escaped on horses AAA Camp was apparently that of a control post AAA No arms captures AAA There is a good pool of water at the camp."
From: A Squadron Time: 11.55
Place: 1 mile west of Hill 450."
War Diary Worcestershire Yeomanry PRO WO95/4566

The second of the three Worcester patrols was D Squadron, who moved north-east with the dual role of observation and to make contact with the right flank of the Australian & New Zealand Mounted Division.

Having completed their role as advance guard, C Squadron under Major WH WIGGIN now moved south-east and took up an outpost position. They remained there in observation until 18.00, their right flank being prolonged by the Warwickshire Yeomanry.

Following in the tracks of the 5/Mounted Brigade on their approach to Kh Sihan were the three regiments of the 6th Mounted Brigade. They too had left Deir el Belah at 02.30 but now, as the Warwick and Worcester Yeomanry's moved off to the east, they continued north to Kh er Reseim.

Far to the north and north-west of Kh er Reseim the Australian & New Zealand Mounted Division had completed the encirclement of Gaza. In the early afternoon however, anxiety over the slow progress of the infantry advance prompted General Chetwode to commit the Australian and New Zealand Mounted Division to the attack.

In anticipation of this action, headquarters of the Imperial Mounted Division [Imp Mtd Div] moved from Kh er Reseim to Beit Durdis at 14.20. Consequently, the Imp Mtd Div was charged with taking over the Australian & New Zealand observation positions in order to protect their rear as they attacked.

The three regiments of the 6/Mounted brigade were those of the Buckinghamshire, Berkshire and Dorset Yeomanry's. At 15.30 one squadron of the Berkshires was sent towards Najd, while another squadron of the same regiment went north-east to Huj; a smaller patrol of one troop was sent to a position just south-east of Beit Durdis. As soon as these patrols were on their way, the rest of the brigade, that is the Dorsets, Bucks and Brigade HQ, moved to a position on a track about one-mile south-east of Beit Durdis.

Under the orders to take over the Australian & New Zealand Mounted Division position's, the 5/Mounted Brigade was to move north-west to Kh Kufieh. However, the order stated that the brigade was not to move until relieved by the Imperial Camel Brigade who held the line south to the Wadi Ghuzze. As the latter brigade did not receive the order at the same time, a long delay resulted which meant that the 5/Mounted Brigade was not fully relieved until after 18.00.

At 16.30 the first reports of enemy reinforcements began to reach the headquarters of both the 6/Mounted Brigade near Beit Durdis and that of the 5/Mounted Brigade still at Kh Sihan.

To the south two officers, Lieutenant-Colonel HA GRAY-CHEAPE and Major AC WATSON, at an advanced post to the south-east of the Warwickshire Yeomanry line, reported a large force of about 3000 infantry marching towards Gaza. C and D Squadrons under Lieutenant J BLACK were sent with machine-guns to try and halt the advance. Deploying on a slight rise a heavy rifle and machine-gun fire was opened up which scattered the head of the column and successfully halted it.

The Berkshire squadron on patrol towards Najd reported a column of three thousand infantry advancing and asked for immediate support. A Squadron of the Dorset Yeomanry was sent to them, while the rest of the Dorset's were despatched with four machine-guns and the Berkshire Battery, Royal Horse Artillery to support the other Berkshire Squadron near Huj.

At 17.15, while waiting for relief by the Berkshire Yeomanry, the Auckland detachment holding Hill 405 south-west of Najd was hit by the approaching enemy force. Overwhelmed, the New Zealanders were driven back from their position, and despite rapid reinforcement by the nearby Berkshires were unable to regain it. In order to reinforce this front further, three troops of D Squadron Worcestershire Yeomanry were sent up from their position three miles to the south.

With the line opposed by such a large enemy force the situation threatened to become critical. The 3/Light Horse Brigade was recalled from their position at Beit Hanun where they were protecting the rear of the Australian & New Zealand Mounted Division attack on Gaza. Leaving one regiment to hold the line, the 8th and 9th Light Horse Regiments galloped back towards Hill 405, but instead of merely reinforcing the hard-pressed holding force, they took high ground to the north-west. With the assistance of two field batteries, they were able to enfilade the Turkish column and effectively relieve the situation.

The enemy continued to try and break through the screen in order to reach the garrison at Gaza. A large force moving north-east from Hariera with the obvious intention of out-flanking the line was observed by the Warwickshire Yeomanry at 18.00. A party of the Worcestershire Yeomanry was sent as reinforcement and the combined troops dismounted and deployed at 18.25.

By 18.30 it was too dark to see. Whilst this fact worked against the infantry who were attacking Gaza, it was an advantage to the mounted troops in the screen for the enemy halted all relieving columns for the night. At 19.00 the line was drawn in and the left flank was held by the 3/Light Horse Brigade north of Beit Durdis. The 6/Mounted Brigade continued the line south and the 5/Mounted Brigade was on the right flank about Kh er Reseim.

With the general withdrawal of all troops later in the evening, the 5th and 6th Mounted Brigades were similarly ordered to retire. From 01.30 on the 27th the long ride back to Deir el Belah was commenced, with the destination being reached at about 08.00, where the opportunity was taken to have breakfast and to water and feed the long-suffering horses. Both brigades were later put on stand-by in the area of In Seirat but neither were required throughout the day.

IMPERIAL MOUNTED DIVISION
3RD LIGHT HORSE BRIGADE
26 MARCH 1917

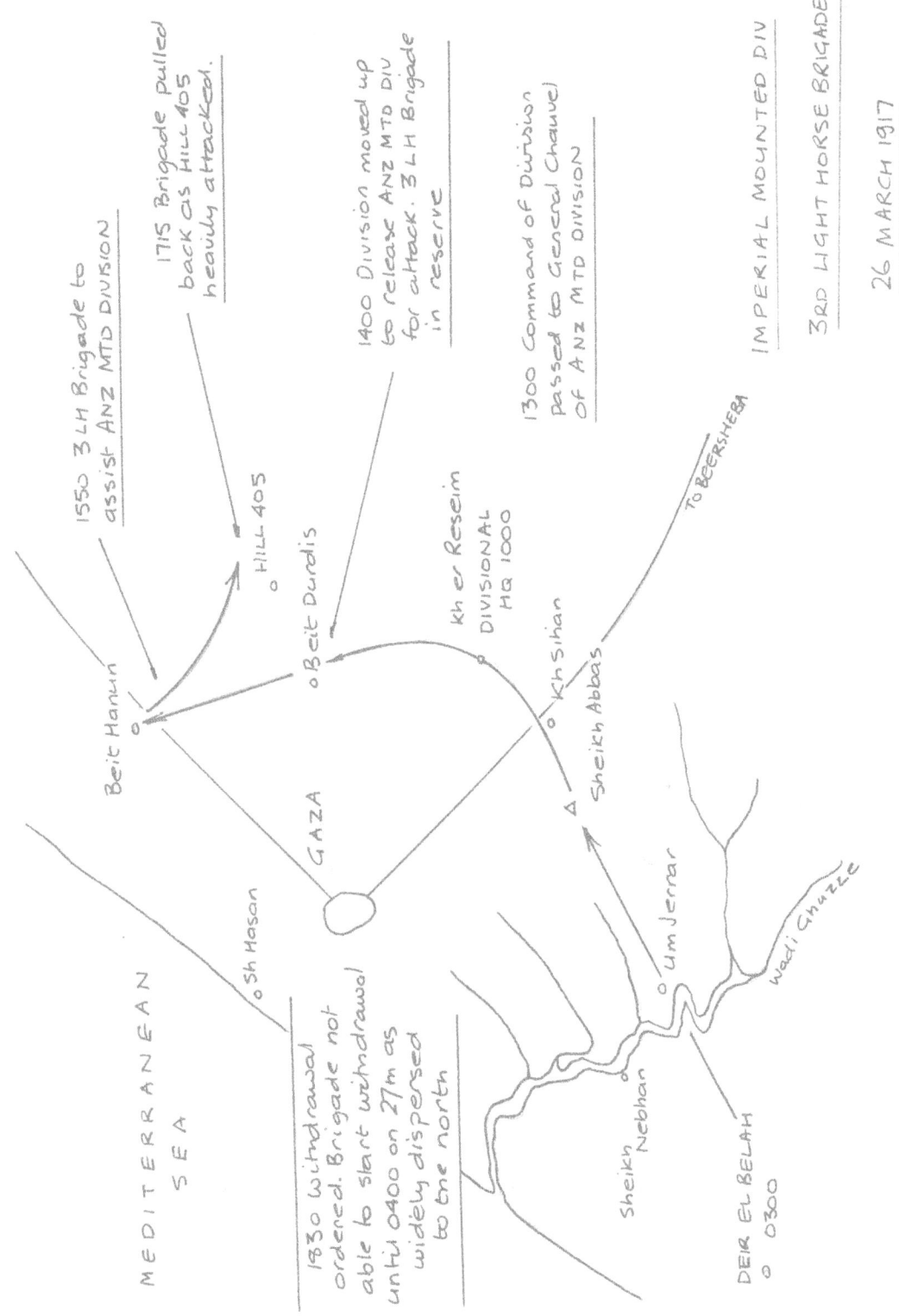

The 3rd Light Horse Brigade

THE SECOND DIVISION TO BE involved in the screen around Gaza was the Imperial Mounted Division. Commanded by General HODGSON it would operate to the east and south-east of the town, thereby extending the line taken by the Australian and New Zealand Mounted Division.

The division left its bivouac at Deir el Belah at 03.00 to follow the Australian and New Zealand Mounted Division to the Wadi Ghuzze. Crossing at Sheikh Nebhan the advance continued through Sheikh Abbas and on to Khirbet er Reseim at 10.00. Divisional Headquarters was established at this point and the brigade was put into reserve.

Some wells had been found on the way up and the opportunity to water the horses was taken. Contact with the enemy was minimal, mainly being encountered by patrols of the division which were sent to the east and south-east. The rest of the morning and early part of the afternoon was passed in anticipation of, and waiting for, the expected enemy reinforcements.

At 13.00 command of the Imperial Mounted Division was passed from General Hodgson to General CHAUVEL of the Australian and New Zealand Mounted Division, in order to release the latter for an attack on Gaza.

At 14.00 preparatory moves to allow this were started when the 6th Mounted Brigade was to take up a position east of Beit Durdis, with the 5th Mounted Brigade continuing the line south around Khirbet Kufieh.

With the Imperial Camel Corps Brigade advancing to Khirbet er Reseim the screen would be maintained and still leave the 3 Light Horse Brigade in reserve. At 15.50, General Chauvel received further word from Desert Column HQ for the need to press the attack on Gaza, with the suggestion that part of the Imperial Mounted Division now be used for this purpose. He was advised also that three batteries of armoured cars were being sent up to support him.

Thus it was that the 3 Light Horse Brigade was sent to directly assist the Australian and New Zealand Mounted Division. Taking up a position south of Beit Hanun, they were between the 6th Mounted Brigade on the right and the 7th Light Horse Regiment on the left. Only two regiments were in the line as the 10th Light Horse Regiment was being held in reserve.

Reports of strong enemy reinforcements began around 15.00; three thousand approaching from Tel el Sheria, with a further four thousand advancing from Jemmame. The latter column struck the 6/Mounted Brigade just as they were relieving the Australian and New Zealand troops, forcing them back from their positions on Hill 405, north east of Beit Durdis, at 17.15.

With the south-eastern part of the line now being threatened, the 3/Light Horse Brigade was ordered back to their defensive role around Beit Durdis, though leaving the 10/LHR behind for observation and as a rear-guard.

As the two regiments arrived back, Brigadier-General ROYSTON, immediately realising the strategic significance of Hill 405, advanced to high ground to the north-west. From here with the 6/Mounted Brigade to his right and coupled with the Nottinghamshire and Berkshire Batteries, Royal Horse Artillery, he was able to take the Turks in enfilade and prevent any further advance.

At 18.30, with dusk fast approaching, the 10/Light Horse Regiment was ordered back to fill a gap between the left of the 6/Mounted Brigade and the Imperial Camel Corps Brigade at Khirbet er Reseim.

It was about this time that orders for the withdrawal of the main attacking force were issued. Because the brigade was so far north however, it was not until 04.00 on the 27 March that they began their long march back to Deir el Belah.

At 05.30 a large formation of Turks attacked the brigade on the Gaza-Beersheba Road near Khirbet Sihan. By good fortune the 7th Light Car Patrol, which had been resting after a very hectic evening, was retiring along the road and was able to give very effective covering fire.

"At dawn we saw we were in a sticky position near (Ali el Muntar) if discovered. We slipped out on to the Gaza-Beersheba road, every now and then meeting small parties of British 'lost ones' whom we directed towards the wadi, and then hit up the pace towards Sihan, where we hoped to meet the armoured cars. They

were not there. Instead, we found the 3rd Light Horse Brigade retiring before a huge enemy force, who were bearing in heavily on them. General Royston galloped over and asked me if I could cover his retirement. This is just the kind of job we are most suited for. We ran the cars into likely position along the ridge, and, while the brigade went by, we waited until the enemy came within range. When they were some 1,200 or 1,500 yards off, we opened fire with five machine guns. It was immense. General Royston was greatly please, and he asked us if we required a squadron to cover our retreat or to stand by in support. We said 'No' so he wished us good luck and galloped after his brigade. We were now on our own. It was the time of our lives. We placed the cars (never attempting to dismount the guns) in such positions that enemy parties, trying to avoid the fire of one, would come under the fire of another; but we could not stem a force of thousands. They kept advancing, and we retired from one ridge to another comfortably, while the 3rd Brigade got clear away across the wadi and was secure. We had targets of mounted men and infantry, and killed at least 150 of them, they must have had very heavy casualties altogether. We suffered no losses."

Lieutenant WHP McKENZIE Commanding 7th Light Car Patrol.

Australian Official History.

AUSTRALIAN AND NEW ZEALAND MOUNTED DIVISION
New Zealand Mounted Rifles Brigade
Early operations on 26 March 1917

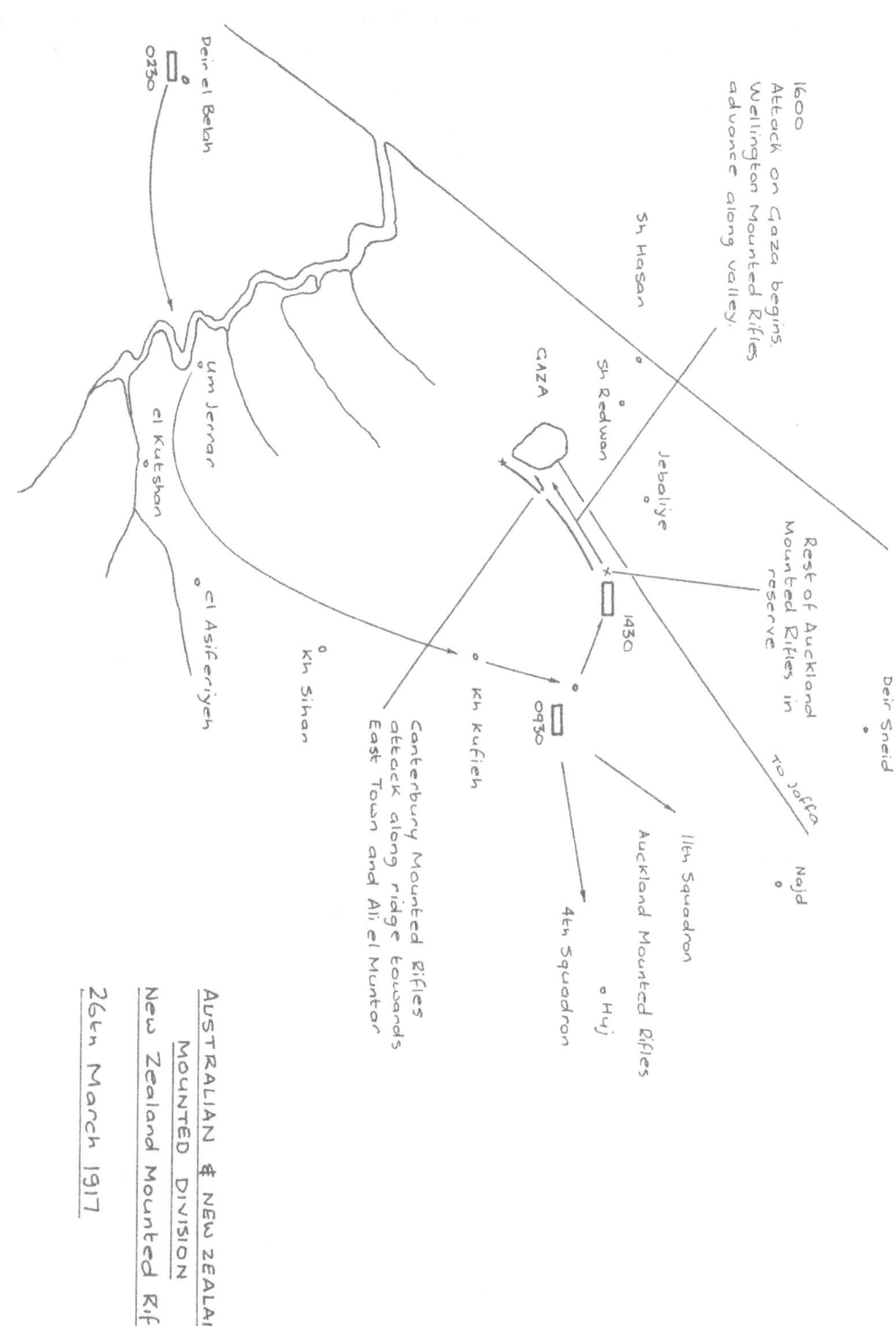

NEW ZEALAND MOUNTED RIFLES BRIGADE
FINAL ATTACK ON GAZA, 26 MARCH 1917

New Zealand Mounted Rifles Brigade
Attack on Gaza 26 March 1917

- Sheikh Hasan
- Sheikh Redwan
- Jebaliye
- Australia Hill
- Chaytor Hill
- Fryer Hill
- GAZA

Auckland Mounted Rifles in reserve (less 4th & 11th Squadrons in screen towards Huj and Najd)

Canterbury Mounted Rifles advance along ridge at 16.00

1st and 8th Squadrons on outskirts of town

18.40 10th Squadron enters Ali el Muntar

1600 Wellington Mounted Rifles attack along valley

Lieutenants Allison & Foley charge trench on left flank and bayonet 32 Turks, half of whom surrendered while rest continued to shoot

Two 77mm Krupps Guns captured by the Wellington Mounted Rifles

SCALE 50mm = 1 mile

The New Zealand Mounted Rifles Brigade

THE NEW ZEALAND MOUNTED RIFLES Brigade followed the 2/Light Horse Brigade from Deir el Belah at 02.30 on the 26 March. The brigade, with a strength of 97 Officers, 1676 men and 2064 horses, crossed the Wadi Ghuzze without incident at 06.00 and continued north-east to Beit Durdis, arriving there at about 09.30. The enemy's awareness of the brigade was apparent when at 10.00 artillery fire from both Gaza and Hareira opened up. No casualties were sustained however and the rest of the morning and early part of the afternoon passed off quietly.

In accordance with the division's role of preventing enemy reinforcements reaching Gaza, two patrols were despatched to the east and north-east of Beit Durdis. Both from the Auckland Mounted Rifles, the 4th Squadron moved east towards Huj at 11.00 with the 11th Squadron moving on Najd an hour later.

At Desert Column Headquarters, General Chetwode had begun to worry that with the main infantry attack only having started at noon, any serious delays might mean that Gaza would be unattainable by nightfall. To assist the infantry he therefore considered the possibility of a limited attack by the mounted troops from the north and north-east.

In readiness for this operation, at 14.30 the brigade was moved to the hills north-east of Gaza and Divisional HQ was established there. At 15.15 orders were issued by Div HQ for an attack by the three brigades of the division. Scheduled to commence at 16.00 the New Zealand Mounted Rifles Brigade would advance along the Gaza-Jaffa Road, with the 2/LHB to their right and the 22nd Mounted Brigade on their left.

Of the NZMR Bde only two regiments were in the front line, the Auckland Mounted Rifles being in reserve. The Canterbury Mounted Rifles were to advance along the ridge towards Gaza while to their right the Wellington Mounted Rifles advanced along the valley.

Despite fairly heavy shell and rifle fire the attack moved rapidly to the edge of the cactus hedges and, as gaps were cut, continued through them. A complete Turkish Field Ambulance was captured on the way and the complement of four Officers, one hundred and twenty-five men and all equipment was sent back to Brigade HQ.

On the left flank of the Wellington Mounted Rifles front a Turkish position checked the advance.

"Lieutenants Allison and Foley with two troops charged a trench situated south-east of The Cemetery and bayoneted thirty-two Turks, half of whom had put up their hands while the other half continued to shoot."

NZMR Brigade HQ War Diary PRO WO95/4544

This part of the line met with further success when they captured two 77mm Krupps Field Guns after a fierce bayonet attack in which some forty-eight of the enemy were killed. However, the advance had been more rapid than that of the other units and the enemy began to counter-attack the salient so formed. The guns were used to good effect though, repelling the enemy before any serious threat could develop.

A stubborn point of resistance was also overcome when the guns were used to blow down a house being used as a sniping post. One shell was enough to cause the surrender of the twenty Turks inside.

The Wellington Regiment, pushing from cactus hedge to cactus hedge and cutting gaps with their bayonets, had captured several trenches and many prisoners, and, finally, by some very fine work they took two Turkish guns with limbers and ammunition all complete. Further progress was held up by several houses filled with Turks from which it was impossible to dislodge them. One large building in particular drew special attention by the incessant fire which came from its occupants, and this prompted the Wellington men to make use of the captured guns to blow the snipers out of the house; and the formation of an extemporised gun crew of mounted riflemen was completed in a moment. The gun was a Krupp, but its intricacies were quickly solved, probably not in conformity with gunnery regulation, but with splendid results. The gun was directed at the house and Corporal Rouse who was "O/C Gun Detachment" looked through the barrel until the target was well in view, inserted a shell, closed the breach and fired the gun. Result, large hole in the house and twenty terrified Turks covered with debris ran out and surrendered. Three shots were fired from the captured gun in the manner described, each of which took effect on its objective. One of the latter in fact caused such destruction of the buildings along the line it traversed that Corporal Rouse was heard to remark that "the New Zealanders had made, at any rate, a new street in Gaza.

The New Zealanders in Sinai and Palestine. Powles. Page 91-92

Meanwhile the Canterbury Mounted Rifles had attacked on the left of the brigade front, the 1st and 8th Squadrons advancing on the East Town of Gaza. At 18.40 the 10th Squadron entered the redoubt on Ali el Muntar, meeting infantry who had successfully assaulted from the south.

"An Officer was despatched to Brigade HQ to obtain teams to remove the captured guns, and defensive position were taken up.

Wellington Mounted Rifles War Diary PRO WO95/4547

Within a very short time however, the now-familiar order to withdraw was received. The diary of the Wellington Mounted Rifles records the time as 18.45, the irony of the time being the simultaneous success of the above squadrons. The darkness made the collection of all men of the brigade a lengthy one, the evacuation of the wounded being particularly time-consuming and difficult. The times that the three regiments left the Gaza area varied from 21.40-23.00, but it mattered little, for the ride back to camp at Deir el Belah was a long and trying one for the exhausted and dispirited troopers. The brigade finally assembled at 08.30 on the 27th March and spent the day on outpost duties.

At Gaza fell Trooper AR FitzHerbert, a well-known settler of Rangitikei, age 64 years, but with the heart of a boy. He was loved by all who knew him and was an inspiration to the whole brigade. He found it difficult to enlist where he was known, on account of his age, but being of a very erect figure and filled with youthful vigour he at last managed to pass for a hale and hearty man of 40; and so got away with reinforcements for the Canterbury regiment, reaching Egypt towards the end of 1915. Immediately upon the return of the brigade from the Peninsula [Gallipoli] he applied to be transferred to the Wellington Regiment and became "No 3" in his own son's section in a troop commanded by a man whom as a boy he had taught to ride and shoot. His great knowledge of horses soon won for him a place in the regiment, and his unfailing cheerfulness under troubles and trials of every kind endeared him to all.

Who could resist that gay laugh or that happy song as he worked away on the horse lines, whether the temperature was 120 degrees in the shade and there blew a khamsin, or the night was shiveringly cold? The story is told of him that once when down with touch of dysentery he was sent to hospital and there fell among a room of "leadswingers", ages well in the early twenties. The consternation he caused was most amusing when after a mere three days in bed he announced his intention of going back to the front, and go he did, though a conspiracy of the matron and nurses managed to keep him in hospital for a week.

Early in the advance on the town through the orchards he was wounded in the neck, but after being bound up he insisted upon going on. Later, however, he was compelled to seek medical aid, and on his way to the dressing station he stopped to attend a wounded comrade, on whom he was tying a bandage when a burst of shrapnel mortally wounded him.

As the regiment was still advancing, and there was no ambulance cart in sight he was bound up carefully and left for the stretcher bearers; but even then he insisted upon having his rifle beside him.

Many times during the campaign in the desert he was asked to take up clerical work for the regiment, such work being thought more suitable to his age, but he invariably refused, saying with a laugh that he had enlisted as a fighting soldier and as such he would remain.

He died as he would have wished in the midst of battle with his rifle in his hand.

The New Zealanders in Sinai and Palestine. Powles. Page 92

53RD (WELSH) DIVISION
158TH INFANTRY BRIGADE
26 MARCH 1917

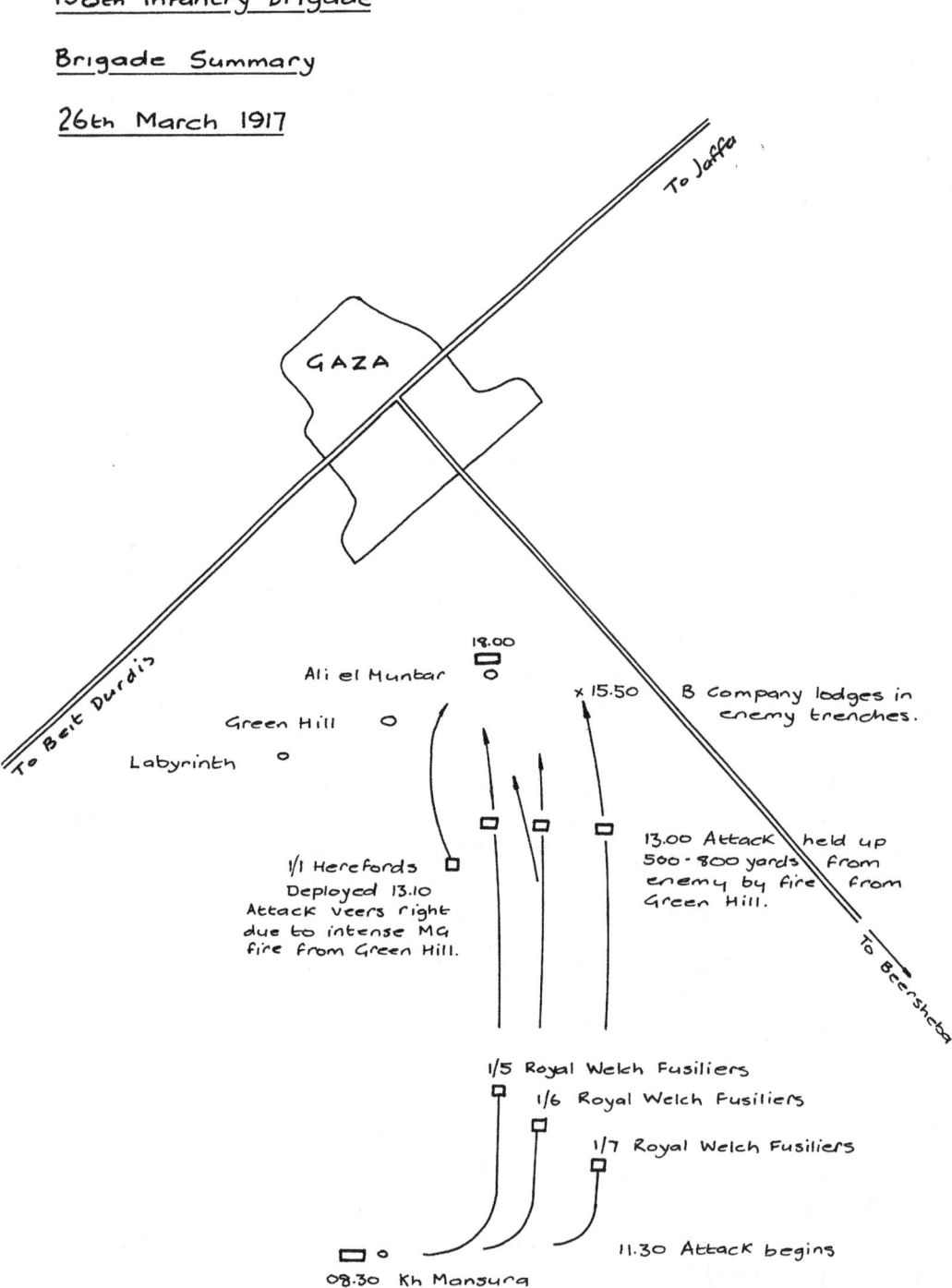

158 Brigade

AT 01.00 ON THE 26 March, the 158 Brigade, along with the rest of the 53rd (Welsh) Division, left its bivouac at Deir el Belah. They marched some four miles to a prepared crossing on the Wadi Ghuzze but due to the guide continually losing his way, were finally led in by the Brigadier General who took an approximate compass bearing; the difficulties due to the featureless terrain were thus exemplified at an early stage. The rendezvous at the el Breij mud hut, three-quarters of a mile from the wadi was eventually reached at 04.00.

At 10.40 pm voluminous orders arrived, some nine pages of closely typed foolscap. We did our best to assimilate this mass of literature and snatch a few minutes rest but without any particular success in either case. However, we hung up the Brigade's red lamp, and punctually at 1am the head of the brigade, 5RWF [Royal Welch Fusiliers] appeared; not so the guide! It was a fine, clear starlit night, with no moon, but not dark, and as we were moving through nearly fully-grown barley and green crops, and there was a heavy dew, we were literally wading, drenched from the waist downwards. Still no sign of the guide, and not till I had rushed vainly hither and yon, for some time, did he appear, very hot and bothered, half an hour late.

The guide, poor soul, was as bad as I had ever met. His canvas marks were not there, and he hadn't really reconnoitred the route properly. We marched in line of battalions, at 50 yards interval, battalion column of route, and the guide completely and utterly lost his way. We alternately cursed and cajoled him, feeling our way along with numerous halts, until the Brigadier decided to march on a compass bearing which eventually brought us to the rendezvous, the el Breij hut, a tumble-down place with a few evil looking Bedouins living in it, about half a mile from the Wadi. Even then the guide lost his way again before we reached the Wadi crossing. However, we did find a crossing of some sort, and got over at 4.35 am, nearly an hour late, and dawn breaking.

History of the 53rd (Welsh) Division. Major Ward. Pages 77-78

It was about this time that a heavy fog formed, destined not clear for several hours. A fog in March was not a common event and no allowance other than a general margin of time had been made for it. However, despite the fact that it's presence made marching a little slower, it also masked the advance from the enemy and later, after daybreak, prevented operations by Turkish aircraft.

"...this was a great help during the further advance as enemy aircraft were useless while it continued."

7/Royal Welch Fusiliers. War Diary PRO95/4627

The brigade reached the Wadi Ghuzze at 04.35 about fifty minutes later than intended and, on crossing, continued to advance onto the Burjabye Ridge en route for Mansura.

The 5/Royal Welch Fusiliers led the advance and deployed into a two-company front with C and D Companies the vanguard under Major W BESWICK. The brigade followed in the order 6/RWF and 7/RWF, with the 1/1 Herefordshire Regiment bringing up the rear. Again advancing on a compass bearing, of 85 degrees, the head of the column reached its initial objective at el Adar - el Burjaliye at 05.45 and a message was sent by the 158 Brigade Headquarters to the 53 Division Headquarters

"Am ready now. Am in position between Burjabye and Adar. Shall I now make good Mansura. Addressed 53rd Division and 160th Brigade."

158 Brigade Headquarters War Diary. PRO WO95/4625

As no instructions for further movement were received and with the brigade concentrated by 06.15, Brigadier General SF MOTT ordered the advance to press on.

The next objective was Mansura at the western extremity of the Mansura Ridge. This was a cliff formed by the edge of a plateau some four-thousand yards wide. From its top there was a clear view across a flat, open plain to the lower slopes on the south-eastern side of Gaza, about 4000 yards distant.

The advance continued in the heavy fog across broken ground, sharply and frequently cut by gullies, or nullahs. The first troops of the brigade began arriving at Mansura at 07.45 and the concentration was completed by about 08.30. At about 08.00 the fog lifted slightly, two Turkish aeroplanes were seen to rise and bugles sounded in the enemy's position, now clearly visible around Ali el Muntar 5000 yards away.

Shortly afterwards the brigade moved to a more sheltered position about 600 yards to the east, and it was here that the morning was passed until the attack began.

Brigade HQ established communication with the 160 Brigade on the el Sire Ridge to the west, and the position of the 158 Brigade was sent by heliograph to 53 Division HQ. At 08.50, the General Officer Commanding 53 Division, Major General AG DALLAS, arrived at Mansura and summoned the brigadiers to a conference to decide the method of attack for the next stage. The Commander Royal Artillery was asked at this meeting, which began at 10.10, how long he required to get his guns into position and he replied "Two hours". It therefore seemed likely that the attack would begin at about 12.30.

Despite this, just after 11.00 Major General Dallas [GOC 53 Division] received a wire from Major General Chetwode of the Desert Column which impressed upon him the importance of time. Accordingly, the 158 Brigade was instructed to advance towards Ali el Muntar, considered to be unoccupied as cavalry of the Desert Column had been seen to the north of Gaza.

Because of this the 5/Royal Welch Fusiliers were ordered to advance, first to the east for a distance of 1000 yards, and then to wheel left on the objective of Ali el Muntar. They were primarily to assess the dispositions of the enemy and were ordered to avoid becoming involved in an attack by themselves. The main attack began at 11.30. Due to the concentration of the brigade it was necessary for all troops to march first in an easterly direction, then wheel left onto the objective. This was achieved by each battalion of the brigade marching 500 yards east of the front battalion, then wheeling to face north, thus extending the right flank of that battalion. The whole deployment was carried out with the calmness and precision of a field-day exercise, the men of each following battalion streaming out past the rear of those who had already turned on to Ali el Muntar.

"The advance was over bare country, and across the open valley which lies between Mansura and the el Sire Ridge, and so up the long, smooth, glacis to the crest, and the Mosque of Ali Muntar. The country was so open that the whole manoeuvre could be seen, not only by the Brigade staff, and the Turks, but by the mounted troops of the Anzac Division picquetting the hills on the far side of the Gaza-Beersheba Road, in the direction of Huj and Beit Durdis.

The three battalions moved out in fine style, and when opposite the various objectives, wheeled left handed and proceeded northwest towards the heights. The 5th RWF naturally completed the wheel first, and advanced rapidly down a slight slope till they reached a small cactus encircled garden, about 800 yards from the crest of Ali Muntar. Thinking that the other two battalions were getting too far to the north, the Brigadier sent me out after them, and I passed the time of day with Rome and Harker, both full of spirits. The only sign of enemy opposition, so far, had been some very high shrapnel. Now rifle fire broke out from Green Hill and Ali Muntar, and the advance slowed down. Captain Ashton."

History of the 53rd (Welsh) Division. Major Ward. Pages 81-82

Even as this movement was being carried out, the enemy opened a heavy fire of both High Explosive (H.E) and shrapnel into the area. Few casualties occurred at this range however, and the advance continued steadily. No artillery support had been given to the attack thus far and at 3000 yards from the objective casualties began to be taken.

At 12.03 a message from the 5/Royal Welch Fusiliers was received by 158 Brigade HQ to say that they were within 1200 yards of Ali el Muntar, but that there was no sign of the enemy as yet. A few minutes later the battalion came under a very heavy rifle and machine-gun fire from both the cactus hedges in front of Ali el Muntar and from Green Hill on the left flank. Being in a completely exposed position, casualties were heavy and they pushed forward to gain some cover while waiting for the other battalions, echeloned to the right, to catch up and prolong the flank. The BGC 158 Brigade spoke on the telephone to the Officer Commanding the 5/RWF, Lt-Colonel BORTHWICK, and asked if the support of machine-guns would be of help. The answer being affirmative, a section of the 158 Brigade Machine Gun Company was ordered up, but unfortunately in the confusion never arrived. The right flank now began to be strengthened as the 1/6 and 1/7 RWF arrived in the line.

"I must point out that the last 1500 yards of our advance was in full view of the enemy and over an absolutely open glacis, the Battalion nevertheless worked a magnificent advance in splendid order and showed the greatest bravery and determination."

7/Royal Welch Fusiliers War Diary. PRO WO95/4627

With this pause in the attack it may be in order to consider what faced the men of the Royal Welch Fusiliers. The term "cactus hedge" may conjure up an attractive, border-type hedge just high enough to conceal the Turks, who were then able to fire through the natural gaps. That was far from the reality. The cactus hedges around Gaza, as elsewhere in Palestine, served to divide the various areas of cultivation from each other. Each plant might be up to ten feet high, with its leaves touching, almost merging, with its neighbour. The thickness of the hedge could be several feet, and the mass of sharp spines which covered the whole surface made as an effective a barrier as the barbed wire entanglements of the Western Front. Certainly the cactus hedges were prized both as natural defences by the Turks and approached with trepidation by the attacking troops.

At 12.15 the 6/Royal Welch Fusiliers were inclined to the left of their line-of-advance to give support to the hard-pressed 5th battalion. A further advance was now made, but as the enemy on Green Hill were not being directly engaged, enfilade fire from that quarter continued unabated in its severity and pinned the 5/RWF down. To alleviate this situation, the brigade reserve of the 1/1 Herefords was ordered up, being deployed at 13.12. With virtually every company of the brigade now in the firing line, the attack was pushed on.

Sergeant Richard PRICE of the Herefordshire Regiment was in this advance and wrote of his experiences in a long letter home to his parents. The initial stages are described thus.

"Of course, I was acting Company Quartermaster Sergeant at this time but as there was not much for me to do in that line I got permission to attach myself to my own platoon which I did. We had now about 2000 yards of ground to cover which lay between us and the enemy's position. It was absolutely flat with not the least cover of any sort, the grain that was very thin was 5 or 6 inches high. Johneys position was on a little rise and he had the ground swept beautifully, we had a few shells over our way but as Johney [Johney Turk-the enemy] did not wish to waste too many shells just then on us we did not grumble as a few shells is quite enough especially if they come straight. We had just enough to show there was no ill feeling. All this time we are advancing first moving out in platoons then sections and eventually when we got under long range rifle fire we got out into what is called extended order. The distance now that we would be away from the enemy about 1400 yards, in this order we keep on at a steady walk until the distance was about 1200 yards then the fire from rifle and machine guns of the Turks was coming into beautiful working order so that we had to advance by short, sharp rushes then we began to have casualties. I had it passed down to me that one of my chaps had been hit, he was about 20 yards away from me so I got up and went to see what was wrong with him and found that he had been hit in the chest just over the heart, but luckily the bullet had turned and was only just under the skin. Meanwhile the rest had gone on and as I had to catch them up again I did what I could for him and told him to stop there for the stretcher bearers. I got to the first line of men which were in a bit of a fold in the ground, there we were fairly safe from the fire coming from the front but we soon found out that they had got a machine gun on us which enfiladed the fold of ground we were in from there[sic] left. Again I went up on my own to the next line to my own company who I thought were further up when I got there, there was men [sic] of our company and also other companies as of course the nearer you get to the enemy so the different companies get mixed up as the supports gradually come up into the different lines. We lay there long enough to get our breath and by now there were a lot of casualties, men dropping right

and left, amongst them my own platoon officer who was killed, then another Captain who had just come and told us that the next time we went forward we were to fill a gap in the firing line about 60 yards in front, off we went and I was in front of the advancing line with the Captain when I got one through the arm. I was at the time about 4 or 5 paces from the line we were getting up to. I did not take much notice at the time as I thought that it was just a couple of bullets that had creased me but I found out when I got up in the firing line that it was one bullets that had gone through my arm and I should think that when I got one I had a whole machine gun to myself as the bullets were that thick. You would wonder how they could miss you, I should think I had a dozen just all sent for me as I got the one in the arm and a dozen others must have whistled by and through my legs at the same time."

Notes in the possession of the author.

As the men of the Herefords advanced against Green Hill, the fire directed upon them was so intense that the attack veered off to the right. Becoming entangled with the left flank of the 5/Royal Welch Fusiliers, their attack became directed upon Ali el Muntar and by 14.00 they were within 500 yards of it. Simultaneously, the other battalions of the brigade were advancing under heavy artillery and machine-gun fire, but even by 15.00 the general line was still some 500 yards short of the objective. The whole attack was now held up and needed a final impetus or reinforcement to succeed.

On the extreme right of the 158 Brigade's line, Captain EW WALKER of the 7/RWF, with several officers from his battalion and from the 5/Welsh Regiment, edged forward to within 200 yards of the enemy position.

"I now sent back a written message to my Commanding Officer, stating that with the help of supports I was in a position to assault, and asking that bombardment be lifted. I afterwards learned that this message did not reach him. This was about 14.30 hours and I waited in the hope of support for about an hour. This delay caused me many casualties but we were not under machine-gun fire."

Captain EW Walker. Records of the Royal Welch Fusiliers. Page 127

It was now apparent that no further support could be expected, confirmed when Second Lieutenant WL ROBERTS, of D Company, came over and reported that he was suffering heavily, despite all brigade supports already having been committed. Consequently, after a brief discussion with his officers, Captain Walker, with Lieutenants C LATHAM and FLETCHER and forty men of B Company, decided to attack along with two officers and forty men of the 5/Welsh Regiment. In a very gallant action, they assaulted and took part of the enemy's position on Ali el Muntar, together with the trenches immediately to the east. Captain Walker was personally responsible for the capture of an enemy machine-gun and the whole party took some forty German, Austrian and Turkish prisoners. During this action, Lieutenant Latham became detached from the main party, and together with an officer of the 5/Welsh, became engaged in heavy fighting at close range amongst the cactus hedges. At this point they captured a great part of the Turkish 53rd Division Staff and several German and Austrian machine-gunners. Soon after this position was taken, Lieutenant Colonel Lawrence of the 7/Cheshire Regiment arrived and, after taking command, both consolidated the position and brought up guns to bear on enemy trenches to the west. Fierce fighting continued in the area, the Turkish troops which faced the Royal Welch Fusiliers now having to protect their left flank from the assaulting troops of the other brigades of the Welsh Division. This breech of the Turkish line changed the fortunes of the whole attack. To the right of the 158th Brigade, Clay Hill was stormed by troops of the 159th Brigade at about 16.30. Soon after this, the 161st Brigade, thrown into the fight at 16.00, captured Green Hill at the point of the bayonet.

At 16.15, the Commanding Officer of the 7/Royal Welch Fusiliers requested that the artillery direct high explosive fire onto the cactus hedges of the enemy position, as machine-gun fire was causing heavy casualties to some sections. The effects of the shell fire were immediately apparent, one particularly damaging machine-gun being taken out at a stroke. Major OWEN of the 7/RWF went back to a battery of guns of the 266th Brigade, Royal Field Artillery, one-thousand yards to the rear and pointed out the desired targets.

The final assault on Ali el Muntar by the 158 Brigade resulted in its capture at about 18.00. By this time it was dark however, and the jobs of consolidation and establishment of an outpost line were not easy ones. The Brigade Major described the situation soon after its capture.

"We found a strange scene of turmoil, masses of dead and wounded of both sides, a lot more people nearly frantic with thirst and excitement, and a great mixing of units.....

Desultory firing was going on the far side - though it was now quite dark - where a certain amount of enemy were still sticking in the gardens and cactus hedges which cover that side."

Records of the Royal Welch Fusiliers. Page 130

The 5/Royal Welch Fusiliers held the west side of the Mosque on Ali el Muntar, holding the line with one company while the rest of the battalion stayed in reserve. The mosque itself and the ground to the east of it were held by companies of the 6/RWF and 7/RWF. The Herefords came up soon afterwards and supported the 5/RWF.

The positions now held by the 158 Brigade, and as we shall see the 53 Division in general, would appear to have been sound and strategic. However, other events had been taking place during the afternoon which would influence the decision of General Sir Archibald Murray, commanding the battle from In Seirat. From early morning the unexpected, dense fog had caused some anxiety to General Chetwode. Although its appearance was, on the whole, an advantage, it was a totally unknown factor over which the commanders had no control. The early achievement of initial objectives did not result in an early attack by the infantry and this led to further worries. The early capture of Gaza was considered vital in order to prevent much of the attacking force becoming isolated in the harsh desert without water. The mounted troops in particular were of great concern as they had last watered their horses and men after midnight on the 25th and the prospect of such a large number facing dawn on the 27th without water was unthinkable. Information obtained before the 26th had given a reasonable estimate as to the dispositions of Turkish troops within striking distance of Gaza. The arrival of Turkish reinforcements from the east would present the real risk of cutting off the retreat of the mounted troops to the north of Gaza, as well as putting the rest of the force under attack from both east and west. Unless Gaza itself had been captured by nightfall on the 26th, withdrawal would have to be ordered.

With the work of consolidation in hand, patrols were sent down the gentle slopes towards Gaza itself. Little opposition was encountered and Turkish troops could be seen retiring north-west into the town. One party under the indomitable Captain Walker and Lieutenant Latham reached as far as the streets on the southern side of Gaza, with other such parties meeting groups of ANZAC mounted troops who had pressed in from the north.

If only this information could have been sent instantly to General Murray!

It was not to be however, for at 22.30 orders were received from 53 Division HQ that the brigade would withdraw and take up a line at Mansura. There was much preparatory work to be done in order to commence movement at the given hour of midnight. The consolidatory work had necessarily dispersed the various units even more than had the attack. Several companies were detailed to search the battlefield for the many wounded who were thus carried to dressing stations and later evacuated. A considerable number of enemy arms had also been captured and, due to the impossibility of carrying them all back, they were either destroyed or rendered useless.

The medical facilities soon began to be overrun and the plight of the wounded became critical. The best course of action for the walking wounded was to make their own way back to dressing stations and even beyond that to the clearing station and hospital. Sergeant Price continues his narrative with his experiences of such a journey.

"When I got down my arm was bleeding rather badly, I asked one of the men on my right about 3 or 4 yards away to get my field dressing out of my pack. I could not hold my rifle in my left hand by this time as it was swollen up and after I had gone about quarter of the way an Officer told me to stop there for stretcher bearers so I had to lie there and the Officer who I had come with on the rush before got killed. Well I lay there for a time and took off my pack while I lay there I had to lie flat as the bullets round me were thick and whistled above and round and fairly knocked the sand up in my eyes. I stayed there for a little while but I can tell you from experience that in an attack of that sort I felt more comfortable while I was rushing forward

than when I was lying down because you have your mind more occupied when rushing forward than when lying still. Well as I say I lay there for sometimes then as it was my arm that was hit I did not require carrying away so I got up when there was not quite so heavy fire from the enemy, put my rifle in my right hand and made my way back towards the emergency dressing station. I did not leave my pack on the field because there was a few little things in it which I did not want to lose. well I got back as far as the fold of ground which I mentioned before on the way up and there was several other wounded men there I sat beside a chap out of the RWF there who had been shot in the right arm, so I bandaged him up and he bandaged me up. There emergency dressing station was in a garden on our right surrounded by cactus and after I had it dressed I sat there for some time to rest as it was about between 4 and 5 by this time, then they told me to go back to what is called the advanced dressing station."

Notes in the possession of the author

Shortly after midnight the brigade began to move out from the positions held and made its tortuous way back across the plain to Mansura. The first men arrived at about 03.45 and, in a state of complete exhaustion after more than twenty-four hours continual marching and fighting, fell asleep in heaps across one another. A couple of hours sleep was all the rest afforded to the men, for at 06.00 on the 27th March breakfast, from the three-day emergency rations, was issued and water bottles filled from the fanatis. At 07.00 orders were received for the 1/1 Herefords to move up to support the 160th and 161st Brigades with a view to reoccupying Ali el Muntar if found to be deserted. The other battalions of the brigade were put on standby, to be ready to move at once if required. Having begun their advance earlier, the 160 Brigade reached Green Hill and the 161 Brigade Ali el Muntar to find them both unoccupied. The Herefords were ordered to continue their advance and to make for Ali el Muntar. At this time -08.30- the three battalions of the Royal Welch Fusiliers were moved to a line 1500 yards NNE of Mansura Bluff, but facing east so as to protect the rear of those advancing on Green Hill and Ali el Muntar. As this move was taking place the enemy had occupied Sheikh Abbas with reinforcements from Hareira and Tel el Sheria, and they were thus able to shell the brigade from a south-easterly direction, which caused much damage in the horse and camel lines.

Although the positions were regained without opposition, the Turks soon launched counter-attacks against both Green Hill and Ali el Muntar. The first was repulsed but subsequent, stronger attacks forced the weary troops to retire. This in turn made the line held by the Royal Welch Fusiliers untenable and they withdrew their left flank. The position thus held faced north towards Ali el Muntar; the 5/RWF were in the middle with the 7/RWF to the right and one company of the sixth battalion to the left.

The brigade remained in this position for the rest of the day, the men laying and watching in the tremendous heat of the Khamsin which had been blowing all morning.

There was much movement by the enemy, their resolve having been stiffened by their escape from apparent defeat only hours before. They assembled in some force in the cactus garden in front of the 5/Royal Welch Fusiliers and the same battalion reported that strong enemy reinforcements were approaching from the east, presumably from the garrison at Beersheba. However, although the atmosphere was one of threat, no serious attacks were made during the day.

At 15.15 the commanding officers of the brigade were instructed to report to brigade headquarters, now at 1500 yards South-east of Ali el Muntar. The Brigadier General had decided that a general retirement was necessary to relieve the congestion caused by the supply camels in the valley between the el Sire and Burjabye Ridges, which prevented further movement of the men of the 53 and 54 Divisions. Instructions at this stage were only verbal and although no directions as to route or timing were given, the battalion commanders conferred and reconnoitred routes in anticipation. Unfortunately, when written orders for the withdrawal were received from 20.30 onwards, the routes given were different from those which had been planned.

Nevertheless, at 22.00 the trenches were evacuated and the men of the brigade assembled on the Gaza-Beersheba Road. The camel and mule transports had already been withdrawn from their positions behind the lines held, and so at the end of a second, gruelling day the men were weighted down with a multitude of equipment from picks and shovels to Lewis guns and magazines.

The march was a very difficult, trying affair although very ably led by an officer of the 436th Field Company, Royal Engineers. At 01.30, on 28 March, the Wadi Ghuzze was reached, the men were given a drink and water bottles filled.

"I must point out that during the two days operations the heat was intense and the men only had one bottle of water each day."

Lieutenant Colonel Harker.
CO 7/Royal Welch Fusiliers War Diary. PRO WO95/4627

After an hour rest the march was resumed and bivouac near Deir el Belah was reached at 06.30, the brigade being put into reserve. Throughout this time there had been the unrelenting struggle to deal with the wounded, most of which had been sustained on the 26th i.e. some forty-eight hours earlier. Sergeant Price's situation has been described from his letter home and we take up his narrative from the early evening of the 26th.

"......then they told me to go back to what is called the advanced dressing station. They showed me which way to go, but to be careful as I went through a certain gap in the cactus hedge, as it was sniped and several had been hit going through it. I got through and felt quite safe going back over the same ground I had come over. There were a few stray bullets flying about but nothing to worry about back there. I just got close to the dressing station which was at the back of a little rise in the ground when someone shouts out to me,
"Hello Sergeant, got another one?"
"Yes, just a little one" I says,
I stand talking to them for a minute when an Officer comes up and says to me you had better get away from here or you will get another. We have had someone killed in the Dressing Station so off I went from there and they sent me to one of the sand-carts to be taken to another DS further back, but I walked there on the way back I met a Captain of the Brigade Staff who had been my platoon officer on the Peninsula [Gallipoli] and he says,
"Hello Price, got another Blighty?"
[Blighty- a wound serious enough to be sent back to England]
"No Sir, only a little one this time" I says.
I stopped to speak to him for a minute or two then I went on to the dressing station. Well when I got there I found it full of wounded, and the Doctors and orderlies were that busy that anyone who was already bandaged up somewhere near tidy was sent to give in his particulars as they had no time to dress only the very worst cases.
It was dark by now and there were camels to take the wounded to the [next] dressing station; they put two men on a camel, the worst cases or men who could not sit up were put on a sort of chair made for the job. They asked men who could walk to do so, as they had not enough camels for the lot, so thinking that by walking we should get away earlier, I and several others fell in to walk as long as we had two legs to stand on. But instead of marching us off straight away we had to fall out again and wait for the camels to be loaded up first. While we waited I went to try and get a drop of water as we had not had much all day, only what we had got in our bottles from the night before and it had been hot all day, and after waiting for some time on my turn I had a drink. I got about half a Gill, [Gill=quarter pint or 150 ml] that's all and lucky to get that as there was scarcely any water at all. However, eventually about 10pm, the camels were loaded up and ready to start, they fell us in and before we marched off the Officer told us that we had 7 or 8 mile to go and if we thought that we could not stick it that we had better fall out there and stay until morning as they had nothing for us if we should fall out on the way. A few fell out, the remainder followed the camels, and we went a little further and the camels stopped, they had lost the way, at least the guide had. Well, I can tell you I did not want much of this as I was that tired that if I sat down for a minute I should fall asleep.
So after sitting there for a while and things did not seem to be getting better I just thought,
"Well, if they are lost so soon, what is going to happen before the end of the journey?"
So as we were not 600 to 800 yards from the dressing station that we started from, I and a couple of others

decided to try and find our way back. We lay down and one of the RAMC orderlies brought us a blanket which we covered ourselves in and slept, it would be about midnight then and when I woke the sun was shining down strong on us. We got up and when all was ready we started off again along with all that had stopped behind the night before. We had no breakfast as there was no rations there. It was burning hot and there was very little water but I managed with the others to get a couple of drinks at intervals on the way down and when we were about one mile from the clearing station I got a ride in a limber waggon that was going that way.

About midday we arrived at the clearing station and got a bit of bully beef and biscuits, a drop of water and later on some bacon and Oxo, which I can tell you was very acceptable. The RAMC orderlies were very good and did all they could for us, but they could not have expected so many as they were not prepared for them. I met some of the boys who had come on the camels that I had started with the night before and they told us that they had not been in many hours before us as they had wandered about the desert all night and at 3am they lay down with the camels and waited until it was light, so I felt glad that I had some luck when I did. We stayed there for the night under a bit of a bivouac which they put up for us, then the same carry on the next day. I got my arm dressed at the place we spent this day in, hanging about and giving particulars, waiting for camels etc until about 7.30pm when I got into a tent to stop there for the night, but no sooner had I settled down than they fetched me and another Sergeant to go further down to the railhead on a camel. So away we went and both of us got onto the same camel one each side, then we had some fun. We were sitting talking when suddenly the camel went to get up and me not thinking of what was coming up went off the camel 4 or 5 yards behind, luckily I kept my feet, that was my first experience in camel riding. Then the Major of the clearing station came up and put the cradles that we could sit down in then strapped us in and away we went to railhead, arrived there about midnight and after giving the usual particulars got down to sleep. We had not quite settled down when one of the orderlies came round and told us that all walking cases could get onto the hospital train which we did. Luckily I got a cot and went to sleep and woke in the morning to find myself no further than El Arish. Here they took us off the train and put us in the 2nd ASH [Australian Stationary Hospital]. It was now Thursday the 29th. On Saturday all walking cases were loaded up in trucks and sent down the line about 10am. We had some breakfast before starting and at Bir el Abd we had some bread and jam and tea, around at Kantara about 6pm we got some cocoa and slept comfortably in tents which had been provided for us. We stopped here until Monday [2 April] during which time my arm was dressed twice. We left here on a hospital train at 12.45 and we had a good time on the train and arrived at Cairo at 5pm. I was taken to the Citadel Hospital which was very full so that we had to be fixed up in some of the quarters belonging to the Barracks. I stayed there until Wednesday [4 April], got my arm dressed a couple of time and from there I went to the Abbassin Convalescent Depot and it was there that I had my arm seen to properly and it was the best show of the lot. I had a good time there for three weeks, plenty of good food and also plenty of attention. As I am finishing this letter Johnny has been giving us a little iron rations [shells] but he can't hurt me as I am sitting comfortable in my dugout.

With Best Love from your Loving Son Richard.

Notes in the possession of the author

"I wish to congratulate the 158th Brigade on their achievements on 26th and 27th inst. On 26th our brigade was completely successful, and in conjunction with 160th and 161st Brigades captured the objective assigned to it after a trying night march of eight miles followed by strenuous fighting in a burning sun from sunrise to sunset.

On 27th, under similar conditions, officers and all ranks showed conspicuous endurance and determination the holding and digging in a line which was vital to the operations of the higher command.

Officers and men I thank you from the bottom of my heart. Notwithstanding your privations your success does not come as a surprise to me, even under the privations undergone by you.

Let us retain our cohesion and spirit as a brigade, supported with the knowledge that we have fought a great fight for the world's great cause of justice and peace.

Your privations have been my constant anxiety during the last three days. Every man must feel proud of his achievements. You have earned the gratitude of the old Country in Wales and Herefordshire.

Officers continue to keep the "care of your men" as your first thought and men "obey your Officer and maintain your discipline".

Please convey this to all officers and other ranks with my grateful thanks, and offer our prayers for the wounded and dead.

The G. O. C. 53rd Division has asked me to convey his gratitude for all you have done.

Your Brigadier

(Signed) S F Mott.

53 Division War Diary Appendices PRO WO95/4614

53RD (WELSH) DIVISION
158TH INFANTRY BRIGADE
27 MARCH 1917

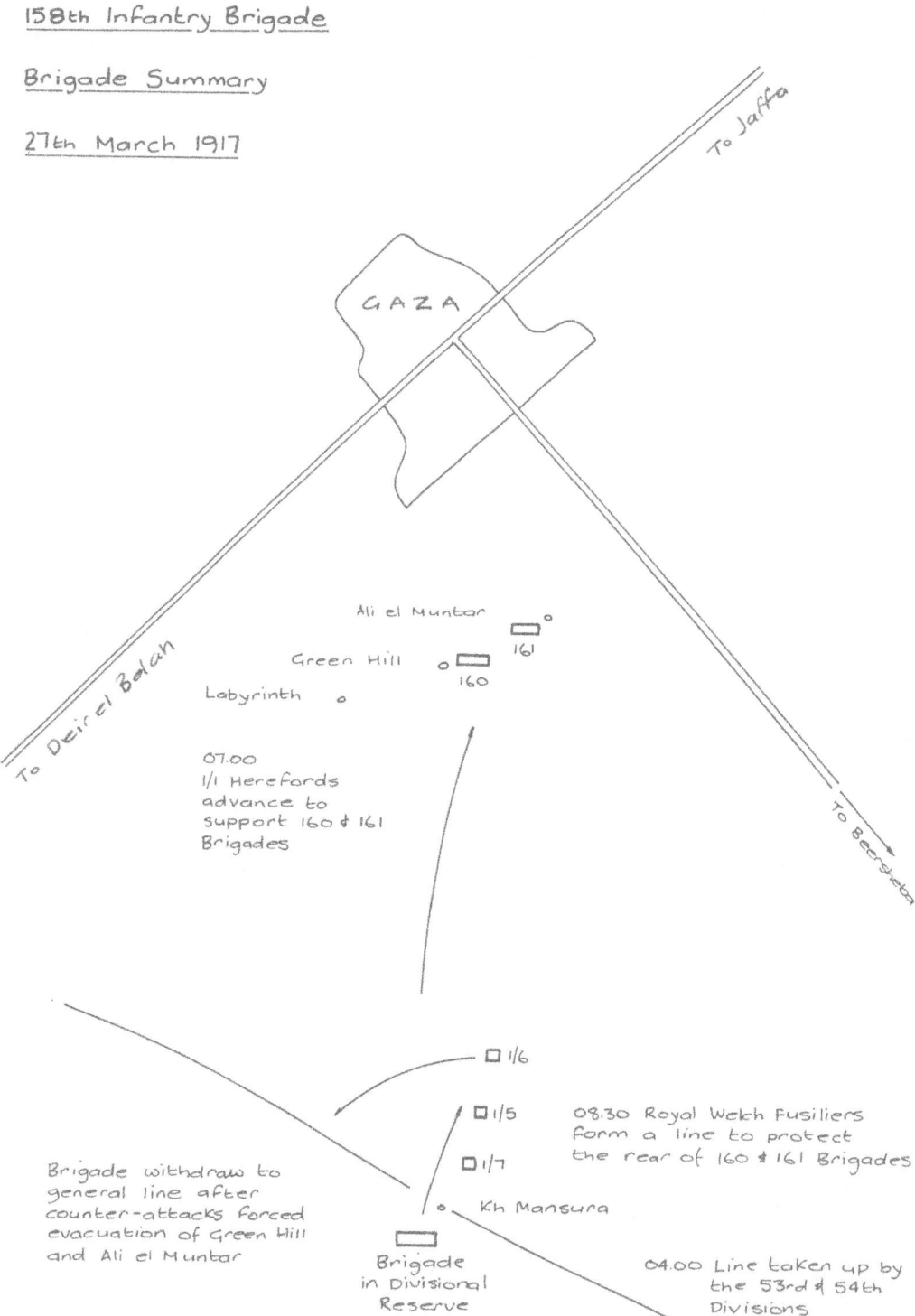

The Casualties

EIGHTEEN/199 OFFICERS AND MEN OF the 158th Brigade were killed in action at the First Battle of Gaza, and a further nine died of wounds during the following three weeks.

Private Joseph BUTLER was born at Greenfield, Flintshire and lived there until enlisting in the 5/Royal Welch Fusiliers. He was in the front line of B Company's attack and was killed aged twenty-four. Twenty-year old Private William EVANS, advancing on the left flank with A Company, was seriously wounded. He was evacuated to hospital at Deir el Belah where he died two days later. In the companies which followed the front line was a Portsmouth man, Private William WHEELER. He was killed with C Company, to leave a widow in Chester to mourn her husband, aged forty-nine. No trace was found of Private William DAVID who was both born and enlisted at Barry, Glamorgan and was killed in action aged eighteen.

With only twenty-two men killed in the two-day engagement, the 6/Royal Welch Fusiliers may have been considered fortunate. A full fortnight elapsed before Mrs Ellen Williams received notification that her husband had died of wounds in hospital at Deir el Belah. Thirty-year old Private John WILLIAMS left five children at home in Pwllheli, Caernarvonshire. Another thirty-year old was Private William WILLIAMS who, being lost without trace, was later commemorated on the Jerusalem Memorial. His spinster sister in Colwyn Bay, Denbighshire was left to mourn. Private Leonard BORASTON had been the senior reporter on the Wallasey News for several years before joining the Cheshire Regiment. After ten weeks training he was transferred to the Royal Welch Fusiliers and sent on active service to Egypt. He died on the 27th March of wounds received in action the previous day and was buried in the War Cemetery at Deir el Belah.

Although the 7/Royal Welch Fusiliers were well echeloned to the right of the attack, they nevertheless sustained the highest number of men killed for the brigade. Two men from the battalion's home town of Newtown, Montgomeryshire (Mont) were among them. Number 290097 Private Cecil DAVIES was twenty-three when killed along with his enlistment pal Private Richard LEWIS 290096, the latter's body never being found. Born and bred in Newtown they enlisted together and died together. One of the youngest men in the battalion to be killed in the attack was eighteen-year old Private David BENNETT. He was the son of William and Mary Bennett of Chapel House, Llandinam, Mont and was buried in Gaza War Cemetery. Welshpool, Mont was another town to lose several men on that fateful Monday. Mrs Margaret Morris lost her son, Mary Morris her husband, when forty-two-year-old Private James MORRIS was killed. Charles and Sarah Watkins had seen their son Joseph enlist as a Private in September 1914. Tempered by service at Gallipoli in August 1915 he was still only twenty-one when killed on the 26th March 1917.

Of the four battalions of the brigade, a further 38/605 were wounded in the two days of the battle on the 26/27 March.

158 Brigade additional narrative.

CAPTAIN WALKER'S ACCOUNT OF THE capture of Ali el Muntar is of particular interest

"He says he advanced with half a company on the right of the 6th Royal Welch Fusiliers, "overlapping with the 159th Brigade, and got on to the ridge running north-east and south-west. On obtaining this position, I found myself facing directly towards the Mosque. I therefore continued that advance in conjunction with the other half of the battalion and the 6th RWF on their left. I advanced very rapidly as the fire on this line of advance was very slight. I did not stop for any length of time till I was 800 yards from the enemy's position. I then called up supports; an officer of the 5th Welch Regiment then brought up two platoons. I then continued the advance to within 600 yards of the objective. Up to this time I had lost only one casualty, as I had drawn no machine gun fire. I lost Mr Thomas, wounded, who had given me great help in every way. I sent a written message to Captain Evans for supports; as a result Mr Westcombe succeeded in joining me. I here again began to suffer casualties, and signalled for further support. Two platoons of the 5th Welch Regiment came up on my right-the remaining two platoons of this company had already come up. I then signalled again and again for support and eventually sent a written message for support which was delivered to the Captain of the 4th Welch Regiment, all my own battalion supports being already up; no supports however came up.

I ordered the two platoons on my right to fix bayonets and move up on to the high ground on my right, where there were some sniper posts which appeared unoccupied, and so proved to be. This enabled me to move forward to within 200 yards of the position. I now sent back a written message to my CO stating that with the help of supports I was in a position to assault, and asking that bombardment be lifted. I afterwards learned that this message did not reach him. This was about 14.30, and I waited in hope of supports for about an hour.

This delay caused me many casualties, but we were not under machine gun fire. Mr Westcombe was hit during this time after excellent work. I was greatly helped by overhead machine gun fire from the ridge behind me, and by the Lewis gun with me, brought up by the 5th Welch Regiment. Mr Roberts from D Company here came over to me and I found that he was suffering more heavily than I was, and could obtain no support. All the supports of his own brigade behind him had come up. Apart from the machine gun in the gully, which I could plainly see firing to my left, there was extraordinarily little fire on our position. Just after this there was a direct hit on the machine gun in the gully, and the artillery bombardment seemed mostly on the foreside of the position. I saw Mr Robert, Mr Lastin and an officer of the 5th Welch Regiment and we assaulted. I was here separated from Mr Latham, who assaulted through the prickly pear hedge, while I went up the gulley to the machine gun, which, however, offered no resistance.

I then sent parties round, and turned out and collected about 20 Austrian and German prisoners, some of whom were officers, and about 12 Turks. Unfortunately, a second machine gun managed to get away into the trenches further to the left, from where it caused us several casualties. I reported capture of the hill, machine gun and prisoners to my CO in duplicate, but I learned that neither message reached him.

The time was, as far as I remember, 15.50, but I subsequently lost my note book. At this time, about five minutes after the capture of the hill, I was reinforced by a strong party of the 7th Cheshire's, under Colonel Lawrence, who then took command and consolidated the position.

History of the 53rd (Welsh) Division. Major Ward. Pages 81-82

53RD (WELSH) DIVISION
160TH INFANTRY BRIGADE
26 MARCH 1917

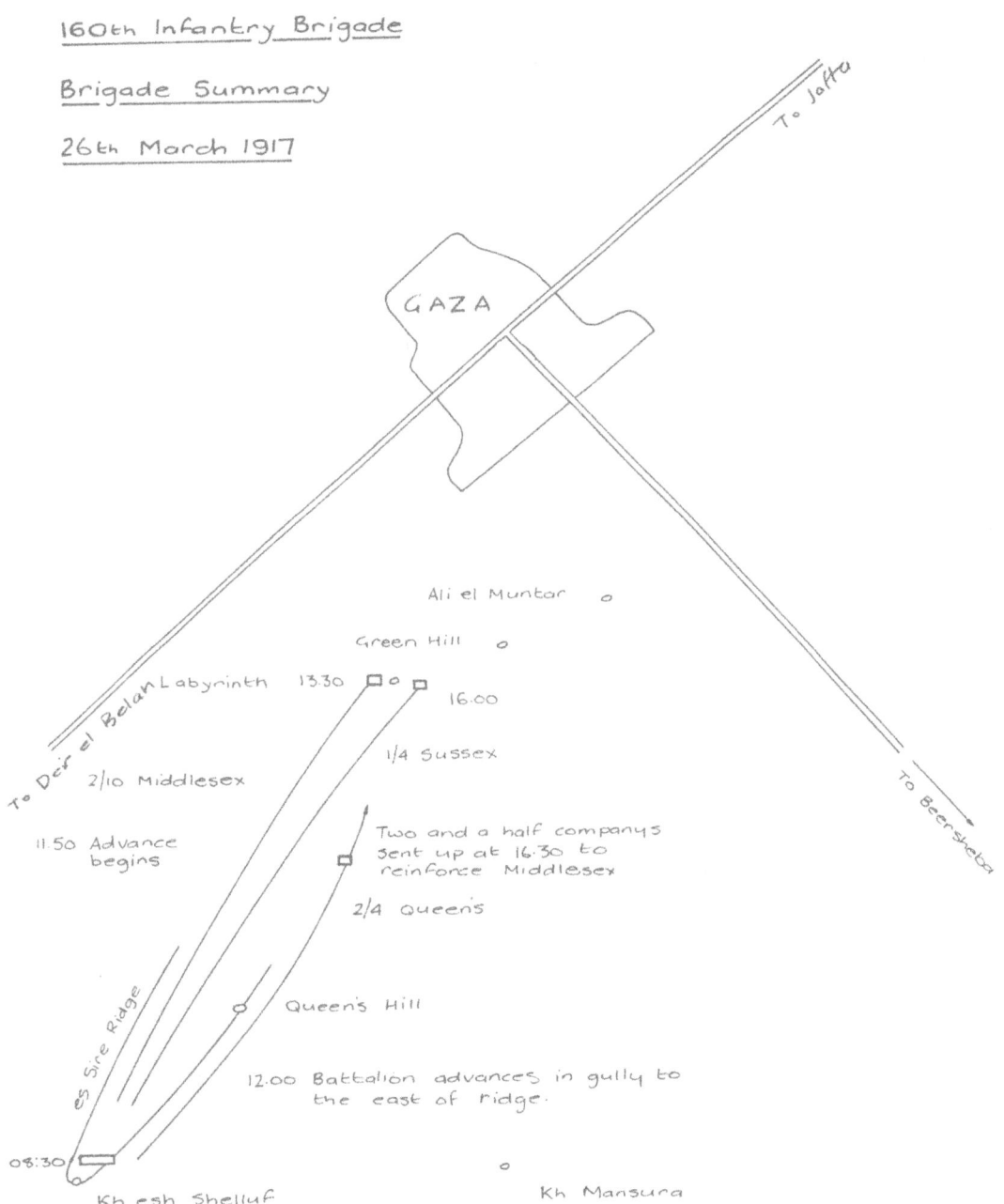

160 Brigade

HAVING BEGUN THE NARRATIVE OF 158 Brigade from the early hours of the 26 March, with the imminent attack dominating the minds of all involved the following description of the approach march is of interest here.

"On the morning of the 24th March, a mixed cavalcade cantered through the old frontier town of Khan Yunis, it was an advance party of British officers seeking out for their units hiding places in the shady fruit groves surrounding the town. It was our first real glimpse of the promised land. On all sides were groves of fig trees, mish-mish, olives and oranges, protected by high impenetrable hedges of prickly pear. On the north this green gem ends abruptly in a bright golden setting of sand-hills, beyond which lies the deep blue Mediterranean. An old crusader's fort raises its tower above the surrounding squalor of mud huts. As we clattered through the lane, for it was scarcely a road, running through the centre of the town, savage looking but stately Bedouins gaze at us with curious eyes, and no doubt spies on the roof tops took a more technical interest in our passing.

The orchards and groves on the Gaza side of Khan Yunis extend for over a mile, and the 53rd Division, moving forward to take up its allotted position, found concealment there from enemy aircraft. Colonel Sinclair Thompson, the GSO 1, pointed out to each officer the definite area for his unit. Roads had to be cut through the cactus hedges, and mud walls, and the troops moved in during the evening. The two mounted divisions were there, and that night the 54th Division marched into Rafah.

The next day, the 53rd Division moved on, late in the afternoon, to Deir el Belah. On the evening of March 25th, the Division left its hiding place amongst the fruit trees of Khan Yunis. Slowly we moved across the plain, columns of infantry, winding lines of artillery, ambulance-carts, camel transport and wagons. It was a beautiful evening with a blood-red sunset and strange but lovely colour effects. Soon the infantry were in thick yielding sand, plunging along, stumbling and cursing in the dark. At midnight we rested for two hours on a sand ridge, just above a tomato patch."

History of the 53rd (Welsh) Division. Major Ward. Pages 76

In accordance with orders received the previous evening, the 160th Brigade of the 53 (Welsh) Division left its bivouac at Deir el Belah. The night march was an uneventful one and the brigade began crossing the Wadi Ghuzze, only slightly behind schedule, at 03.45. The brigade consisted of only three battalions as the fourth, the 2/4 Royal West Kent Regiment, had been detailed to cover a diversionary manoeuvre along the sand-dunes on the far-left flank. Thus, it was the 4/Royal Sussex Regiment who led the 2/10 Middlesex Regiment and the 2/4 Queen's (Royal West Surrey) Regiment across the dry riverbed and onto the el Sire Ridge beyond. At this point, timed at approximately 04.30, the brigadiers of both 160 and 158 Brigades decided, in the absence of further orders to push patrols forward towards their respective destinations. The 160 Brigade continued its advance onto the el Sire Ridge and in doing so allowed Brigade HQ to be established on the south-western end of the rise. By 05.20 the leading battalion, the 4/Sussex, reported that they had occupied a prominent position on the ridge and were pushing patrols towards esh Shelluf; at 06.00 orders were received from General Dallas for the brigade to advance to esh Shelluf. One battalion, the 2/4 Queen's, was held at el Sire as Brigade Reserve. There were only two battalions which therefore reached esh Shelluf, the 4/Sussex at 07.55 and the 2/10 Middlesex about fifty minutes later.

At 08.00 the Divisional HQ was moved up to el Burjabye and it was about this time that the fog cleared. The Brigadier-General, Colonel WJC BUTLER, proceeded to a conference at Mansura to discuss the final details for the attack with the other senior officers. The brigade was later instructed to push troops towards Ali el Muntar to reconnoitre, reiterated at 11.00 and 11.20 and advising the troops to await artillery support where required. In spite of these reservations about an attack, the consideration of time had become an over-riding factor, and consequently at 11.30 orders were received by 160 Brigade HQ to attack the Labyrinth. The other two front-line battalions were to attack alongside one another, each on a two-company front; the limits of the assault were bounded by the mosque of Ali el Muntar on the right and a niche between two hillocks that appeared to be to the north of the mosque, on the left.

The 4/Sussex advanced on the right of the brigade front, and moved off at 11.50. Almost at once the enemy opened up with a heavy shell-fire onto the ridge and at 12.22 a message was sent to Divisional HQ to say that Ali el Muntar and Labyrinth appeared to be strongly held and artillery support was required. By this time the scouts of the 4/Sussex were within 1200 yards of the enemy trenches and were being fired upon. Shortly afterwards the same battalion captured the first enemy trench, the attack being pushed down through the next hollow to the crest beyond. Further progress was now limited by the enemy barrage and the Officer Commanding the Sussex, Lieutenant Colonel HS ASHWORTH, stopped the advance at this point.

The 2/10 Middlesex, to the left of the brigade attack, met with less opposition and were able to achieve lodgements in the enemy trenches to the left of the position by 13.00. By 13.30 the whole position at Labyrinth had been cleared by the battalion and a further advanced position on a grassy slope, which overlooked Gaza at 800 yards distant, was reached.

The Brigade Reserve battalion had meanwhile been ordered into the attack. The 2/4 Queen's began to advance at 12.00 and due to heavy shelling of the es Sire Ridge they continued forward in a gully to the east of the ridge. The battalion was able to progress to within 1300 yards of the enemy and were held at this point as support. Captain HERBERT of the 2/4 Queen's took command of the brigade at 14.30 as both the Brigade Major and Staff Captain had been wounded by a shell.

We shall now pause for a moment to consider the positions gained and the situations which faced the troops. The 2/10 Middlesex had achieved their objective in clearing the left of the Labyrinth and held high ground overlooking Gaza. The 4/Sussex had met with considerable opposition, being enfiladed by fire from Green Hill to the right as well as direct fire from the front. They had suffered heavy casualties, including Lieutenant Colonel Ashworth, killed, shortly after the halt, and were now held up. Finally, the Brigade Reserve of the 2/4 Queen's had been sent up and held a supporting line some 1300 yards from the enemy.

The heavy shelling of the front line had caused the 4/Sussex to fall back from their position at 15.30, taking up a stand on a ridge immediately to their rear. The advance of the battalion up to this point is graphically described by one of the officers.

"The ground is very rough, we rush some Turks out of a forward position at which we are machine-gunned heavily when we reach. We rush by sections over this and under heavy fire, to a gully on the other side. Sergeant Tribe is hit in this rush and I fall over, but get up and under cover safely. Here I saw the last of Tyrell-Green. Captain Weekes goes on and I follow with more men later. The line gets to a ridge about 400 yards from the Turks and I with Partridge and a number of men in a gully just behind. We are in a bad position; heavily shelled and under awful Machine-Gun and Rifle fire. About 2.15 I go into the firing line.

The position gets worse.

We are enfiladed by High-Explosive, shrapnel and machine-gun fire; many get killed and wounded including Tyrell-Green, Tappenden and the Colonel. We stay here for about an hour and it is hell. My platoon lose heavily. We are ordered to retire and retire back through trees and across the plain east of Gaza. We are shelled. I gather a party together and cross the ridge, where I meet Captain Gray, Johnson, Patching and about 70 men. The Colonel has been killed. We are shelled and so decide to move to our starting point at El Sire. Meet Paddon, all tired out and thirsty - no water, no rations."

Lieutenant PW Lovering 4/Sussex Regiment.
From an account held by the Imperial War Museum Documents 6696
By permission of IWM

At 16.00 the 2/4 Queen's reported a considerable number of wounded men were streaming back from the front line, men of the 4/Sussex, being shelled the whole time. One company from the reserve was sent up to reinforce the right flank which was then gallantly pushed to the attack, recapturing the hill just lost. This impetus was sufficient to enable the whole line to surge forward and the brigade objective was taken.

The new priority was now that of consolidation. At 16.30 two-and-a-half companies of the 2/4 Queens were sent up to help the 2/10 Middlesex in this work. The remainder of the reserve battalion did not have an easy time or escape lightly however.

"The enemy heavily shelled with HE [High Explosive] *every ridge and nullah in the neighbourhood. Numerous casualties occurred at this time. Several heavy HE shells burst within ten yards of the three machine-guns and the position held by the Queen's, covering everyone with gas fumes and fragments of earth and shell."*

2/4 Queen's War Diary. PRO WO95/4631

As darkness fell, at around 18.00, desperately needed supplies of water and Small-Arms Ammunition (SAA) were despatched to the firing line. This work fell to the reserve battalion and the first party carried up eleven fanatis and ten thousand rounds across the broken ground in the dark.

About this time contact was made with the 4/Essex Regiment who, along with the rest of the 161 Brigade, had captured Green Hill. This meant that the right flank of the 160 Brigade was no longer open. The left flank however was still being subjected to a hot fire from concealed enemy positions amongst the cultivated areas to the north-west. So damaging was this fire that at 19.00 the flank was necessarily thrown back, with the Officer Commanding the 2/10 Middlesex advising Brigade HQ that the position was untenable unless reinforcements were sent up.

At 19.20 the 4/Sussex were relieved by men of the Essex Regiment, and were then able to fall back and take the opportunity to reorganise. Consolidation and support work continued throughout the evening, being an especially arduous task at the end of a period of eighteen hours marching and heavy fighting.

At 23.00 orders were received from Divisional HQ for the whole division to withdraw to a line extending from Tel el Ujul on the left, through a point one mile north of esh Shelluf and then across to Mansura and Sheikh Abbas. This required the 160 Brigade to withdraw their front to cover the section from esh Shelluf to Mansura. In the same way that supply and reinforcement had been difficult due to the widely disposed troops, the passing of orders for the withdrawal was necessarily as difficult a task. In fact, one party of the 2/4 Queen's arrived at the front line with further supplies of water and SAA around midnight only to find that it had been evacuated! It was thus a somewhat disorganised withdrawal that took place between the receipt of orders and about 04.30. The 4/Sussex and 2/10 Middlesex took up outpost positions around esh Shelluf. The order to withdraw, in the form of an untimed message, was not received by the Officer Commanding the 2/4 Queen's until 05.30, further illustrating the problems of communication.

The respite afforded to the brigade was however to be a very short affair. Orders were received at 06.00 for strong patrols to be pushed forward and reconnoitre the positions so recently evacuated with a view to reoccupying the same. Accordingly, the 2/10 Middlesex were despatched.

This return to the offensive was carried out with the 161 Brigade moving up on the right to the positions at Ali el Muntar, Green Hill and the Labyrinth. By 08.15 the latter position was reoccupied by the troops of the Essex Brigade and at this time the 2/4 Queens were ordered to move up and consolidate the position to their left. The 2/4 Queen's moved off and crossed a deep nullah to the north of esh Shelluf and were clear of it by 09.30; continuing to advance across the broken country the battalion picked up the outpost men as they went. To the north and north-east the troops of the 2/10 Middlesex and 161 Brigade could be clearly seen advancing on the enemy positions. Shortly afterwards however, that attack came to a halt and the troops were soon forced to retreat under a heavy fire. The 2/4 Queen's held their line and lay down as the retiring troops passed through them.

The morning then alternated between short advances by isolated platoons and companies, to retirements by whole sections of the line. Desperate company commanders urged their men on as they dug in, often on completely exposed positions then led them forward as opportunities arose. The whole time the area was subjected to an intense shrapnel and high-explosive fire from the enemy to the north-west; the fire was highly accurate and "methodically searched" along the areas held by the harassed troops. One of the officers who took part in the morning's advance gives an insight into the exhaustion and confusion.

53RD (WELSH) DIVISION
160TH INFANTRY BRIGADE
27 MARCH 1917

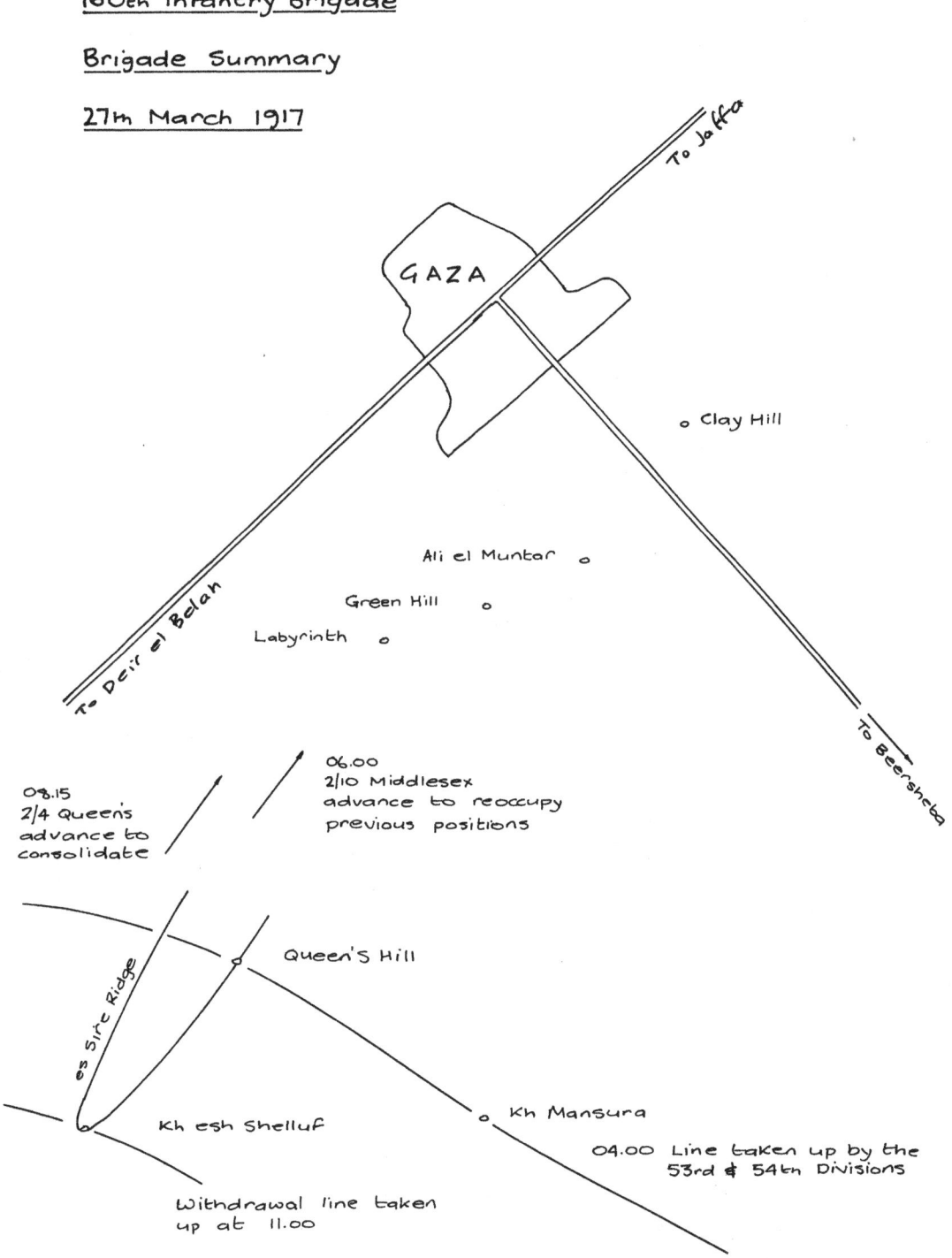

"We rise at daybreak. Weekes, Gray, Warren, Johnson, Patching, Read, Paddon, Partridge, Major Goodman, Major Beale, Peskett turn up. We reorganise, eat and get a little water (one bottle between six men). We move forward not knowing what we are to do and everybody is <u>done.</u> The Turks counter-attack and reinforcements are trying to get in on the right from Beersheba. We dig in and get a little water which saves us."

Lieutenant PW Lovering 4/Sussex.
From an account held by the Imperial War Museum Documents 6696
By permission of IWM

By 11.00 it had become clear to General Dallas that the forward positions of the 53 Division, along with the 161 Brigade, were too far forward to be safely held. Consequently, orders were issued for a withdrawal to a line facing NNW from esh Shelluf. The 2/4 Queen's, with the 2/10 Middlesex to their right, were to take position on a ridge to the rear of 161 Brigade and thus cover the left flank of that brigade.

"The heat during this period was intense; the men suffered severely from the want of water and there were numerous casualties."

2/4 Queen's War Diary. PRO WO95/4631

Late in the morning, Brigadier General G DAWNAY of the General Staff at Eastern Force Headquarters, telephoned General Dallas to see if the positions occupied by the 53 and 54 Divisions could be held for three or four days. It was felt that unless the pressure from the enemy batteries on Sheikh Abbas could be relieved, defence of the present positions would be difficult. General Dobell then had to make a decision as to the future course of action. The enemy at Sheikh Abbas were inflicting steady losses and were causing considerable disruption to the supply lines from the Wadi Ghuzze. The 52 (Lowland) Division could be sent up from In Seirat to attack this position but the reorganisation of supply lines would take time; all the while the troops of the 53 and 54 Divisions would continue to be under fire from both front line and rear with no cover whatsoever. Water supply to the front-line troops, difficult at the best of times, would become a major problem in the intense heat and with the constant bombardment from Sheikh Abbas. After consulting General Sir Archibald Murray, General Dobell therefore concluded that the fight would have to be broken off. Orders were issued by telephone at 16.30, later confirmed in writing, that both divisions should be withdrawn to the left bank of the Wadi Ghuzze.

On receipt of these orders, General Dallas accordingly directed that retirement should begin at 19.00, cover being provided by 158 and 163 Brigades. Once again, the relaying of this order to all the troops in the field proved a difficult task, so much so that the 2/4 Queen's were still moving forwards, to retake ground previously held, as late as 21.00. On the whole though, the retirement was unhindered and was completed by about 04.00 on 28 March. The brigade took up an outpost line near Sheikh Rashid the 2/10 Middlesex being on the left and in touch with the 159 Brigade and supported by one Machine-Gun Company. The 2/4 Royal West Kents, back with the brigade after having operated under Colonel Money on the left flank, were in the centre, also with one Machine-Gun Company, with the 4/Sussex to the right with machine-guns. The 2/4 Queen's with the remainder of 160 Brigade MG Company was in reserve with Brigade HQ at Sheikh Rashid.

With no immediate prospect of resumption in the attack, there was now a chance for the brigade to rest. Many men used the opportunity to write home to tell their families that despite the inevitable casualty lists they, at least, were safe. The following letter was written on the 3 April and, in a few sentences, captures much of the atmosphere of the day.

By the time you get this letter you will no doubt have heard that we have been in action and, I regret to say, lost heavily. I was in the third line of advance and although we never had many fellows hit, the bullets were whizzing past my head and throwing the dust up all around us. Shrapnel and High Explosive shells were bursting about every fifteen yards and it was simply a miracle that not many fellows were hit, although our CSM was nearly the first chap of our company to get hit, being shot in the stomach.

We still kept advancing and it was a lovely sight to see the lads under that terrible hail of lead carrying on just as if they had been on a field day and with our bayonets fixed we drove the Turks off the ridges where they retired into their redoubt which was very strongly built and also very strongly held.

The ridge which we captured about 12.30pm in the afternoon we held until 3.30 pm. They were popping away at us by thousands whilst several shells burst close to where I was lying, smothering me in dust and one piece of spent shrapnel dropped about an inch from my arm whilst another piece hit the back of my helmet.

One of our worst enemies was the lack of water, our lips were all cracking and our tongues were parched as it was terribly hot but the crying and groaning of the wounded and dying was awful.

Our Officers were splendid and their casualties were eighteen including our brave and gallant Colonel who was killed not more than fifteen yards from where I was lying, whilst I was expecting every minute to be my last.

Please, dearest ones will you all pray to God to thank Him for his gracious mercy in preserving and delivering me out of that terrible battle on March 26th and 27th. I can honestly say that whilst I was on that ridge under that terrible fire I offered up to God a little prayer and He has kept me safe and sound."

Private RH SIMMS 4/Sussex Regiment.

From an account held by the Imperial War Museum.

By permission of IWM

The Artillery Action on the 26 and 27 March.

THE ARTILLERY SUPPORT FOR THE attack was provided by four brigades of the Royal Field Artillery [RFA]. With three batteries each, 265 and 266 were to primarily support the attacking battalions of the 53rd Division, while 270 and 271 were attached to 54 Division. Each of the Field Artillery Brigades comprised three batteries, A and B being equipped with 18-pounder guns, while C Battery was the Howitzer battery with 4.5" Howitzers.

On the morning of the 26th, the headquarters of the artillery was moved up to EL BURJALIYE at around 08.30 and by 10.30 had been pushed forward to MANSURA. Up to this point the infantry advance had been without opposition and no artillery support had therefore been called for.

The 265 Brigade was moved along the EL SIRE Ridge with orders to support the advance of the 160 Infantry Brigade. This was due to begin at 12.30 with the objectives of Middlesex Hill, Labyrinth and Green Hill to be attacked before the final assault on Ali el Muntar. However, due to pressure from General Chetwode of the Desert Column, this was brought forward to 11.30.

Forward Observation Officers [FOO] were sent up as follows;

Lieutenant CULLIMORE   A/265 Battery
2/Lieutenant BARTON   B/265 Battery
2/Lieutenant MATTHEWS C/265 Battery

It was not until 12.30 that the first rounds were fired however, the exhausting job of getting the batteries into position having taken close to the original estimate given at 10.10. According to the war diary of the 265 Brigade, targets were selected by the FOO's and were as varied as cactus hedges, the mosque on Ali el Muntar and the red-roofed houses, at ranges of between 3800 and 6000 yards. (No further written orders were received from Artillery Headquarters until the early hours of the 27th). This fire was maintained through the afternoon with advances by the infantry noted but followed by retirements around 16.00. At 18.10 all batteries were ordered to cease firing and the diary notes the following ammunition expended;

A/265	470 rounds of Shrapnel	38 rounds of High Explosive
B/265	432 " "	177 " " "
C/265	96 " "	298 " " "

The second brigade, 266 RFA, operated in much the same fashion, but although the bombardment was to primarily cover the attack of 158 Infantry Brigade, it would also have responsibility for the 159 Infantry Brigade. During the infantry withdrawal in the late afternoon, the barrage was directed on the reverse slopes of Ali el Muntar and Green Hill to give the maximum chance for the men to get away. A total of 190 rounds were fired during the operations on the 26th and 1/7 casualties were sustained, all wounded.

Artillery Action on 26th March 1917
270 AND 271 BRIGADES RFA

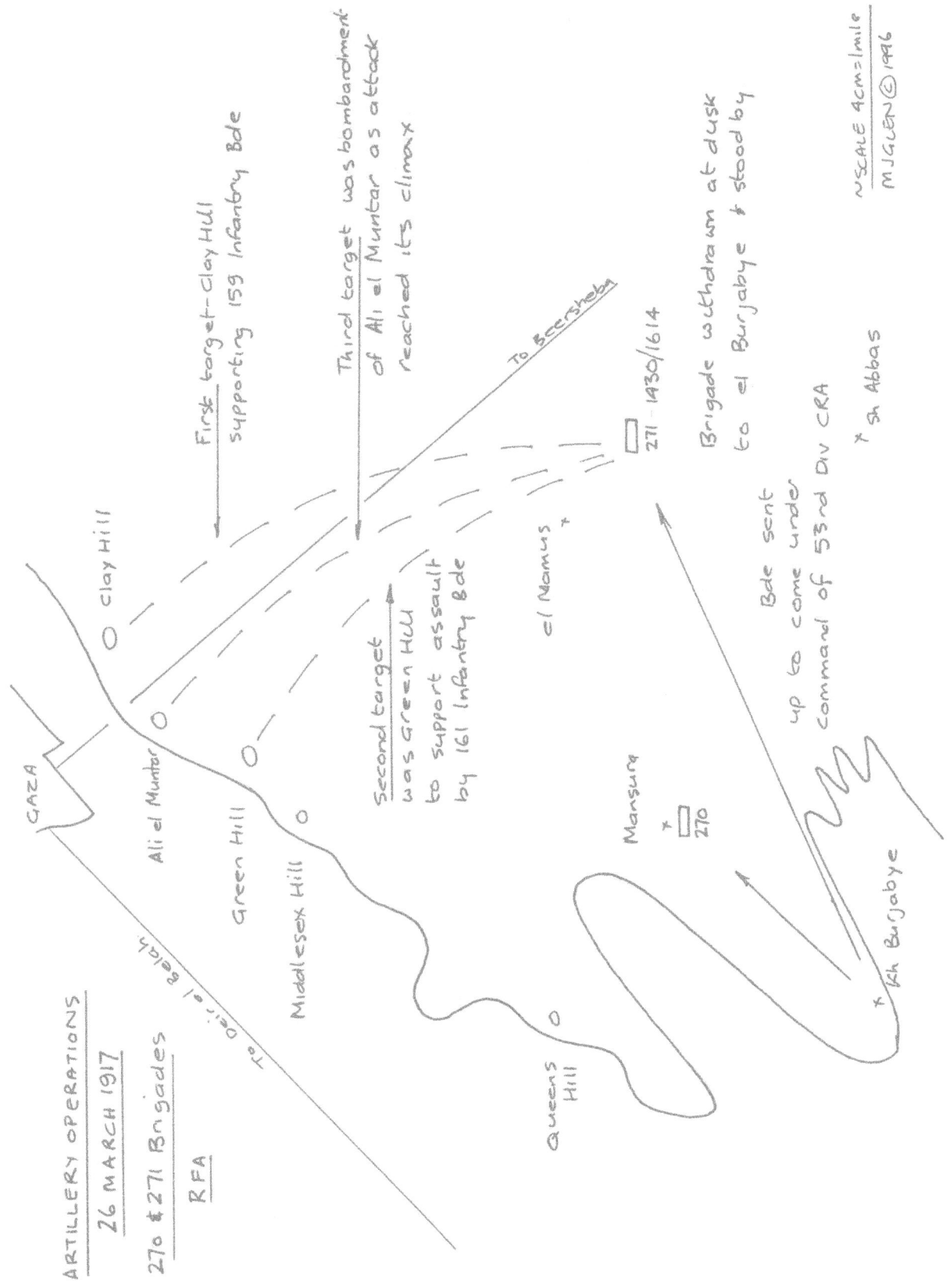

Artillery Action on 27th March 1917
270 AND 271 BRIGADES RFA

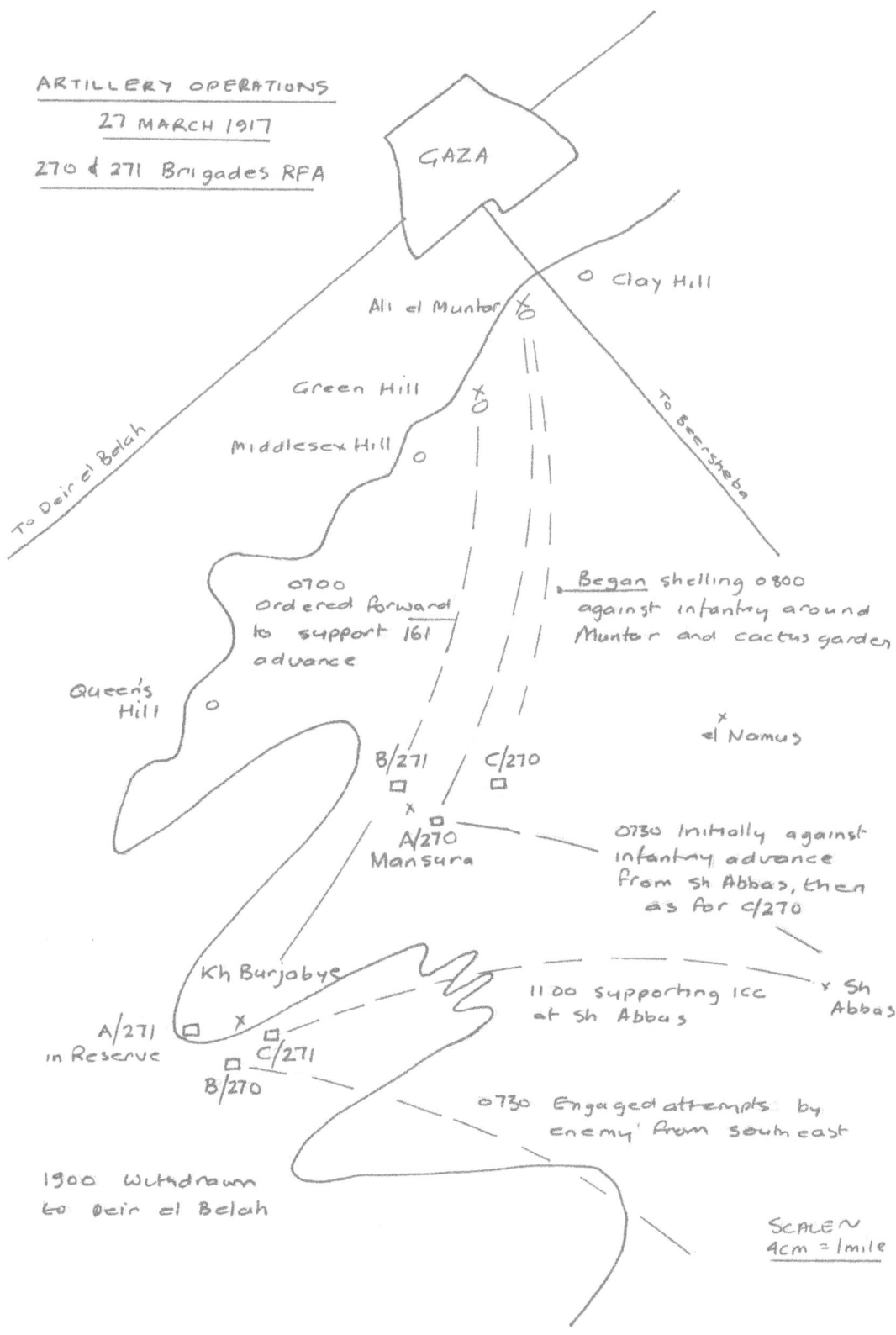

Artillery Support by 265 Brigade, Royal Field Artillery on 26 March 1917.

For the first three hours of the battle artillery support had not been good. Colonel Rome (6th RWF) had sent repeated messages for artillery support against the crest of Ali Muntar, and comments that "the artillery was very slow indeed in picking up targets, and it is suggested in future that a Forward Observation Officer in direct communication with his battery is sent with each battalion commander".

The 266th RFA Brigade at Mansura, and the 265th between the el Sire and Tel el Ahmar ridges, had commenced to fire about mid-day, while on the banks of the Wadi Ghuzze one section of the 10th Heavy Battery was in action at the end of the el Sire Ridge, and the other near the Gaza-Rafa Road. Their task it must be admitted was not easy. Because of difficulties of ammunition supply, only the Cheshire Brigade (265) and the 4th Welsh Brigade (266) were brought up to support the attack of the three infantry brigades, and the dispositions were such that the 266th had to support two infantry brigades in line. There was no pre-arranged plan beyond that "the mass of the artillery will be employed in enfilading the enemy's work, which face south-east and east of Ali Muntar, which it is intended to attack"; enemy positions which were unknown.

The 265th RFA Brigade had crossed the Wadi Ghuzze in rear of the 160th Infantry Brigade. Their instructions were that they would have to work through divisional headquarters, but they do not seem to have done so; they had officers forward, and were in communication with the infantry Brigade Headquarters; they had no further orders from or communication with divisional headquarters, or the CRA [Commander Royal Artillery]. Captain Barton, acting as Forward Observation Officer for B/265, says there was a shortage of telephone cable. "I reported to Colonel Pearson (Middlesex) and when the order to advance was given, followed the battalion laying my cable and pausing from time to time to send information to the battery which was shelling the Labyrinth. For a time all went well; then I found myself at the end of my cable and no reserve to call for. We tried running out an extension by means of an enamelled wire, about the thickness of stout thread and about as much use. Finally I went on ahead of the telephonist and signalled back to him, but the difficulty of getting orders through in time to be effective by this means will be easily understood. During the battle my battery occupied no less than six different positions, lying far apart, and in exceptionally difficult country. Getting guns round or across the numerous wadis was the devil of a job. They expended 1,511 rounds during the day.

The 266th RFA Brigade had the more difficult task, with two brigades of infantry deployed in front of them. Perhaps it was for this reason that General Dallas "gave personal instruction to the BGC (Mott) that the artillery support would be under Divisional control, and that all requirements were to be made to Divisional Headquarters through brigade". On the other hand the diary of the Divisional Artillery Headquarters states that "time did not admit of any detailed programme. All that could be done was to trust to information from the F.O.O.s to bombard whatever parts of the enemy's works were holding up the infantry's advance. Neither the full extent of the enemy's line, nor his flanks had been accurately located". The complaint of all Commanding Officers of the 158th and 159th Infantry Brigades was, however, that the F.O.O.s were conspicuous by their absence and it is not to be wondered at, with seven battalions in line. [author's boldening] It seems as though all information came from the infantry through brigade, and so to the artillery. The diary complains that "during the whole afternoon conflicting reports as to the position of our infantry were received." Owing to this fact, and the fact that the amount of equipment available for communication between Divisional Artillery Headquarters and units was altogether insufficient, and to there being no accurate maps on a fairly large scale, it was very difficult to keep units informed of the situation.

The Divisional Signal Company declare that they laid cables to four infantry brigades, two artillery brigades, and divisional ammunition column. Be that as it may, the 159th Infantry Brigade had no artillery officers forward, and were much hampered by the lack of support at critical moments.

History of the 53rd (Welsh) Division. Major Ward. Pages 76

The Casualties

Seven/65 Officers and men of the 160 Brigade, mainly of the three battalions, were killed in action at the First Battle of Gaza, and a further 1/6 died of wounds in the following three weeks.

Of the fatalities sustained by the 4/Sussex all but four were killed in action on the first day. In the front line of the attack on the Labyrinth was twenty-year-old Private John IZZARD, of Ifield, Sussex. He was with A Company on the left of the battalion attack and was lost without trace. Also in the front line, but on the right with B Company, was Lance Corporal George HARMSWORTH aged twenty-three. Born at Chittoe, Wiltshire his parents moved to Northampton to run the Dairy at Althorp Park; he too was lost without trace. Although any battalion would have had a number of eighteen and nineteen-year olds among its ranks, many of those with the 4/Sussex were killed that day. Private Ernest CROOK, Private Victor CHAMP, Private Ernest POTTER all eighteen; Private Charles ORTON, Private Alfred DAWS, Private Percy BURGESS were but a year older. The list goes on, but more than just names, for each was a son to parents from all parts of Sussex. The part played in the advance by Sergeant Frank TRIBE has been noted. He joined the Territorials before the war and on mobilisation was forced to give up his business as a blacksmith and wheelwright at Stedham, Sussex. Following service at Suvla Bay, Gallipoli his time as a Territorial had expired but he re-enlisted and was sent to Egypt from where he met his death.

Of the 22/333 Officers and men wounded, nearly half of them were from the 4/Sussex, the accounts of Lovering and Simms bearing this out.

Although he had been born at Coventry, Warwickshire Private Algernon HORSWILL enlisted at Chelsea, Middlesex in the 2/10 Middlesex. His parents learned of the death of their only son, aged twenty-five, at Gaza, never being able even to see a grave for he was lost without trace. No 291292 Private Arthur COOTE was born at Whitechapel, Middlesex, while No 291287 Private George SALMON was born south of the river at Kew, Surrey. They were drawn together by the war, enlisting at the same time at Stamford Brook, Middlesex. Both were killed in action on 26 March and are commemorated on the Jerusalem Memorial, neither of their bodies ever being found. For whatever reason, many men enlisted in the Army under false names, often using a middle name of their surname or, conversely, retaining the surname when adding another. Private William HERBERT was only twenty when killed at Gaza and was probably under age when he joined the 2/4 Queen's using the name ALLEN. He trained as a Lewis Gunner and was with A Company's Lewis Gun Section when the battalion advanced along the southern slopes of the el Sire Ridge. Although his body was never recovered, it is believed he was wounded and died in the field. He was the only child of Susannah Herbert of Victoria Road who was thus left alone, as her husband William had died previously.

53RD (WELSH) DIVISION
159TH INFANTRY BRIGADE
26 MARCH 1917

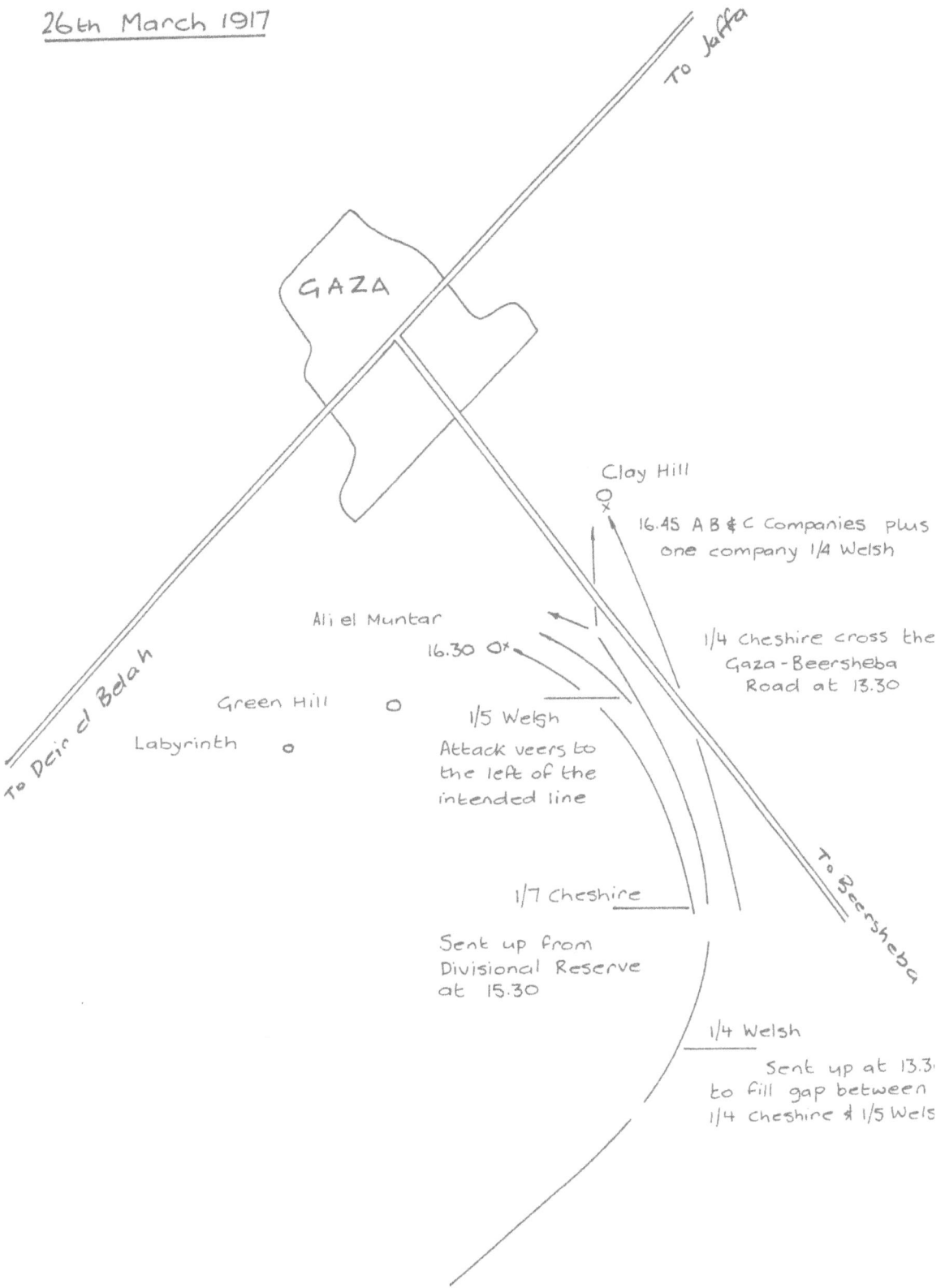

53RD (WELSH) DIVISION
159TH INFANTRY BRIGADE
27 MARCH 1917

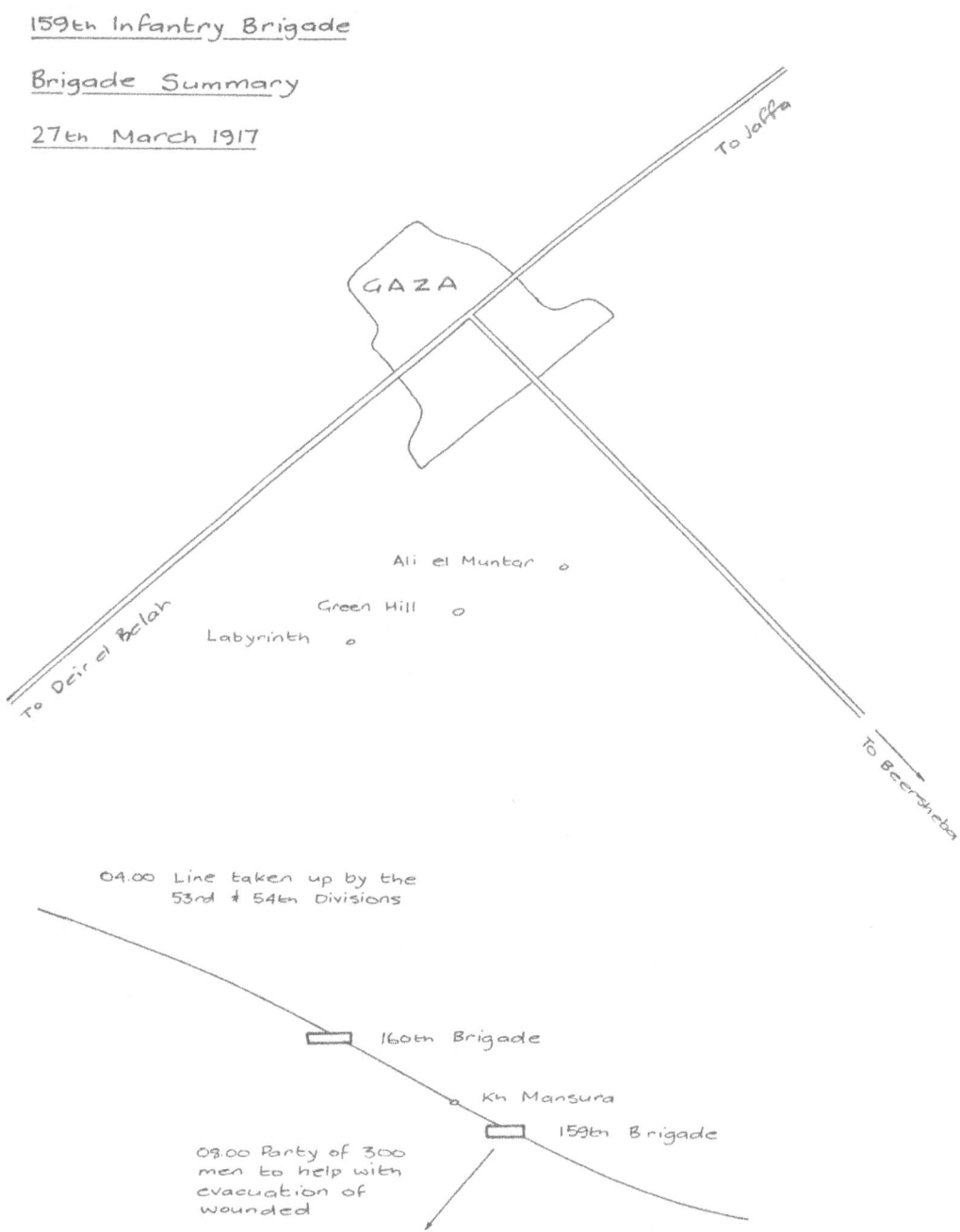

159 Brigade

THE DIVISIONAL OPERATION ORDER FOR the 26 March, 1917 detailed the 159th Brigade as support, primarily to the 158 Brigade attack on the south-east approach to Ali el Muntar. The brigade left its bivouac at Deir el Belah at 02.45, having had to wait for the160 Brigade to clear first of all, and marched via el Breij to the Wadi Ghuzze. Brigade Headquarters was established at the crossing, and communication was opened with both 53 Division Head Quarters [HQ] and the 158 Brigade by telephone. At 05.40 Brigadier General JH DuB Travers Commanding Officer [CO] of 159 Brigade asked for further orders but was advised to stay in position on the Wadi Ghuzze until ordered to move. Thirty minutes later information was received from Brigadier General SF Mott, CO 158 Brigade, that he had reached el Burjabye unopposed and that 160 Brigade was at el Sire. The 159 Brigade remained in position, the request for further orders was repeated at 08.25 but the answer was as before.

The waiting ended at 09.30 when the brigade was ordered forward to Mansura to support 158 Brigade. The General Officer Commanding 53 Division, Major General Dallas, was now at Mansura and the Brigadier Generals were to meet him to discuss the final preparations for the attack. The meeting took place at 10.10 and the 159 Brigade was allotted to the right of the 158 Brigade in the attack on Ali el Muntar from the southeast. Not having received orders to move up until late, Brigadier General Travers advised the meeting that he would not be in position for about one and a half hours, thus 12.00 at the earliest.

The attack was set for 12.30 - 13.00.

As we have seen however, anxieties over the lateness of the infantry attack were expressed by the commanders of the two cavalry divisions during the morning. Consequently, at 11.50, Brigade HQ received the order to attack.

Arriving at the starting point some forty minutes late, after their four-mile march across the broken ground, the men of the brigade could see the Welsh Territorials of the 158 Brigade moving across the open plain towards Ali el Muntar. The attacking orders had not detailed brigade responsibilities, and so it was on the move that the Brigadiers Generals mutually agreed a plan. Brigadier General Travers felt that the position was too strong to be taken by a single brigade and so the 159 Brigade would extend the front to the right, coming under his direct command.

The ridge on which Ali el Muntar stood continued northeast to a position, just over the Gaza - Beersheba Road, known as Clay Hill. The brigade was to take this hill then work back along the ridge, thereby assisting the attack on Ali el Muntar itself by the 158 Brigade.

The 4/Cheshire Regiment was to be on the right of the brigade front with the 5/Welsh Regiment on the left and in contact with 158 Brigade. The 4/Welsh Regiment was to follow as brigade support, while the remaining battalion, the 7/Cheshire Regiment, would stay at Mansura as Divisional Reserve. A section of machine-guns was attached to each of the front-line battalions, the other two sections being held in reserve.

Marching rapidly across the rear of the developing attack, the 159 Brigade extended and then wheeled left to face the objective. The 5/Welsh and 4/Cheshire's were to each attack on a two-company front; the second line was to follow at 400 yards. Frontage of the companies was 200 yards, which gave a total attack frontage of 800 yards.

At 13.00 the advancing troops were met with shrapnel fire from the left on Ali el Muntar, but very few casualties occurred up to this point. Pressing on, a ridge some 1200 yards was reached about half an hour later. The attack now came under very heavy rifle and machine-gun fire and casualties began, including the CO of the 5/Welsh, Lieutenant Colonel Bowen. Due to the intense fire, the 5/Welsh had been drawn to the left, towards Ali el Muntar, and a large gap had appeared between them and the 4/Cheshire's. Consequently, at 13.30 the 4/Welsh were sent up from brigade support to fill the void, one platoon being retained to carry up ammunition. This reinforcement was not, however, enough to carry the attack. The advance was now held up and the Commanding Officers of both 158 and 159 Brigades again conferred to consider the next move.

Private Victor MANSELL of the 1/5th Welsh took part in this attack and his experience was to irrevocably colour his life. His son takes up the narrative.

"He told me of the "terrible pasting" they had at Gaza on the 26 March. Countless times he'd mention little Danny BEYNON from Tylorstown, a particular pal of his, who fell at his side from a machine gun burst. They had been told they must not stop on any account, but had to keep going on. I don't think he ever forgot not being able to stop for his pal.

...Recently I got the Commonwealth War Graves Memorial Register and the first name I looked up was little Danny Beynon whose name I had heard so many times. We were three boys and if we were complaining about anything we'd hear the same old thing. You boys don't know you are born. Poor little Danny Beynon, not much older or bigger than you are, was cut in half by a Turkish machine gun, you've got nothing to moan about."

Letter to the author 1984

The casualties and situation of the troops in the frontal attack on Ali el Muntar bore ample witness that it was strongly held. The decision to push the right flank from Clay Hill, which appeared to offer less resistance, and then to advance along the ridge now took on greater significance. The main responsibility for this attack fell to the 4/Cheshire's, who moved steadily forward from about 13.30 onwards. Artillery support was very weak as the brigade battery was at Mansura; the range was therefore long and communication with it most difficult.

"It must be remembered that the Maps in our possession were not very accurate and there was the greatest difficulty in explaining exactly where artillery support was required."

159 Brigade HQ War Diary. PRO WO95/4628

Simultaneously with this advance, the men on the ridge to the southeast of Ali el Muntar were reorganised for the final assault. This group consisted of the 4/Welsh and 5/Welsh and was strengthened by D Company 4/Cheshire's, detailed from the left of their battalion's advance.

"13.45. It was now reported to 53rd Division HQ that all reserves were in.
The battle was now being fought out in grim earnest."

159 Brigade HQ War Diary. PRO WO95/4628

As the fight continued, valuable support was performed by the various sections of the Machine Gun Companies. One section under Lieutenant CS SPENCE attached to the 4/Cheshire's, and another under Second Lieutenant PR EVANS with the 5/Welsh, "managed to push on and with great initiative reached the ridge which was the objective." From here Lieutenant Spence engaged an enemy battery at 1000 yards and succeeded in silencing it.

At 15.30 came two events of crucial importance to the fortunes of the brigade. Firstly, with the arrival of the 161 Brigade at Mansura, the Divisional Reserve of the 7/Cheshire Regiment was placed at the disposal of the GOC 159 Brigade. They were immediately sent up to support the 5/Welsh who were still meeting fierce opposition.

The second event was the message received at 15.52 by Brigade HQ to say that 271 Brigade RFA had been ordered up to support the right flank. This brigade opened fire at 16.14 and was immediately successful in silencing the enemy machine-guns on Clay Hill; it was later found that a direct hit had destroyed one of the guns.

"Had this brigade (271 RFA) arrived an hour before it is not too much to say that the two brigades attacking the position would have been saved many casualties"

159 Brigade HQ War Diary. PRO WO95/4628

The turning point of the battle had been reached.
The north-east edge of the Ali el Muntar position was reached by a mixed force composed mainly

of the 4/ and 5/Welsh, together with one company of the 7/Cheshire's and D Company 4/Cheshire's who had been diverted left as previously described. With the 158 Brigade to the left of the brigade, the outlying portions of the citadel on Ali el Muntar were stormed at 16.30.

> "To Headquarters, 159 Infantry Brigade.
> 26 March
> We captured Citadel (Conical Shaped Hill) at 16.30 also the trenches immediately NE. AAA. Our Artillery is now causing many casualties it is an HE Battery I think. Can you communicate at once to Division AAA
> From O/C 1/7 Cheshire Regiment
> 17.15 By Runner Private Webb 1/7th Cheshire Regiment.
> 7/Cheshire War Diary. PRO WO95/4630

Simultaneously with this advance, the enemy position on Clay Hill, successfully bombarded by the 271 Brigade RFA, was assaulted. Three companies of the 4/Cheshire's attacked from the south-east, while the southern slopes were taken by one company of the 4/Welsh, the whole position being over-run by 16.45.

As with the other brigades, steps were at once taken to consolidate the ground won. The 4/Cheshire's, with a section of machine-guns, took up a position facing north-west and north-east on Clay Hill. The ridge between this hill and Ali el Muntar, known as Delilah's Neck, was held by men of the 4/ and 5/ Welsh, supported by two sections of machine-guns. This was the extent of the achievements as seen by Brigade HQ in position between Mansura and Ali el Muntar. Information to say that the cactus hedges to the south-east of Ali el Muntar and outlying parts of the citadel had been captured was not received until 18.15. This was immediately passed by telegraph to 53 Division HQ. Communications had been good until this point but wires failed and a joint line used by the 4/ and 5/Welsh became faulty.

It was about this time, 18.00, that the possibility of withdrawal was first heard; Brigade HQ received a message to this effect. The feeling at Brigade HQ was that this would be a move to be avoided if at all possible, as the men would be very disappointed to give up the hard-won gains of the day. It was for this reason that no hint of the message was conveyed to the battalions at this stage.

However, at 21.30 definite orders were received to withdraw all troops to Mansura, subsequently confirmed by telegram. As with other brigades, the process of communicating these orders to the widely dispersed companies was a long and tedious one. Consequently, the actual withdrawal did not start until midnight. The 4/Cheshire's and 4/Welsh Regiments on Clay Hill came away first and then the men, of all battalions, on the ridge north-east of Ali el Muntar. Finally, the party of some 200 men under Captain IRWIN of the 7/Cheshire's who had taken the outskirts of the citadel, took up the rear.

The march was a very slow affair, as machine-guns, Lewis guns and ammunition had to be brought in. Coupled with the task of carrying in the many wounded it was a trying time at the end of an exhausting twenty-four hours. Mansura was reached at about 03.30 by the first troops and the withdrawal was completed about an hour later.

So great was the number of wounded that at 08.00 on the morning of the 27th the brigade was asked for a party of 300 men to help carry away the injured from the positions near brigade head-quarters to the Wadi Ghuzze. This work was carried out under a heavy shell-fire, with many wounded having to walk due to the shortage of sand-carts and camels.

During the early morning, moves were made by both 161 and 160 Brigades to reoccupy the positions abandoned during the night. While this took place, the 159 Brigade took up an outpost line between 158 Brigade on the left and 163 Brigade on the right, and facing south-east. Only two battalions, the 4/Welsh and the 7/Cheshire, were actually in the line, left and right respectively; the 4/Cheshire was in Brigade Reserve while the 5/Welsh were detailed Divisional Reserve. Brigade HQ was east of Tel el Ahmar, and at 11.30 received a message to say that 53 Division HQ was moving to Burjabye. Heavy shelling continued intermittently throughout the early afternoon and no part of the brigade was ordered to advance.

At 17.30 Brigade HQ received a combined 53 and 54 Divisional Order for the withdrawal of all troops across the Wadi Ghuzze. The first stage was to commence at 21.00 and would be the Royal Field Artillery

Brigades, Field Companies Royal Engineers, together with 159 Brigade. The remainder of both divisions would withdraw an hour later at 22.00. The brigade was detailed to take up an outpost line on the high ground at Tel el Shabani. From Burjabye the brigade followed the southern slope of the Burjabye Ridge to el Adar. Continuing south to the Wadi Nukhabir, the Wadi Ghuzze was reached in the vicinity of Sheikh Nebhan. Crossing at el Breij the brigade passed Sheikh Rashid and thence to el Shabani, arriving at 02.00. The line was taken up to the west of the Khan-Yunis Road exclusive, and the 160 Brigade continued the line to the right.

"That march was a nightmare. Our battalions were the last to move and marched down the sandy bed of the wadi, running down Happy Valley until it joined the Wadi Ghuzze until finally they emerged near the Cairo Road. The troops were terribly depressed by this incomprehensible retreat. The night was very dark and it was impossible to see. The bed of the wadi was soft and its course very winding. There were constant checks. Everyone was very tired and most of the men were asleep as they marched, and at every check, bumped into the man ahead. At one point a company commander fell asleep on his horse and promptly fell off, causing a mild diversion."

The Cheshire Regiment in the Great War. Page 186.

The retirement march has been referred to in many accounts of the battle. With heavy casualties to the pack-animals, many machine-guns, ammunition and other equipment had to be carried for the nine-mile journey. Incredibly, there had been no water issued during the day and only a quarter-issue prior to the start of the march had to suffice for the whole time. The problem of water supply at anywhere but a short distance from the railhead at Deir el Belah was thus constantly reiterated. Although attributed to a particular battalion, perhaps the following extract may serve as a tribute to all who endured the march.

"The 1/5 Welsh Regiment did particularly good work in this march having lost heavily in men and pack saddlery. In spite of want of sleep (this was the third night in succession the men had had no sleep) and almost continuous marching an fighting, there was not the slightest sign of demoralisation."

159 Brigade HQ War Diary. PRO WO95/4628

[N.B. The 5/Welsh had 2/69 killed; 18/165 wounded; 0/5 died of wounds.]

Amidst the more obvious emotions felt by the men in the desert about to face battle, for many not for the first time but nevertheless with apprehension or fear, the subsequent grief of losing friends and comrades and the pain of physical wounds, the following letter shows a less expected feeling.

"Memories of nearly three score years ago are difficult to express, when nostalgia creeps in, and figures and faces take on a somewhat ethereal appearance.
One memory will live with me as long as I do however.
We were bivouacked at a place many miles beyond the firing line in the Sinai Desert and under a wonderful starlit sky. I believe a Welsh regiment was in bivouac a mile or so to our left.
Neither before or since have I been so moved as those voices sounded across those wastes of sand, brought up as I was in a good Christian home, and influenced by a good Father and Mother.
The hymn Guide me Oh thou (Great Jehovah) was wafted on a gentle breeze coming from the Mediterranean a few miles distant, and Land of my Fathers etc I shall never hear without this memory recurring.
I prefer this to all others I experienced in this campaign, for many I'm certain it was a moving experience."

Private R C SILLITOE to the author in 1984

The bond forged by their experiences on the 26 March was to last a lifetime. Private Alf HAWKINS lived in Barnet, North London in his retirement, but kept in touch with his friends and comrades of the 5th Welsh until he was the last known survivor of those incomprehensible days. From having served in A Company with Victor Mansell, he became a good friend of his son and travelled down to Mountain Ash in the Welsh Valleys until his death in the late eighties. In contact with the author in 1984, Alf Hawkins was reluctant to say too much in case he "got it wrong" and said things which hadn't happened, but it was clear that he had gone through such a traumatic experience during his time with the Welsh troops in the wastes around Gaza, that it was impossible not to respect his integrity and to believe that here was a survivor of one of the most devastating battles of the whole war. May this be his epitaph.

The Casualties

THERE WERE 9/158 OFFICERS AND men of the 159 Brigade were killed in action at the First Battle of Gaza and a further 1/15 died of wounds during the following three weeks.

Private David DAVIES was working at Senghenydd colliery, in 1913 the scene of the country's worst mining disaster in which 439 men died, when war broke out. He immediately enlisted in the 4/Welsh and took part in the landing at Suvla Bay, Gallipoli from where he was evacuated to Egypt with frostbite. Just over a year later, aged nineteen, he died of wounds received in action at Gaza. A full month after the battle Mr Picton, of Pembroke Dock was informed that both his sons were missing in action in Palestine. Unlike his brother, Sergeant William PICTON never returned when the battalion advanced to support the 5/Welsh and the 4/Cheshire's. Another Gallipoli veteran was Corporal Rupert WASHER, a Llanelli man born and bred. Working in the docks he was a well-known Rugby Football forward, captaining the New Dock RFC for several seasons; he too was lost without trace in the attack on Ali el Muntar. Although the battalion did not take part in the advance on the 27th, several men were killed on that day. Twenty-two-year-old Sergeant Frederick GIBSON of Milford Haven was one such casualty, probably being caught by a direct hit during the heavy shelling of the brigade lines.

During the 5/Welsh advance against Delilah's Neck, A and C Companies in the front line sustained many casualties from rifle and machine-gun fire. Nineteen-year-old Lance Corporal John BRADY from Penydarren, Glamorgan was with C Company, Private Benjamin DAVIES of Merthyr Tydfil, also nineteen, was with A Company; neither of their bodies was ever found. Although many had enlisted at the outbreak of war, Sergeant John JONES had joined the Army in 1901, at the end of the Boer War! He was wounded at Gallipoli and spent three months in hospital before coming home to Penrhiweceiber, Glamorgan on leave. It was the last time he saw his wife and three little children, for just over a year later he was killed in action. A second Penrhiweceiber man to lose his life at Gaza was twenty-one-year-old Lance Corporal Benjamin ROPER. He too, had been wounded at Gallipoli and spent seven months in a Liverpool hospital. Although left with a weak heart, he rejoined the battalion and was sent to Egypt. Eight days after landing he was killed in action, the only son of Mr and Mrs Roper of Morris Avenue. Private Henry PEARMAN lingered for many days before finally succumbing to his wounds on the 4 April. He had joined the Territorials in 1912 while working as a collier, and in 1915 was sent to Gallipoli with the 5/Welsh. He was still only nineteen years old when he died and had not been home for two years. Private James HALSALL has been born in Southport, Lancashire in 1884 and had remained in the town when he remarried. He was killed in action on 26 March, probably in the heavy rifle and machine-gun fire which met the 4/Cheshire's attack on Clay Hill. One who survived the advance was Private John CLARKE. As he dug in with A Company on the northern slopes of Clay Hill, he would have been able to see Gaza in the foreground to the Mediterranean Sea. He was never to enter the town for, after the night withdrawal, he was killed when the outpost lines were heavily shelled. Aged twenty-five, his body was never recovered. Twenty-four-year-old Corporal William HOLMES was wounded and evacuated to the hospital at Deir el Belah. Two days later he was buried in the War Cemetery there, another of the young men who had enlisted in the first weeks of the war to lose his life. The only NCO of the battalion to be killed at the First Battle of Gaza was thirty-one-year-old Sergeant Fred HODGES. He enlisted at Birkenhead, Cheshire but it was in his home town of Bournemouth that his parents received the news of his death.

Lance Corporal James COLLINS was thirty-five years old when he enlisted in the 7/Cheshire's. Married with four children he was a member of the Volunteer Fire Brigade in Macclesfield, as well as working in the local slate industry. He was killed in action on 26 March 1917. When Mr and Mrs Gay of Oldham Street, Bollington, Cheshire received news that their only son had been killed in action, a mistake on the notification led them to hope that he was still alive. A week later, on 21 April, Private Robert GAY aged twenty-two was confirmed killed in action, a cruel irony for his now grieving parents. After being initially sent to Gallipoli, Private Fred MATHER was transferred to the column sent to relieve Kut el Amara in Mesopotamia, where the force under General Townsend had been besieged by the Turks. He was subsequently sent to Egypt and was killed on the first day of the attack on Gaza. Only three days previously, he had written home to say that he was well, and this letter reached his parents about the same time as news of his death. Lance Corporal Fred CATHERALL moved to Macclesfield when he was six years old and was educated there at Christ Church School. Proficient at running from an early age he became a well-known member of the local Athletic Club. After his death on 26 March aged twenty-three, his parents returned to live in his home town of Manchester.

Of the brigade's four battalions, all of which were in action on the 26/27 March, 42/472 were wounded. In addition, one officer and 16 men of the 159 Brigade Machine Gun Company were wounded.

159 Brigade additional narrative

Captain Lee, who described his command as a mixed grill from all units in the Brigade, his own, the 5th Welch, predominating, gave a fuller account of the charge through the cactus hedges.

"Our great concern was a certain cactus hedge, from which machine guns might wipe us all out as soon as we got level with it. A small party was sent off to investigate, and all being reported well we got on a few yards further, leaving some behind (hit) at every rush forward. Worn out and heavily laden (besides their packs the men carried extra rations, a second water bottle, and extra bandoliers of ammunition) the prospect of having to rush the entrenched and steep slopes was not a pleasant one, but with bayonets fixed and revolvers cocked, off we went with a cheer. The Turks vacated their trenches and ran. The top of the hill was reached and we rounded up many Turks. Those who ran were fired at and some bowled over.

On looking round we found ourselves behind Turks who were still firing on other oncoming troops, and we got some fine firing at their backs, until they withdrew. Our party had reached the top, I suppose unobserved, at any rate for a while, for we were troubled by British shells and rifle fire from the converging troops. These troubles soon ceased, and Colonel Lawrence of the Cheshire's came along and took command of the situation. Water shortage was serious, and parties were sent off to collect water bottles from the dead, and ammunition from the wounded and dead.

On the latter point, Captain FS Harries wrote, "the lack of water and only seven hours sleep in nearly four days were almost the worst features. The men were splendid and up to a point it was more like a sham fight, but the machine guns stopped us and as we lay we suffered terribly."

History of the 53rd (Welsh) Division Major Dudley Ward Pages 88-89

54TH (EAST ANGLIAN) DIVISION
161ST INFANTRY BRIGADE
26 MARCH 1917

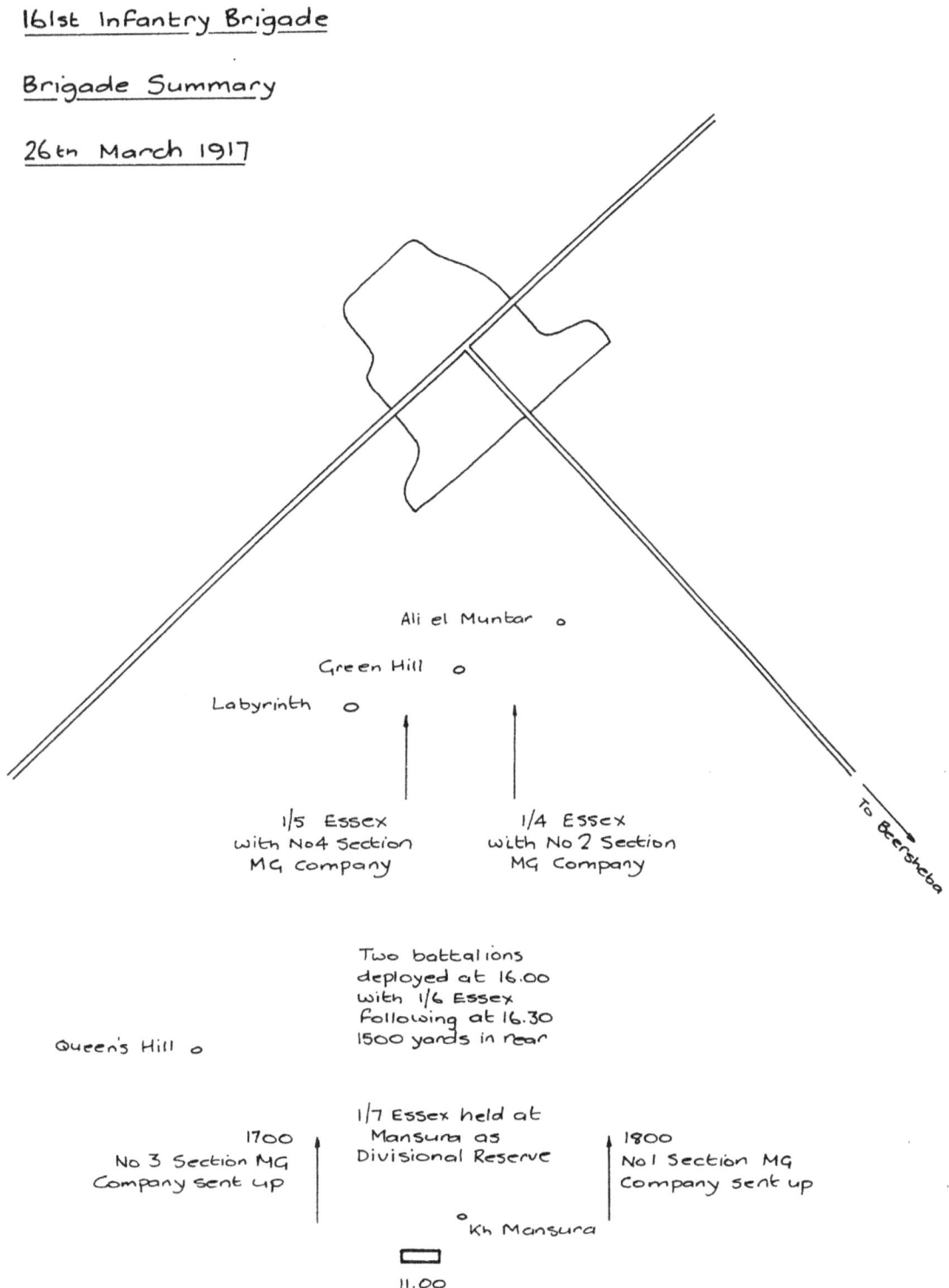

54TH (EAST ANGLIAN) DIVISION
161ST INFANTRY BRIGADE
27 MARCH 1917

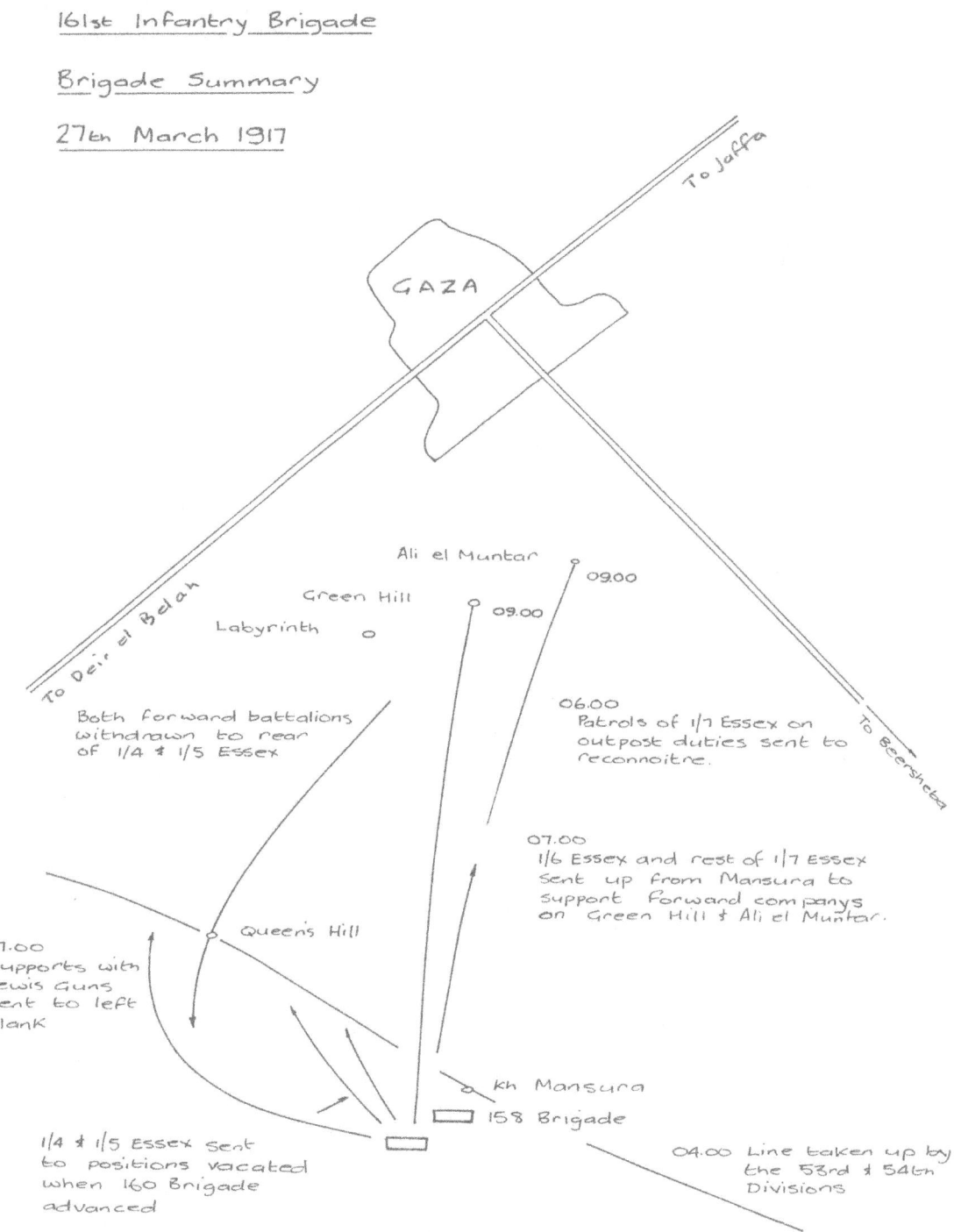

161 Brigade

FOR THE ACTIONS ON THE 26th March 1917 the 54th (East Anglian) Division was to have a split role. The 162 and 163 Brigades were to follow the cavalry screen moving to the east and north of Gaza, in a position to support where necessary. The 161st Brigade, or the Essex Brigade as it was composed of four Territorial battalions of the Essex Regiment, was attached to the 53rd Division as general support.

In the early hours of the 26th March the stillness was broken by the sound of cavalry and their batteries passing the division in wait at IN SEIRAT. The thick sea fog helped to muffle the clatter of hooves and the crunch of wheels as the mounted troops made their way towards the WADI GHUZZE, over an hour passing before the silence returned.

As day broke the brigade began to move, following the tracks of the cavalry through the wet green corn to the Wadi Ghuzze at Sheikh Nebhan. Several armoured cars arrived at the crossing but became stuck in the soft sand of the dry river-bed and were helped on their way by the efforts of the brigade! The halt was just long enough for some bully-beef to be eaten but no time for breakfast; the march was resumed to the north-east along the Wadi Nukhabir, a tributary of the Wadi Ghuzze. Moving along the wadi afforded some measure of cover from the enemy artillery which had opened up and eventually the brigade arrived at the southern side of the el Burjaliye Ridge.

By this time it was 10.00 and the heat had become intense as the march resumed, being very heavy going in the soft sand. An hour later the brigade came in sight of MANSURA RIDGE and it was here that the remainder of the morning and early afternoon was passed.

At 16.00 Brigade Major WRIGHT galloped back from the ridge with orders for Company Commanders to report to the Brigadier at once. The brigade was to be sent to support the attacking 53rd Division, which was fully committed to the assault on The Labyrinth and Ali el Muntar, but was held up by heavy enfilade fire from an area known as Green Hill. The Essex Brigade was to therefore assault this position and thus enable the attack to be pushed to a speedy end. The 1/4th and 1/5th Battalions of the Essex Regiment formed the front line of the brigade attack, with the 1/6th Battalion following some fifteen hundred yards behind.

"The frontage of the attack was determined by Ali el Muntar to the right and the sandy slope of the Labyrinth to the left. On the right slope of Green Hill stood a lone tree which became the point of direction for the inner flanks and divided the frontage equally."

With the 1/5th Essex in the East. Page 67

The enemy positions were not visible from the place of deployment but the trenches were thought to lie at the foot of the slopes to be assaulted. Some three-thousand, seven hundred and fifty yards of totally open ground had to be crossed and it was intended to push the attack as quickly as possible to minimise the inevitable casualties.

The 5/Essex were to the left of the brigade front, the 4/Essex to the right, extending at three paces interval as they came under rifle fire. Each battalion was supported by a section of the 161st Brigade Machine Gun Company: No 2 Section under Lieutenant RHS COLEMAN attached to the 5/Essex and No 4 Section under Lieutenant AHF HARWOOD detailed to the right with the 4/Essex.

"The casualties began to mount, but no time was wasted searching for cover where none was to be found."

With the 1/5th Essex in the East. Page 72

Despite the heavy losses the attack continued to move steadily forward, and the 6/Essex, in close support, advanced its B and C Companies to the front line to give impetus. At 17.00 No 3 Section of the Brigade MGC under Lieutenant RDF HALL was sent up to the left flank, now partially held up, but as two guns failed the support was effectively halved. The last reserve of machine guns was thrown into the fight as No 1 Section under 2nd Lieutenant JN COKER moved up on the right flank around 18.00.

The advance of the centre companies of the 1/4th and 1/5th Essex was rapid and unhesitating. "Mansura Ridge," wrote Captain Bittles "was about 30ft high and was not easy of ascent, but I remember Colonel Jameson doubled up it in his eagerness as he urged us on. He had no fixed headquarters, but moved between the firing line and supports. The attack was absolutely as laid down in the drill book. We had practiced the movement so often on the Canal that we could extend with the utmost precision, the men being hardly a fraction of a foot out in their intervals. When we reached the plateau we extended and were met with terrific rifle and machine gun fire. There was not a particle of cover, the ground being like a billiard table. The Lewis gun mules were hit and the men took the weapons and ammunition forward by hand. There was some shrapnel at the commencement, but later it was all machine gun and rifle fire; it came like peas at you. By the time the front companies had got within 150 yards of Green Hill the support companies had closed up. Within 100 yards of the trenches I was hit and could not go on, but I could see what was happening ahead. When the long lines were close to the Turkish wire they found a shred of cover caused by a slight rise. It was very slight, but it was just sufficient to protect them from fire."

Lying in the centre of the attacking line was Harvey Capron, adjutant of the 5th Essex, who had played his part with the greatest zest and eagerness. Nearby him was Captain Colvin of C Company, with a sergeant and one or two others. The line thickened as the supports came in and then Capron said to his colleague that the time had come to take the trenches. He made a movement as if to rise, which, apparently, was instantly detected by a Turkish sniper and he was shot through the heart. The sergeant had barely time to call Captain Colvin's attention to the casualty, when, as if animated by the dead officer's resolve, the whole line rose and went through the Turkish wire into the trenches. The men of the two companies of the 6th Essex, hurrying up to the fray, had just time to reach the firing line when the forward move began, and they gave impetus to the last decisive rush. [Lieutenant Thomas Harvey Overbury Capron. Age 21. From Grays, Essex.]

The Turks, already withdrawing, left hurriedly. A few brave men remained and were bayoneted as they stood, whilst others were shot down as they ran down the communication trenches. "The barbed wire" wrote Captain Bittles, who was watching this final episode, "was a great trouble, for men who were caught in it and killed whilst extricating themselves. 'Dicky' Richardson behaved most gallantly; he was last seen in the barbed wire firing his revolved at the Turks. [2/Lieutenant Geoffrey Oliver Richardson. Age 20. From Buckhurst Hill, Essex. Served in France with the London Rifle Brigade from 1914.]

Colonel Jameson met a brave man's end. The ardour of the advance took him to within two hundred yards of Green Hill, carrying a rifle and bayonet, when he was shot down. As he lay desperately wounded, he refused to let RSM Howard do anything for him until everyone else in the vicinity had been looked after. He said "You can do nothing for me; look after the others". Happily we were able to move him, but he died the next day. [Lt Colonel Edmund Jameson DSO. Age 41. From Ardmore, Dublin Served in the 14th Hussars in the Boer War]

The second in command (Major Barrington Wells) was hit in the arm early on, but nevertheless carried on until after the trenches were taken; all the company commanders went down. Gidley dashed forward and no one heard of him again". [Lieutenant Frederick Gidley. Age 23. of Shirely Park Road, Addiscombe, Surrey.]

Essex Territorial Infantry Brigade Volume 5. Burrows. Pages 156-157

As fierce fighting under a storm of rifle, machine-gun and artillery fire continued, eventually the determination and courage of the men paid off. Lodgements were made in the enemy lines and as hand-to-hand fighting ensued, trenches were cleared with the bayonet. A and C Companies of the 5/Essex took Green Hill while B and D Companies established themselves further to the left on Labyrinth. To the right of the brigade front the 4/Essex were still bravely struggling forward and to help them, one further company of the brigade reserve of the 6/Essex was sent up.

By 18.10 the whole position had been won. The two front battalions had lost nearly three hundred men killed, with a further two hundred from each being wounded. The determination and urgency of the two-hour attack was afterwards described by one of the senior officers with the 5/Essex.

"Then the machine guns started a cross fire from both flanks; men fell thick and fast; and still they went on, utterly regardless of anything else but getting there. This was all I was destined to see, as I was either picked off or ran into a chance shot at long range. The bullet, which went through my thigh, did not hurt me but it stopped me, and I could only lie there in the open and watch them as they disappeared into the dust and smoke. The fire became more intense. Private George BUERS, my faithful batman, applied the field-dressing and bound up my wound, quite indifferent to the bullets which fell thick around us and whistled and whined past our ears. The 6th Essex came following steadily one. My friend, Alexander, their second-in-command, passed me.

"How are the 5th going?" I said.

"Oh, top-hole" he replied, and swung on gaily, to meet his death in the open, like the gallant soldier that he was. The deadly monotony of the machine gun fire went on, but I could hear that our Lewis Guns were firing pretty continuously too. At last I heard a cheer and then another and another, and I knew that victory was won. Elated as I was by that cheer, it made me feel strangely small when I heard it, as those splendid fellows swept over the barbed wire and into the enemy's trenches - while I lay on the ground with my head in a hole."

Lieutenant Colonel T GIBBONS DSO
With the 1/5th Essex in the East Pages 68-69.

As soon as the forward troops had taken the positions, the Turks opened up with a heavy fire of high explosive shells. Unfortunately, although the range was too long to inflict casualties on the positions themselves, considerable damage was done to the signal wires. Signallers made valiant, but vain attempts to regain contact with the headquarters; most of the Brigade Signallers became casualties. Corporal AE RUFFLE of the 5/Essex volunteered to go back to HQ to get news of the overall situation and further orders. Braving the intense Turkish artillery and machine-gun fire for a second time, he reported back to Major WE WILSON on Labyrinth two hours later with the news that Captain A COLVIN was established on Green Hill, but that battalion headquarters could not be found.

At dusk, B and D Companies of the 5/Essex additionally took over the line held by the 4/Sussex, who had suffered very serious casualties, including their Commanding Officer Lieutenant-Colonel Ashworth. The casualties to the brigade were mainly caused by the well-placed Turkish machine-guns, the fire from each supporting the other to create an intense field of fire from which it is incredible that any survived. The severity of the machine-gun fire is referred to time and again in accounts of the battle, survivors of Gallipoli and the Somme stating that it surpassed even the terrible fire encountered on those occasions. The realisation that machine-guns were in use would first have come from the distinctive sound, its effect being described by an onlooker with the Signal Company.

"The enemy had a clean sweep over the plain and the hideous tat-tat seemed almost incessant. Of all the horrible sounds of war, I think the devilish tat-tat of a Maxim is the most fear-inspiring. There is something vicious in its rattle which goes straight to the heart. Rifle fire is altogether different - it has a dull rolling sound - but clear and sharp above it are the spiteful bursts of machine-gun fire. Perhaps a gunner will be content with spurts of four or five shots as he searches the enemy, then there comes burr, burr, burr as a whole belt of ammunition goes through at a target which suddenly presents itself."

Essex Territorial Infantry Brigade Volume 5 Page 151.

The Brigadier and Brigade Major visited the position during the evening, consolidation of which was well in hand. Company Commanders were summoned to Brigade HQ at 21.00, there being informed of the heavy casualties and that a withdrawal was being contemplated. A second meeting would take place at midnight on Green Hill to discuss the situation further.

"On my way back I visited Colvin on the Green Hill position and I then saw what strong one it was, the Turks in addition to the ordinary wire entanglements having still further protected the position by pits some four feet deep by six feet wide, filled with barbed wire. A and C Companies must have wrought havoc with the bayonet, the ground being literally covered with Turkish corpses, their white uniforms shewing up strongly in

the moonlight. Undoubtedly A and C Companies had borne the brunt of the attack."

Major Wilson.
With the 1/5th Essex in the East. Page 73.

From the positions on Labyrinth the confusion of the Turks could be clearly heard. The general noise, the clatter of wheels and sounds of the animals seemed to indicate that a withdrawal was taking place, later confirmed as patrols of the 5/Essex met no opposition as they advanced all but into the town.

The planned meeting on Green Hill went ahead at the appointed hour, the result being that an immediate withdrawal of all troops was ordered. All wounded men were to be brought in by the retiring troops, but stretchers proved to be so scarce that most casualties were carried on waterproof sheets. The 4/Sussex on Labyrinth had been so reduced in numbers that a party of fifty men under Captain EB DEAKIN of the 5/Essex took over the task of bringing in their wounded. Once again, all of this took place in the darkness and over rough, totally featureless ground.

It was around 02.25 on the 27th March that three companies of the 6/Essex left their positions as rear-guard to the brigade; dawn had already broken before the last of the weary troops crossed the outpost line of the 7/Essex on the way to Mansura. The necessary duties of filling water-bottles and cleaning rifles had barely been completed when orders were received for an immediate advance. The 7/Essex had already been sent forward from their outpost line into the positions so recently abandoned and the 6/Essex were to support them. The 5/Essex were in reserve with the 4/Essex but at about 09.00 both were ordered onto a north-east facing line from Mansura to Queen's Hill.

The 7/Essex had moved forward quickly and with little opposition, with A and B Companies of the 6/Essex following them onto Ali el Muntar. C and D Companies, 6/Essex were further west supporting the remainder of the 7/Essex on Green Hill. Each of the two columns had one section of machine-guns accompanying it, as well as the Lewis Guns of each company.

CSM FJ Rolph, of A Company, 6th Essex, tells in considerable detail the story of the day's eventful and tragic happenings: "About 6am we were issuing water, when Captain Tee rushed up and said, 'We have got to go up at once.' It seemed a great pity, for we were without water, some poor beggars had drained their bottles in anticipation of getting them filled. Up we went and were soon moving over the plain which we had crossed the day before. There were a few shells about, also machine guns, but they did not do much damage. There were rows of casualties from the previous day, which seemed to be all from Welsh regiments - it was on the extreme right of our line. I don't think there were any Turks to stop us of they would have enfiladed us as we passed along in waves in front of their trenches. I saw Captain Tee to the left so we went over to him. He was standing under a tree, telling some men off for bunching just in front. We were held up for a while, as the artillery was shelling [the] Mosque on the top of Ali el Muntar.

When the shelling ceased, I pushed on with Lance-Corporal Barry, and explored a trench on the right, by means of which we were the first at the Mosque. Seeing a little fort in front, we rushed over, but beyond machine guns we found nothing. When we got back to the Mosque men were put into the trench. Lance Corporal Gibbs and a few men pushed after the Turks, who were located in some rows of cacti a few fields in front of us. I called him back, but he did not respond and it was the last I saw of him. The enemy were easily visible and we saw some of them go into Gaza itself, which lay to our left. After a while we saw something which appeared to be sheep or goats coming over the hills from a direction which we later knew to be Beersheba. Then through glasses they were identified as troops, but we were uncertain of their nationality, some of us thinking they were Indians. The Turks in front waved a white flag, which we thought was in token of surrender, but it was probable they were signalling the oncoming Turks, concerning whom we were then under no illusions.

Essex Territorial Infantry Brigade Volume 5. Burrows. Pages 162-163

By about 09.00 the two battalions held the key positions of Ali el Muntar and Green Hill, this being a much larger frontage than that previously held.

Turkish counter-attacks did not take long to develop however, with artillery and machine-gun fire supporting them. Attacks came from the south-east and simultaneously against the north and north-east slopes of Ali el Muntar while the artillery fire extended across the front to Green Hill. The Turkish works to the south of this position were unoccupied at this time and to avoid being cut off by the enemy troops now on two sides, both battalions fell back. One Lewis Gun of the 6/Essex, A Company, was lodged in a small salient to the north-east of Ali el Muntar and inflicted heavy casualties on the Turks who were on three sides of them. The retirement to the works was completed just in time as the enemy was barely thirty yards from the last parties who left. Captured enemy arms and equipment obviously had to be abandoned under this pressure, but all were rendered useless before doing so. The counter-attacks were thus narrowly foiled. CSM Rolph continues the story

"Events moved rapidly and a written message came from colonel Bowker, 'Withdraw fighting westward,' brought by Private Swift, to whom many of us owed our safety. It was high ground where we were and we could see right over the plain. There was a good deal of machine gun fire from the extreme left of the Turkish line, which caused casualties, among them Private Dick Freeman. Private G Brazier was firing from behind a cactus hedge when a bullet came through one of the thick leaves and the juice spurted over his glasses. He had something very emphatic to say about the Turks. Another little incident I always remember when we were busy getting away I noticed one private lying back in a trench pulling cactus thorns out of his knees. To get from the mosque we had to cross the sunken road and it was there that poor old A Company and some of B Company, who had reinforced us, caught it, for I shall always believe 'Jacko' had a machine gun on the plain and another from the town trained on that spot. We went over one at a time and it was whilst standing on the other side that I saw the last of Lance Corporal Skinner. We made our way along the Turkish front-line trench for some way and then a few of us crossed over towards the sea -still inside the defences- and sheltered, as we thought, in some hollow ground, but soon found that the enemy had got the range, apparently with a machine gun from the Mosque. Several men were hit and some of us rushed out and after a time observed some of our troop holding a hill (Queen's Hill) on our half right I made my way over and found a line composed of Essex and 53rd Division. It was a good job we left the trench when we did, for most of those who remained there were either killed or captured. The Turks sprayed us with shrapnel and as I had not got an entrenching implement, I lay in a little gully. It was funny, but on the plain the previous day I had waited on the wounded for one. I got one, but gave it away and could not get another. The Turks did not seem inclined to attack, so the order was given 'Essex get back to Mansura.' Back we went - hot, tired and thirsty. I ran across Colonel Bowker, who took the saddle off a Lewis gun mule and rode it. Presently we saw a crowd round a well, who called us over. Found they were Essex, who were lowering mess tins on puttees and fetching up dirty, muddy water. I filled myself until I bubbled over. We then reached Mansura and found the 5th holding the line across the plain. There Colonel Bowker organised us into two companies."

Essex Territorial Infantry Brigade Volume 5. Burrows. Pages 163-164

As the Turks had begun to threaten the line, the 4/ and 5/Essex were moved to establish a line facing north-east from Mansura to Queen's Hill. Both battalions had lost heavily on the previous day and the strength of the 5/Essex was only about two hundred and fifty men. These were reorganised into three companies; B under Lieutenant B ARCHER, with C and part of D under 2nd Lieutenant A COLVIN, with the remainder of D, remnants of A and Headquarters under Lieutenant B CARLYON-HUGHES. The Lewis Guns and final eighty or so men were held about three hundred yards to the rear, the 4/Essex being similarly disposed, although not as strongly.

The rest of the day was more or less peaceful, with isolated groups of men passing back through the lines in the early afternoon. There was uncertainty as to the position of troops to the left of the line. Men of the 53rd Division had evidently been there earlier but by the afternoon it became apparent that the flank was exposed. The supports with Lewis Guns were sent up at about 17.00.

"From that hour until dark perfect stillness reigned - it seemed almost unreal."

With the 1/5th Essex in the East. Page 75.

Between 19.00 and 20.00 the Turks launched an attack against the left flank with about two hundred men. Advancing to within calling distance they were initially mistaken for men of the division, uncertainty being further maintained by the fact that they were calling out "Essex! Essex!" and wearing Essex Service dress. Only when one of their number, over-enthusiastic to impress, called out "Royal Essex!" was the ploy realised. Opening fire at such a short range, the Turks were forced back with over a hundred casualties.

Shortly afterwards, orders were received for the withdrawal of the brigade to Mansura at 22.30. Just after midnight the march was resumed, the destination this time being In Seirat, a very slow and arduous journey over the difficult terrain. The way was lost after about three hours and a halt was called until daybreak, when the position was found to be near Sheikh Nebhan on the Wadi Ghuzze. A short march was all that was needed to conclude the journey to a very welcome rest at In Seirat.

Although the Essex Brigade played an important part in the operations against Gaza in November, the following quote seemed most appropriate at this stage, given the staggering casualties that were sustained on the 26 and 27 March, but which received scant attention at home.

The following quote is unnervingly prophetic.

"The war story of the 161st Brigade must become ever more precious to Essex men and women as the years pass. We were so near to the mighty conflict in France and Flanders that great "sideshows" like those of Gallipoli and Palestine are dwarfed by comparison. Yet we must expect that in time our descendants will turn with increasing interest and respect to the deeds of the army which gloriously failed and to those of the army which gloriously conquered and entered Jerusalem, for of those armies the Essex Territorial Infantry Brigade formed part. Their gallantry will stir imagination in days to come; quicken and deepen the spirit of devotion to the county. They were our own kith and kin and we would not forget, though immersed once again in the trials and tribulations of post-war life, that those who suffered the daily perils and discomforts of Gallipoli and Palestine must many a time have been heartsore for sights and scenes of the old county.

Essex Territorial Infantry Brigade Volume 5 Burrows.

Last night I lay at Good Easter
Under a hedge I knew;
Last night in wood by High Easter
I trod the may-floor blue.
****

Roding, that names eight churches
(Banks with paigles pight),
Chelmer, whose mill and willows
Keep one red tower in sight.
****

Ah! I may not go back now,
Neither be turned nor stayed,
Yet should I live, I'd seek her,
Once that my vows are paid.

Arthur Shirley Cripps.

[Author's note. Good Easter and High Easter are villages near the 5th Essex home-town of Chelmsford. The Chelmer is the river on which Chelmsford stands. The Roding is another river in the area along which are eight villages, (disputably nine among long-time residents of the area) hence the eight churches. Paigles are primroses. Pight is local for covered.]

The Casualties

IN ALL **27/405** OFFICERS AND men of the 161st Brigade were killed in action at the First Battle of Gaza, and a further 2/45 died of wounds during the following three weeks.

Private Joseph TRAPP was born at Loughton, Essex and was a well-known member of Loughton athletic Club. He worked as a gardener at Warren House in Epping Forest until enlisting in the 1/4 Essex early in the war. He served in the Gallipoli Campaign and although he suffered greatly from dysentery, stayed with the battalion until being seriously wounded at Gaza. He died in hospital at Deir el Belah on 29 March 1917 aged twenty-five. Since its inception, the New Town of Harlow, Essex has slowly engulfed the scattered hamlets which once bore that collective name. In one of these, Private Herbert CORDELL had been born and raised but left to join the army early in 1915. On the 26th March, 1917 whilst advancing with A Company on the right flank, he was killed in action aged twenty-six, and was buried in the Gaza War Cemetery. B Company was also in the front line, and formed the left flank of the battalion's advance. Although only twenty-five, Harold DRAKEFORD had risen to the rank of Company Quarter Master Sergeant, having seen service at Gallipoli eighteen months previously. He survived the assault on Green Hill on the 26th but was lost without trace the following day, probably during the heavy shelling from Sheikh Abbas Ridge. Private Victor VANDY was born at Leyton, Essex and served with the Royal Navy on board "HMS IMPREGNABLE". Transferring to the 4/Essex he was killed in action on the 26 March still aged only twenty. The seemingly endless casualty list of the 4/Essex for the two-day engagement brought news of a double loss for Mr TF Elliott of Ilford, Essex. His two sons, Private Frank Thomas ELLIOTT aged twenty-three and Private Robert Thomas ELLIOTT who was younger by two years, were both lost without trace on the 26 March.

After the death of their son, Mr and Mrs J Death moved from their home at Colchester Road, Halstead, Essex to Felixstowe on the Suffolk coast. A Gallipoli veteran aged eighteen, Private Albert DEATH had enlisted in the 1/5th Essex when only sixteen and was killed in action on the 26 March 1917. Private William FELL was in the front line of the 5/Essex advance when an enemy machine-gun stopped his company. Moving out onto the flank alone, he located the gun thus enabling the Lewis Guns to engage it and press the attack on. He was severely wounded in this gallant action however, and died the following day, the third of five serving brothers to become a casualty. Young men of the battalion continued to fall by the score as the attack crossed the barren plain. Private Arthur BELL, nineteen, of Great Bentley, Essex; Private Harold DARBY, twenty, and Private Frederick OLLEY, eighteen, both from the battalion's home town of Chelmsford, were all lost without trace. Corporal Herbert STOCK, Private Herbert STONE, Private George THEADOM from the Essex villages of Little Bardfield, Matching Green and Kelvedon; all aged twenty, all killed. As men in front of them fell, those in the following companies pressed on without pause. Sergeant Henry HALLS of Dunmow was in B Company, with Private Frederick MALYON of Writtle in A Company to his right. As the ranks closed up both were killed in the storm of machine-gun fire. As the young men died to leave grieving parents and friends, so too fell the older men to leave widows and children too young to grieve. Sergeant Frederick HART, thirty-eight, lived with his wife at Church Lane, Bocking, while twenty-eight-year-old fellow Sergeant Alfred MANN's wife lived further to the north-east at Colchester. Their loss on the 26th March was noted by Lieutenant Colonel T Gibbons, commanding the battalion who paid tribute to them as "good section leaders all". Two young children were left fatherless when Private Rodney WIGGINS was killed on the same day. Born at Little Baddow near Chelmsford in 1887 his wife and family were left alone in nearby Danbury.

Several men who originally enlisted with the Bedfordshire Regiment and subsequently transferred to the 1/6th Essex were killed in action at the First Battle of Gaza. Private Ernest DOWNHAM was one such case having travelled to Bedford from his home in Bishop's Stortford, Hertfordshire to enlist. The son of Charles and Mary Downham, he was killed on the 26 March, aged thirty-one. Despite a minimum age of eighteen for enlistment, Private George GENTRY was only seventeen when killed on the 27 March. He came from West Ham, Essex and, like virtually every other one of those killed with the battalion, was lost without trace. Another example of the eagerness to serve in the army was that of Private David VOISEY. Born in East Ham, Essex he volunteered in the first days of the war aged but fifteen. Three years later, having served with the battalion continuously and been wounded at Gallipoli, he was killed in action on the 27 March 1917. Mrs Clara Tallack had already lost her husband in the war when she was informed that her son, Private Frank TALLACK, had been killed in action in Palestine. Aged twenty, he fell on the 27 March. Private Francis RICKS was born in Hertfordshire and lived in Church Hill, East Barnet with his parents. He was with C Company as they advanced in support of the 4/ and 5/Essex on the 26 March. Aged twenty, his body was never recovered and he is commemorated on the Jerusalem Memorial.

In reserve on the 26 March, the 1/7 Essex was the first to advance the following day, reoccupying the deserted enemy trenches in the early hours. Arthur and Rebecca Hart of Walthamstow lost their only son on that day. Nineteen-year-old Private Arthur HART was seriously wounded when the reoccupied positions were heavily counter-attacked. He died on the 28 March and was buried in the cemetery at Deir el Belah. Sergeant Walter SLADE enlisted in the 7/Essex at Leyton, Essex but had seen active service several years earlier during the Boer War. Aged thirty-eight he lived in Grove Road, Walthamstow and was married. Often, men who enlisted together also died together. No. 301095 Lance Corporal Bertie AUGER was born in Suffolk at Stoke-by-Nayland and met No 301097 Private Frank BEETON when both joined up at Colchester. No 300890 Private Richard SMITH lived in Barnaby Street, Stratford with his parents; his brother William was also killed in action. He joined up in nearby Walthamstow, the battalion's home town, and there met No 300891 Private Albert CHRISTIE. All four were killed in action on the 27th March. In the advance Sergeant Frederick FORSTER was with D Company who were ordered to reoccupy The Labyrinth on the left of the front. Aged twenty-four he was killed, probably during the heavy counter-attacks which forced withdrawal from the position.

A further 37/630 were wounded on the two days, a staggering total which was almost identical to those sustained by the 158 Brigade.

161 Brigade Additional narrative

THE LEFT OF THE 1/5TH kept resolutely upon its objective, the Brown Hill, on the skyline. The bulk of D Company, when they entered the trenches, found a series of broken gullies and on the top of the farther rise were men of the Royal Sussex Regiment, who had been holding on since early morning. They had suffered severe losses from what they thought to be minenwerfer fire, but Major Wilson was inclined to think that 5.9" H.E was responsible. The enemy put down a barrage from these guns just as the objective was reached by the 5th Essex on Brown Hill, but fortunately the range was just too long to do much injury, though it caused casualties among the last men in. From that point patrols were sent out to ascertain the enemy's whereabouts and touch was sought with the companies on the right.

In the centre of the objective of the 1/5th Essex was a small stone hut and this proved a great attraction, for it was the focus of enemy resistance. Three platoons of B and D Companies concentrated there, suffering considerable casualties in so doing, for at least one machine gun, resolutely handled, operated therefrom. They got within fifty yards of the structure, when further progress was stayed. Captain J F Finn, then commanding No 5 Platoon of B Company, recalls, "I straightened out the line, but many more men were hit as the bullets continued to fall about us like hail. Windsor [2nd Lieutenant] called out to me that he was hit, so did Gilmore [2nd Lieutenant] who was some way off. Not only did he give this information, but he shouted out the details; this despite the fact that he dared not move for fear of being hit again and that the engagement was continuing vigorously. A few minutes later Womersley [Signalling Officer], who was near me on the left, got up and said that he was going to try and get in telephonic communication with the gunners to see if they could fire on the stone hut. This was very desirable, as in this part on the line we had no artillery support during the operation. Womersley, I heard afterwards, only got a little way before being hit twice. Those of us who were not wounded kept up a brisk fire in an endeavour to get shots in the windows of the hut, but we were not in a position to do much. I sent a man back to battalion headquarters to report, but I discovered afterwards that, owing to casualties, it did not exist. A little while later we heard a loud cheer from the right. This was afterwards discovered came from A and C Companies of the 1/5th, the remnant of the 1/4th and the three companies of the 1/6th, when they attacked the works with the bayonet and captured the Green Hill defences. Following this, the Turkish fire ceased and doubtless those on our immediate front retired owing to the fall of Green Hill. Darkness fell and we commenced to dig in.

Whilst this was being done, Lieutenant Calverley came along and volunteered to take a small patrol to the front. This he did and returned later with three Bedouins, whom he had taken prisoner, and also reported he had proceeded well to our front without observing and body of the enemy. Our work of entrenching continued as a reply to my message to battalion headquarters was awaited. It was done to a most heart-rending accompaniment of groans and cries from the wounded, who were lying, it seemed, everywhere. No one could be spared to take these poor fellows back and no stretchers were there even if this could have been possible. The RAMC arrangements were inadequate for a sudden advance over practically two miles of open country. "The heavy casualties of March 26th were mainly caused by the steady fire of three Turkish machine guns and one automatic rifle," wrote an officer, "but it was their protected position and perfect lateral field for cross fire that made the effect so deadly. This fact was proved by the number of men hit below the chest in the course of the advance."

As night fell, therefore, the whole of the defensive position on the south-eastern side of Gaza was in the hands of the British troops. The 1/4th, and the 1/5th and three companies of the 1/6th occupied Green Hill, and the survivors were busily employed in adapting the trenches on the crest facing Gaza for the purpose of defence. The remaining company of the 1/6th Essex was brought up and Colonel Bowker, commanding that battalion, took charge of the line. The 1/7th Essex were retained in divisional reserve at Mansura. Several patrols were sent out to feel for the enemy. Lieutenant Harold Durell, 1/6th Essex, who led one of these parties, writes; "When we settled down in the Turkish positions my left was on the track, which, upon the map, runs nearly due north from the "R" in Mansura Ridge. In the night my patrol went out along the track due north towards Gaza. We left the track once to examine a Turkish camp on the west and returned to the track again at its northern end. I have a distinct recollection then of passing buildings and at the time I had no doubt that I had reached the outskirts of Gaza. I should not like to say after this time how far north we patrolled from our posts in the old Turkish line, but if I had to guess at it I should put it at about *half a mile. Looking at my route by the map, it seems probable that I skirted the south-eastern edge of Gaza.*

Essex Territorial Infantry Brigade Volume 5. Burrows. Pages 158-160

Epilogue

THE APPEAL SOUNDED GENUINE, INTERESTED and sincere. As the sunshine broke through the window and as the kettle began to whistle, he could see them. The tears began to flow as the sand was flicked up around his feet, the bullets miraculously missing him but ripping into those nearby. He heard his name and turned to see his school chum clutching his leg, blood flowing through the tightly-squeezed fingers. The agony flooded back, for he knew he couldn't stop and the life-long tears burned his face. Maybe, just maybe, the stretcher bearers would get to him in time, but he knew, of course, they wouldn't.

The whistle from the stove grew and the shell, as if held by a debating hand, struck the machine-gun just ahead. As the sand and smoke rose the tap-tap-tap stopped, but his relief was short-lived when he saw Johnny Turk laying there in the same agony as his pals. The sun glistened on the shell-cases piled around and with an angry kick he sent them flying, the tinkling muffled by the ever-present sand.

Maybe he could now tell his story.

Conclusion

THE FIRST BATTLE OF GAZA should have been a resounding success despite the high casualties. The withdrawal at the moment of capturing the high ground which overlooked the town was a cruel blow to the triumphant men. The following is more a review of the factors which had influenced the course of actions during the day, rather than an attempt to excuse or condemn the decision.

The early-morning fog was proposed as a major factor in the delay of the attack on the town, which began around mid-day. However, several sources have indicated that the fog was of benefit to the Desert Column, as it helped to muffle the sound of movement of the mounted troops. Additionally, it assisted the Eastern Force, as enemy aircraft were unable to take off until mid-morning, thereby delaying the spotting of troop movements.

One crucial factor was the difference in the perceived positions of the 53rd and 54th Divisions late in the afternoon, and their actual positions. At 18.10 General Chetwode, GOC Desert Column, decided to withdraw the mounted troops as no news of infantry captures had been received; the prospect of the infantry being committed to a night's fighting amongst the cactus gardens while enemy reinforcements built up was too much to contemplate. At 19.00 the order to General Dallas of the 53rd Division was to withdraw his right flank "to make touch with the 54th Division", in the assumption that the latter division was around the Burjabye Ridge, as previously ordered. General Dallas however, had not been told of this move by the 54th Division and believed them to still be at Sheikh Abbas, some four miles further to the south-east, rather than only a mile or so away around the strong position of Green Hill. Despite protests at the order to withdraw, the true position of the 54th Division was not realised until around midnight, and not until 05.00 on the 27th did General Chetwode fully appreciate the implication of the withdrawal. The attempts to regain the abandoned ground have been documented in the text. **The distances and difficulties of communication, together with the human error of the exhausted and hard-pressed headquarters staff conspired produce to the fateful result. The maps available at the First Battle of Gaza were also very basic, the more detailed versions not being produced until much later; this has been reflected in the maps shown in the text.**

The ever-present spectre of water shortage cannot be ignored. It is clear from many quotes that the pitiful water ration for the men was of major concern to the officers. On one notable occasion during the campaign, astute work by the General Staff enabled a water convoy to be sent up to isolated troops who had been without water for thirty-six hours. On the 26th March the failure of definite information that Gaza had been captured posed the question; Withdraw, or leave men and horses isolated over many miles without water and at the mercy of inevitable Turkish reinforcements from the east?

Finally, and perhaps most difficult to appreciate, was the factor of the types of communication as well as the distances involved. While it was true that the battle was not led by generals who were close to the front, in Palestine the distances were immense. As has been seen, the men of the 53rd and 54th Divisions had attacked across the open plain of over two miles. There was no enemy to be seen at that range, but when contact was made amongst the cactus hedges and entrenchments all vestiges of battalion command broke down, thereby compounding the task of those at brigade and division levels. Company commanders did their utmost to send messages and reports back however, several have been quoted in the text, but although the runners who undertook this duty were determined to get through many were killed or wounded. Under these circumstances, it is clear there was a very disjointed and incomplete picture of the day's events available to the commanders; in many cases the advances and gains made were due to the initiative and courage of the officers and men in the firing lines.

In conclusion then, it comes down to a battle fought under conditions which today's technologically incomparable troops would find difficult to execute. The men of 1917 fought the battle, with the loss of many of their comrades and pals then returned home to be first ignored and then forgotten.

No 4 Platoon A Company
1/5th Essex Regiment
161st Brigade 54th Division

Names of men: left to right.
Back Row.   Taylor F: Wiggins: Butler: Brooker: Marshall H: Barker
            Boreham: Brunwin: Deeks: Wilshire: Clayton.

Middle Row. LCorp Halls: Porter: Corporal Cooper: Sergt Price:
            2nd Lieutenant H K Chester: Sergt Mitson: Corpl Stapleton:
            Corpl Beard: Farren: Everard

Front Row. Collins: Partridge: Harden: L Corpl Cowell: Piper:
            Marshall GM: Bowers: Hanwick: Gaffey.

Cherry & Co. St Albans, Hertfordshire. 10/7/1915

1/7th Battalion Essex Regiment July 1915 Before sailing for Gallipoli

Back Row (Left to Right) Lt & QM R Warner; Lt E Whur; Lt EW Broadberry; Lt A Young; Lt SA Mackie; Lt LFH Bailey; Lt J Schofield;

Third Row 2nd Lt W Sharkey; 2nd Lt G Heatherington; 2nd Lt L Champ; Lt G Jones; 2nd Lt DM Penrose; Lt SCW Hearn; 2nd Lt E Lewis; Lt JR Eve.

Second Row Capt DH Pearson; Capt. R Jenner Clarke; Capt FR Waller; Capt WR Johnson; Major HF Kemball; Lt & Adjt RA Stubbings; Capt GC Ewer; Capt G Shenstone; Capt A Graham.

Front Row 2nd Lt JG Kemball; 2nd Lt FLl Thomas; 2nd Lt AR Carpenter; 2nd Lt AHF Harwood; 2nd Lt AG Johnson; 2nd Lt C Needell

ALI EL MUNTAR 26th March 1917

BROKEN GROUND SOUTH-EAST OF GAZA

This photograph gives some idea of the extremely rough terrain which faced the troops; both for the Mounted Brigades on their way to establishing the screen around Gaza, as well as the infantry in the assault on the town itself.

    The scale can be judged from the figures to the left-centre of the picture. It is likely that the Wadi Nukhabir is to the foreground, with Sheikh Abbas and Mansura Ridge on the horizon, right and left respectively.

By permission of IWM Copyright No Q12755

Middlesex Hill Green Hill Ali el Muntar   Fryer Hill   Anzac Ridge

ALI EL MUNTAR FROM MANSURA RIDGE

Once the broken ground between the Wadi Ghuzze and Mansura Ridge had been crossed, a flat, open plain lay in front of the advancing troops. The objective, as this photograph clearly shows, was visible some **3750** yards distant.

By permission of IWM Copyright No Q7646

GAZA FROM ALI EL MUNTAR

The tantalising view of Gaza which would have met the weary but exultant men of the 53rd Division, as well as those advanced men of the Australian and New Zealand units, when Ali el Muntar was taken late on the 26 March 1917. The sand-dunes of the coast are visible between the Mediterranean Sea, on the horizon, and the town.

By permission of IWM Copyright No Q47645

Captain Harry Keppel CHESTER

1/5th Battalion Essex Regiment. Died, 28th March 1917, of wounds received at Gaza on 26th March. Age 22. Son of Harry and Mildred Mary Chester, of Broome End, Stansted, Essex. Buried in the Deir el Belah War Cemetery.
Educated at Eton College and King's College, Cambridge, a member of the Officer Training Corps at the latter in 1913. Commissioned into the Essex Regiment in October 1914 and served at Gallipoli from August to December 1915. Upon evacuation of the Peninsula, served in Egypt and Palestine.

"...It was now 10 o'clock and the attack started on our left, on the other side of the ridge. The Turkish gunners got busy and searched our slope of the ridge with shrapnel, which burst very high, but made it advisable to get into a gully close by.
...The enemy continued to shell the wadi, and we continued on our way by platoons. The leading platoon of 'A' Company was caught by a shell which wounded Willmott, the Company Commander, in the head, severely wounded CSM White and Chester, the platoon commander, and caused several other casualties among the rank and file. Poor Chester died the next day, mourned by Officers and men alike. He was never a barrack-square soldier, but probably had more brains than anyone else in the Battalion, having had a brilliant career at Eton, which promised great things-alas, never to be realised. A little hesitating in his manner and careless in his outward appearance, he had nevertheless the heart of a lion and a true sympathy for his men which earned him alike their affection and their esteem."

With the 1/5th Essex in the East. Lt Colonel Gibbons. Page 67

Postcard to
Mrs M Davies,
97, Brynmor Road
Llanelly

Private Thomas Henry DAVIES, Egypt 1918

Private Thomas Henry Davies, 1/4th Welsh Regiment, was wounded at the First Battle of Gaza.

Private Alf HAWKINS

1/5th Welsh Regiment

Hewson Camp, Pembroke; three miles from Neyland. 1916.

[Back Row, Second from the right.]

Wounded at Gaza with "a slight wound on finger next to my trigger finger and to this day [1984] the nail is still split."

Sergeant Richard Edward PRICE. Taken at Llangollen by Lellsome & Sons. One wound stripe indicates after Gallipoli but before Gaza.

Born 13 November 1887. A carpenter by trade, he enlisted in the 1/1 Herefordshire Regiment with the Number 8023 202872 on 5 April 1908 at Rhyader, Radnorshire, Wales. Served at Gallipoli and was badly wounded in the chest and lungs at Suvla Bay, being sent back to Britain to recover. On 12 December 1916, he was awarded the Territorial Force Efficiency Medal [TFEM] A while later, a Medical Board decided he was fit enough and he served overseas again, taking part in the Battles of Gaza in 1917, being wounded in the arm on 26 March rest and recovery this time being completed in Egypt. In 1918, he returned to England where a further Medical Board decided against active service, and much to his disgust he was transferred to the Cheshire Regiment to see out his Army Career. He was discharged, disabled in consequence of lung damage, on 11 June 1919 and the following details are recorded on his discharge certificate;
Height 5' 3". Eyes-blue. Hair-brown.
Scars to right forearm, nose, chest, back, left arm.
He resumed his work as a carpenter. He died on 25 April 1981.

Farrier and General Smith

Sidney George TUCKER.

Cairo 1915

Farrier Corporal Sidney George TUCKER

Number 903 on enlistment in the Dorset (Queen's Own) Yeomanry at Sherborne, Dorset on 7th September 1914, aged nineteen years.
Went out to Egypt in March 1915, with a change of number to 230271.
Initial rank was Farrier and General Smith but was promoted to the above rank in September 1916.

ORDER OF BATTLE FOR 26 March 1917.

DESERT COLUMN: Formation and support troops

    Australian and New Zealand Mounted Division

    Imperial Mounted Division

EASTERN FORCE: Formation and support troops

    52 Lowland Division

    53 Welsh Division

    54 East Anglian Division
    74 Yeomanry Division

THE ORDER OF BATTLE FOR 26th MARCH 1917

DESERT COLUMN
Major General (Lt-General) Sir PW CHETWODE. Bt. CB.DSO.

AUSTRALIAN AND NEW ZEALAND MOUNTED DIVISION
Major General Sir HG CHAUVEL. KCMG. CB

IMPERIAL MOUNTED DIVISION
Colonel (Major General) HW HODGSON CVO. CB

SUPPORT TROOPS

Royal Horse Artillery
Leicester Battery
Somerset Battery
Inverness Battery
Ayr Battery

Royal Horse Artillery
1/1 Nottinghamshire Battery
1/1 Berkshire Battery
A and B Batteries Honorable Artillery Company

Field Ambulances
1st Light Horse
2nd Light Horse
New Zealand Mounted
1/1st North Midland Mounted

Field Ambulances
3rd Light Horse
4th Light Horse
1/ 1st South Midland Mounted
1/ 2nd South Midland Mounted

Engineers
1st Australian Field Squadron

Engineers
Imperial Mounted Division Field Squadron

ORDER OF BATTLE FOR 26 March 1917.

AUSTRALIAN and NEW ZEALAND MOUNTED DIVISION

2nd Australian Light Horse Brigade
Colonel (Brigadier General) G de L RYRIE CMG

5th Light Horse Regiment
Lt Col LC WILSON
6th Light Horse Regiment
Lt Col WHITE
7th Light Horse Regiment
Lt Col GM Macarthur ONSLOW
2nd Australian Machine Gun Squadron

New Zealand Mounted Rifles Brigade
Colonel (Brigadier-General) EWC CHAYTOR CB

Auckland Mounted Rifles
Lieutenant Colonel CER MACKSEY
Canterbury Mounted Rifles
Lieutenant Colonel J FINDLAY
Wellington Mounted Rifles
Lieutenant Colonel W MELDRUM
New Zealand Machine Gun Squadron

22nd Mounted Brigade
Colonel (Brigadier-General) FAB FRYER

1/1 Lincolnshire Yeomanry
Commanding Officer unknown
1/1 Staffordshire Yeomanry
Commanding Officer unknown
1/1 East Riding Yeomanry
Major CE REYNARD
18th Machine Gun Squadron
Captain WINTRINGHAM

ORDER OF BATTLE FOR 26 March 1917.

IMPERIAL MOUNTED DIVISION

3rd Australian Light Horse Brigade

Colonel (Brigadier General) JR ROYSTON CMG DSO

8th Light Horse Regiment
Lt Col LC MAYGAR VC

9th Light Horse Regiment
Lt Col WH SCOTT DSO

10th Light Horse Regiment
Major ACN OLDEN

3rd Australian Machine Gun Squadron

5th Mounted Brigade

Colonel (Brigadier-General) EE WIGGIN DSO

1/1 Warwick Yeomanry
Lt Col HA GRAY-CHEAPE

1/1 Gloucester Yeomanry
Major AJ PALMER

1/1 Worcester Yeomanry
Colonel HJ WILLIAMS

16th Machine Gun Squadron

6th Mounted Brigade

Lieutenant Colonel (Brigadier-General) TMS PITT

1/1 Buckinghamshire Yeomanry
Lt Colonel JP GRENFELL

1/1 Berkshire Yeomanry
Commanding Officer unknown

1/1 Dorset Yeomanry
Commanding Officer unknown

17th Machine Gun Squadron

THE ORDER OF BATTLE FOR 26th MARCH 1917

EASTERN FORCE
Major General (Lt-General) Sir CM DOBELL KCB.CMG.DSO.

Imperial Camel Brigade
1st [Australian & New Zealand] Battalion   Hong Kong & Singapore Camel Battery
2nd [Imperial] Battalion   1/1st Scottish Horse Field Ambulance
3rd [Australian & New Zealand] Battalion   Brigade Signals:
Engineers: Machine Gun Company

| 52 (Lowland) DIVISION
Brevet Colonel WE SMITH | 53rd (Welsh) DIVISION
Major General AG DALLAS | 54th (East Anglian) DIVISION
Colonel SW HARE | 74th (Yeomanry) DIVISION
Brevet Lt-Colonel ES GIRDWOOD |
|---|---|---|---|

Support Troops

C Squadron Glasgow Yeomanry	A Squadron Duke of Lancaster's Own Yeomanry	A Squadron 1/1st Hertfordshire Yeomanry	A Squadron 1/2nd County of London Yeomanry
Royal Field Artillery
261 Brigade A/B/C Batteries
262 Brigade A/B/C Batteries
263 Brigade A/B Batteries	**Royal Field Artillery**
265 Brigade A/B/C Batteries
266 Brigade A/B/C Batteries
267 Brigade A/B Batteries	**Royal Field Artillery**
270 Brigade A/B/C Batteries
271 Brigade A/B Batteries
272 Brigade B/C Batteries	**Royal Field Artillery**
No Artillery
Royal Engineers
410th Field Company
412th Field Company
413th Field Company	**Royal Engineers**
436th Field Company
437th Field Company
439th Field Company	**Royal Engineers**
484th Field Company
486th Field Company
495th Field Company	**Royal Engineers**
No Engineers
Field Ambulances
1/1st Lowland
1/2nd Lowland
1/3rd Lowland	**Field Ambulances**
1/1st Welsh
1/2nd Welsh
1/3rd Welsh	**Field Ambulances**
2/1st East Anglian
1/2nd East Anglian
1/3rd East Anglian	**Field Ambulances**
229th Brigade
230th Brigade
231st Brigade

ORDER OF BATTLE FOR 26 March 1917.

52nd (Lowland) DIVISION

155 Brigade
Lieutenant Colonel (Brigadier General) JB POLLOCK-M'CALL CMG

1/4th Royal Scots Fusiliers
Lieutenant Colonel H THOMPSON

1/5th Royal Scots Fusiliers
Major JB COOK

1/4th King's Own Scottish Borderers
Lieutenant Colonel JMB SANDERS

1/5th King's Own Scottish Borderers
Lieutenant Colonel SIMSON

155 Brigade Machine Gun Company

156 Brigade
Lieutenant Colonel AH LEGGETT

1/4th Royal Scots
Lieutenant Colonel FH GOLDTHORPE

1/7th Royal Scots
Lieutenant Colonel WC PEEBLES

1/7th Scottish Rifles
Lieutenant Colonel JG ROMANES

1/8th Scottish Rifles
Lieutenant Colonel JM FINDLAY

156 Brigade Machine Gun Company

157 Brigade
Colonel (Brigadier-General) CDH MOORE DSO

1/5th Highland Light Infantry
Colonel F MORRISON

1/6th Highland Light Infantry
Lieutenant Colonel J ANDERSON

1/7th Highland Light Infantry
Lieutenant Colonel JH GALBRAITH

1/5th Argyll & Sutherland Highlanders
Lieutenant Colonel B MATHEW-LANNOWE

157 Brigade Machine Gun Company

ORDER OF BATTLE FOR 26 March 1917.

53rd (Welsh) DIVISION

158 Brigade
Major (Brigadier General) SF MOTT

1/5th Royal Welch Fusiliers
Lieutenant Colonel FH BORTHWICK

1/6th Royal Welch Fusiliers
Lieutenant Colonel CS ROME

1/7th Royal Welch Fusiliers
Lieutenant Colonel TH HARKER

1/1st Herefordshire Regiment
Lieutenant Colonel G DRAGE

158th Brigade Machine Gun Company

159 Brigade
Colonel (Brigadier General) JH DuB TRAVERS

1/4th Cheshire Regiment
Lieutenant Colonel GH SWINDELLS

1/7th Cheshire Regiment
Lieutenant Colonel HM LAWRENCE

1/4th Welsh Regiment
Lieutenant Colonel HJ KINSMAN

1/5th Welsh Regiment
Lieutenant Colonel HR BOWEN

159 Brigade Machine Gun Company

160 Brigade
Colonel (Brigadier-General) WJC BUTLER

1/4th Royal Sussex Regiment
Lieutenant Colonel HS ASHWORTH

2/4th Royal West Surrey Regiment
Lieutenant Colonel H St C WILKINS

2/4th Royal West Kent Regiment
Lieutenant Colonel NE MONEY

2/10th Middlesex Regiment
Lieutenant Colonel VLN PEARSON

160 Brigade Machine Gun Company

ORDER OF BATTLE FOR 26 March 1917.

54th (East Anglian) DIVISION

161 Brigade
Lieutenant Colonel (Brigadier General) W MARRIOTT-DODDINGTON

1/4th Essex Regiment
Lieutenant Colonel EJ JAMESON

1/5th Essex Regiment
Lieutenant Colonel T GIBBONS

1/6th Essex Regiment
Major HP ALEXANDER

1/7th Essex Regiment
Lieutenant Colonel LS DELAMERE

161 Brigade Machine Gun Company
Major JA WALKER

162 Brigade
Brevet Lieutenant Colonel (Brigadier General) A MUDGE

1/5th Bedfordshire Regiment
Lieutenant Colonel EW BRIGHTEN

1/4th Northamptonshire Regiment
Colonel JC BROWN

1/10th London Regiment
Commanding Officer unknown

1/11th London Regiment
Commanding Officer unknown

162 Brigade Machine Gun Company

163 Brigade
Major (Hon Colonel Brigadier-General) T WARD

1/4th Norfolk Regiment
Lieutenant Colonel WA YOUDEN

1/5th Norfolk Regiment
Lieutenant Colonel BS GRISSELL

1/5th Suffolk Regiment
Lieutenant Colonel FA WOLLASTON

1/8th Hampshire Regiment
Major JFH MARSH

163 Brigade Machine Gun Company

ORDER OF BATTLE FOR 26 March 1917.

74th (Yeomanry) DIVISION

229 Brigade
Colonel (Brigadier General) R HOARE

16th Devon Regiment (Royal 1st & Royal North Devon Yeomanry's)
Lieutenant-Colonel RA SANDERS

12th Somerset Light Infantry (West Somerset Yeomanry)
Lieutenant-Colonel FNQ SHOULDHAM

14th Royal Highlanders (Fife & Forfar Yeomanry)
Sir J GILMOUR Bart M.P

12th Royal Scots Fusiliers (Ayr & Lanark Yeomanry's)
Lieutenant-Colonel JD BOSWELL

4th Machine Gun Company

Second Battle of Gaza

Introduction 98

Desert Column operations from 17 April 99
3rd Light Horse Brigade. 100
5th Mounted Brigade 103
4th Light Horse Brigade 113
6th Mounted Brigade 116
New Zealand Mounted Rifles Brigade. 118
22nd Mounted Brigade 122
2nd Light Horse Brigade 123
1st Light Horse Brigade 125

Eastern Force operations from 17 April 127
162nd Infantry Brigade 127
163rd Infantry Brigade 133
161st Infantry Brigade 145
155th Infantry Brigade 146
156th Infantry Brigade 160
157th Infantry Brigade 165
159th Infantry Brigade 172
160th Infantry Brigade 177
158th Infantry Brigade 183

Photographs 187
Trooper Arthur Henry NOAKES 187
Corporal John COMMON 188
Private John Henry BOSSINGHAM 189

Appendix 1 192
Order of Battle for 19 April
Appendix 2 203
Casualty list criteria
Appendix 3 204
Casualty total charts for the First Battle
Appendix 3 204
Casualty total charts for the Second Battle
Appendix 5 213
Gallantry Awards for the First & Second Battles
Appendix 6 241
Bibliography
Appendix 7 243
Appeals for information
Appendix 8 244
Appreciation
Appendix 9 247
Conventions and abbreviations

Second Battle of Gaza

Introduction

Following the events of 26 & 27 March, all troops were withdrawn to allow rest and reorganisation for a fresh assault on Gaza. Commanded by Lieutenant-General Sir Archibald Murray at Khan Yunis, it was decided to attack with two Corps. The Eastern Force would attack from the south-west, while the Desert Column would extend a covering screen to the south-east of Gaza to prevent Turkish troops circling round from the town or stop reinforcements advancing from Beersheba. The build-up was to be slow and thorough, with initial movements beginning on 16 & 17 April, to allow a strong line from which to launch the main attack.

The Eastern Force was to advance on a front with three Divisions.

52nd (Lowland) Division was to attack along the El Sire Ridge, which ran through a series of hills from the south-west. to its highest point at Ali el Muntar overlooking Gaza; Outpost Hill and Green Hill would become the scenes of bitter and protracted fighting to take and re-take them during the course of the 19 April.

The 54th (East Anglian) Division would both cover the right flank of the 52nd Division and attack two main targets on the Gaza-Beersheba Road; Road Trenches and Tank Redoubt would see enormous casualties being suffered.

Finally, the 53rd (Welsh) Division would advance along the coast, thus protecting the left flank of the 52nd Division, and take two the objectives of Sheikh Ajlin and Samson Ridge.

The Desert Column was to advance with two Divisions.

As well as providing a screen to the south-east to protect the right flank of the troops attacking Gaza, there were two objectives at Atawineh Redoubt and Sausage Ridge/Hairpin Redoubt

GENERAL PLAN of movements by CORPS & DIVISIONS

19 April 1917

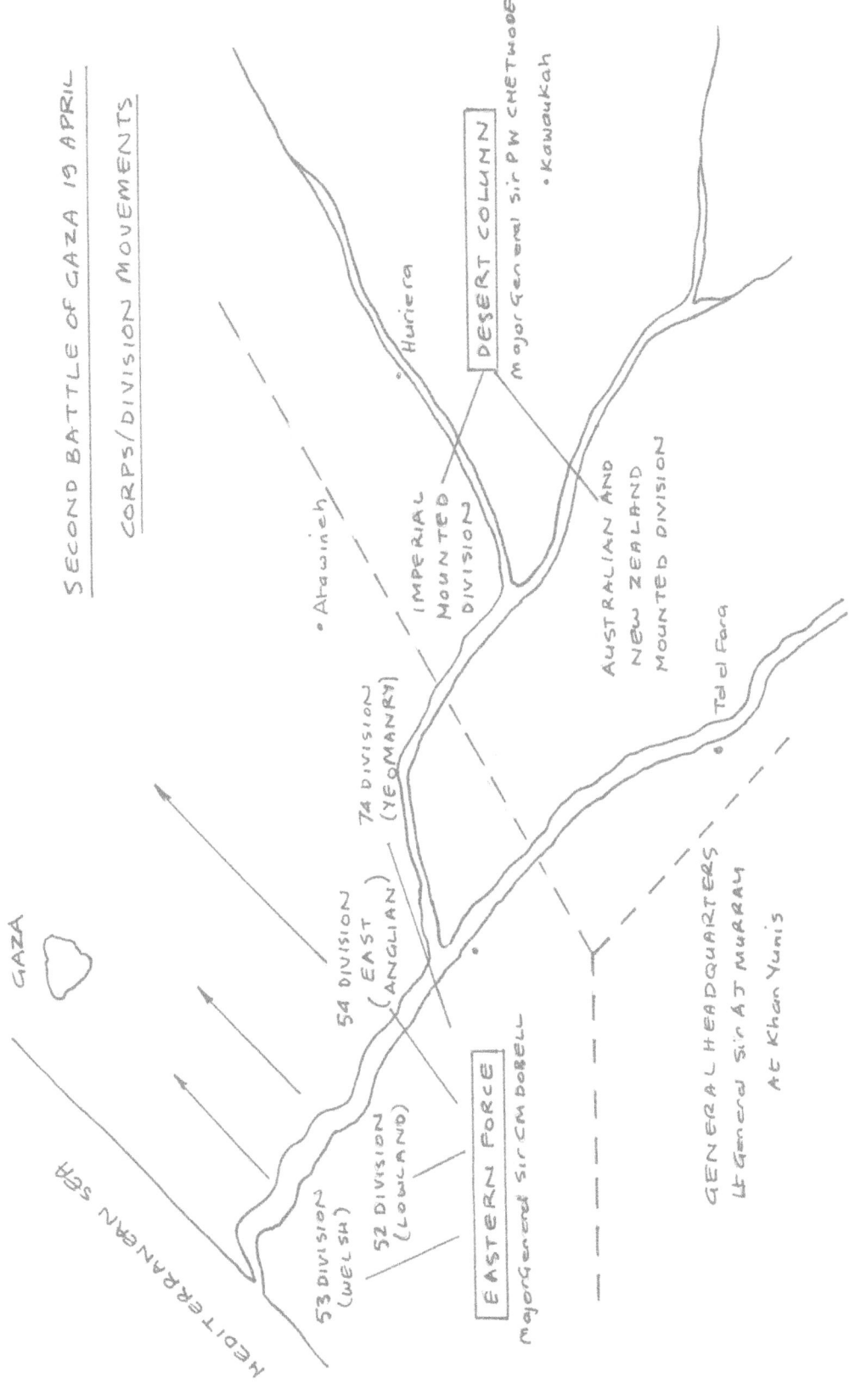

Second Battle of Gaza
3rd Light Horse Brigade.

FOR THE FIRST PHASE OF the battle on the 17th April, the 3rd Light Horse Brigade shared the common role of the IMPERIAL MOUNTED DIVISION, namely that of observation towards ASIFERIYEH and thereby protecting the right flank of the 54th Division's advance against Sheikh Abbas. Moving from TEL EL JEMMI in the early hours, the brigade made its way to EL MENDUR and took up a position to watch for reinforcements moving towards Sheikh Abbas. The 54th Division's objectives were taken against little opposition and upon relief around 1500 the brigade was free to return to Tel el Jemmi.

At 02.00 on 18th April the brigade commenced similar moves to the previous day, but this time they were to support the 6th Mounted Brigade who was on outpost duties about el Mendur. There was little movement by the enemy and by 10.00 the brigade once again returned to Tel el Jemmi. The rest of the day passed without incident until 17.00, when orders were received for the following day's operations. The Imperial Mounted Division was charged with taking the Turkish positions about the Gaza-Beersheba Road. These consisted of two redoubts, each at the summit of a ridge which rose to the north-east, the occupation of which would prevent enemy reinforcements moving along the road towards Gaza.

The 3rd Light Horse Brigade left its bivouac at Tel el Jemmi at 20.00 and rode north-east for two miles before crossing the Wadi Sheria near el Mendur. After a two hour halt on the northern bank of the wadi, the column took the course of the Wadi SIHAN to Asiferiyeh and dismounted before taking up positions for the attack. Of the two regiments in the line, the 10th Light Horse Regiment was on the right, with the 8th Light Horse Regiment in close support. Extending the division line to the right was the 5th Mounted Brigade and shortly before dawn the 4th Light Horse Brigade arrived to take up a line in contact with the left flank.

As the watery dawn broke, the objective of the 3rd Light Horse Brigade became visible. Over two miles of gently rising ground lay before them, the spine of Atawineh Ridge running in a north-easterly direction to the Atawineh Redoubt, at its summit on the Gaza-Beersheba Road. The redoubt commanded an extensive field, for although both flanks were open for some 2000 yards, to the front the ridge descended, any movement on either side being clearly visible.

The advance started at 07.00. With the spine of the ridge marking the left flank of the brigade, the two front-line regiments led the way, each being accompanied by two sections of the 3rd Australian Machine Gun Squadron. A gap soon developed on the left flank however, and the 8/Light Horse Regiment was ordered up from support to maintain contact between the 10/Light Horse Regiment and the 4/Light Horse Brigade.

By 08.40 the firing-line had approached two Turkish advanced trenches and prepared to assault them. The sight of the approaching Australians was sufficient in itself for these particular Turks however, and white flags were quickly raised. Regrettably, this signal had been used deceitfully in the past and had cost several Australian lives, so on this occasion the line was held until the Turkish intention was clearly that of surrender. Advancing slowly, the first two trenches were occupied and a third, previously unknown, trench was also captured, with about sixty prisoners in all being taken. After a short halt the advance was resumed and under heavy rifle fire, progressed to a line which varied between 1500 and 2000 yards from the Gaza-Beersheba Road. From concealed positions off to the right, enemy artillery took the brigade in enfilade and caused many casualties. Enemy resistance at this point also proved stubborn and totally held up the 5th Mounted Brigade, consequently preventing any further advance by the 3rd Light Horse Brigade which was forced to hold its position under constant fire while awaiting orders. The precarious situation of the 8/Light Horse Regiment was compounded when

"Two armoured cars came into the firing line at 10.30 with no doubt the best of intentions. They were of very little if any assistance to us, but in fact were the cause indirectly of increasing our casualties. The machines took up a position in the firing line, consequently enemy fire was concentrated on them. Our men

in the vicinity suffered and in addition one man was actually run over by a car and is in hospital. The cars were put out of action, the tyres being riddled and one gun damaged."

8/Light Horse Regiment War Diary. PRO WO 95/4560

At midday, the 8/Light Horse Regiment on the left was withdrawn in order to swing the brigade line to face north. Simultaneously, the 5/Mounted Brigade was similarly aligned, the intention being a combined assault on Atawineh Redoubt. The latter move resulted in a heavy counter-attack against that brigade, who asked for support from the 9/Light Horse Regiment on the right flank of the 3rd Light Horse Brigade, but they in turn were also being heavily engaged and were unable to assist. Under such condition the brigade was forced to retire, but fortunately the arrival of one squadron of the Warwickshire Yeomanry at 12.45, and a second shortly afterwards, allowed this withdrawal to be limited. For nearly two hours the situation in the line remained critical and only when three squadrons of the Berkshire and Buckinghamshire Yeomanry's arrived at 14.30 was the area finally stabilised.

The offensive now resumed as the 3rd Light Horse Brigade made a valiant attempt to advance and succeeded in establishing a line which was only 500 yards from the enemy position. Once again though, the sheer volume and intensity of the fire proved too great and the line was halted, under continued heavy enfilade artillery fire from the left and right flanks.

Orders to withdraw from the field were received at dusk and at 19.45 the men moved out to re-join their horse which had been left at Asiferiyeh. The final withdrawal line was taken up between Asiferiyeh on the left and Munkheileh on the right, at which point it joined up with the 6th Mounted Brigade.

IMPERIAL MOUNTED DIVISION
3RD LIGHT HORSE BRIGADE
19 APRIL 1917

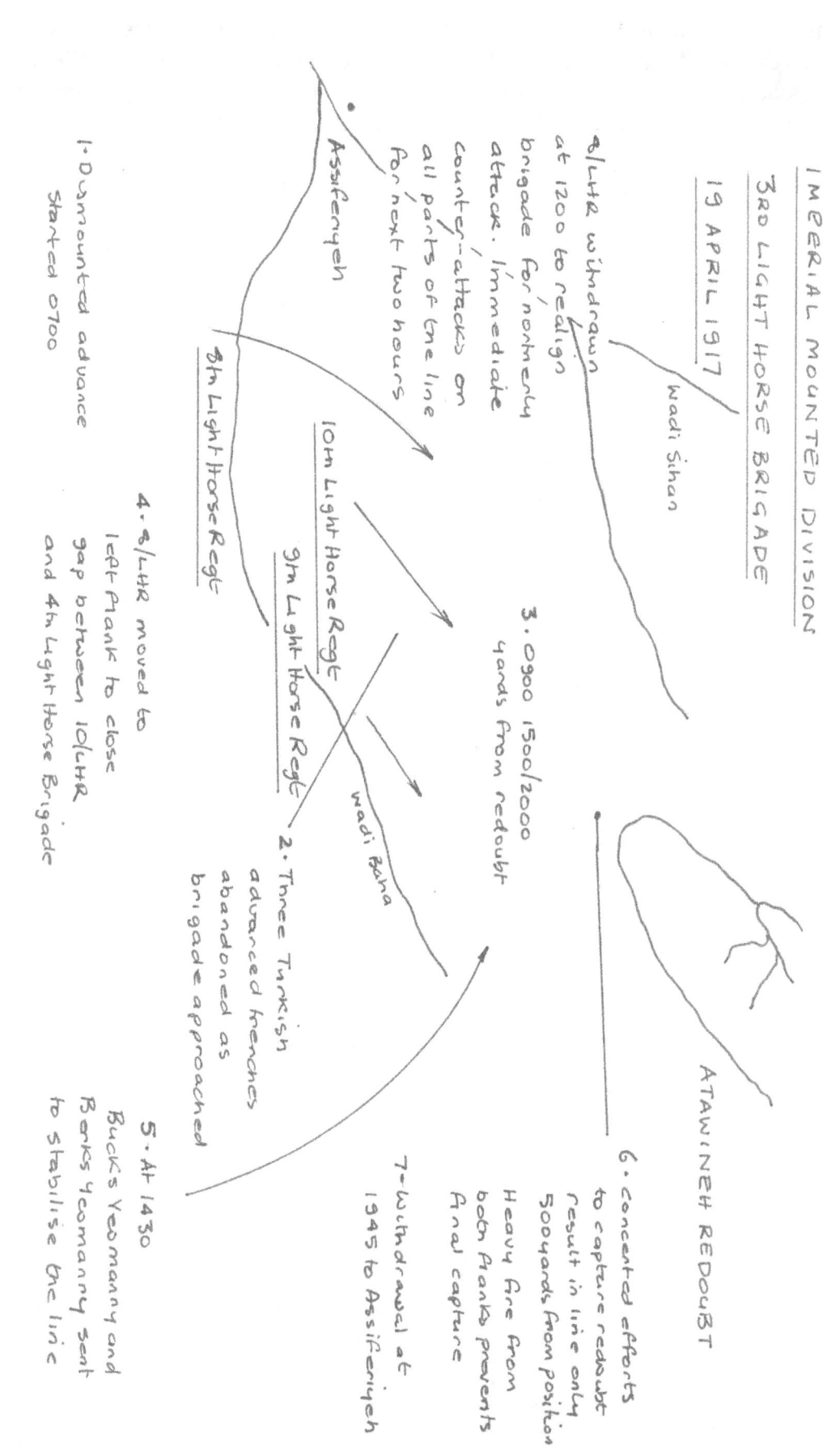

Second Battle of Gaza
5th Mounted Brigade.

THROUGH MANY OF THE ACCOUNTS and sources of the mounted troops it seems clear that many of the men had served for many years; no doubt that may be true of the infantry but the documentation for the yeomanry seems to emphasise this fact. Familiarity with conditions and the development of personal routine are two consequences of this experience, typified by the following quote.

"During the periods when the Regiment was many miles ahead of railhead, rations and forage reached it by means of the wonderful system of camel transport which was one of the many marvels of this campaign. Coarse large-meshed nets, like those used to deal with cargo on ships, were employed, slung on either side of the unsavoury beasts and so carried safe to the required destination; at least the quantity usually arrived as it had set out, though some thought the quality deteriorated on the journey. But camels will be camels. No doubt the irritation caused by the flies swarming about their sore eyes and slobbery mouths was considerable, and the sharp corners of the loaves of bread protruding through the net provided obviously a heaven-sent opportunity for a good scratch in the world of sand. Captain Teichman always peeled his bread ration with surgical precision, but then doctors often are a bit squeamish.

Another feature of warfare demanded attention at this time in the shape of lice and other creeping things. Hitherto, since Gallipoli, the army had been singularly free from this particular plague, but when it arrived at el Arish and encamped on ground long occupied by Turkish troops, it was not long before clothing became infested. While at El Burj, Corporal Foster of D Squadron, who had been through he South African campaign with the 18th Hussars, pointed out that the same ants which they had employed in South Africa to rid their clothing of vermin were to be found in the sand-hills. Experiments were made and it was quickly found that these ants provided the most efficient delousers imaginable, a very fortunate discovery, though unluckily these useful little insects were not found in many localities.

Yeomanry Cavalry of Worcestershire 1914-1922. Page 82

Along with the rest of the IMPERIAL MOUNTED DIVISION, the 5th Mounted Brigade began its preparatory moves on the evening of the 16th April. From IN SEIRAT the brigade rode to a new camp near TEL EL JEMMI on the Wadi Ghuzze, arriving at about 21.00.

At midnight two small patrols of the Worcester Yeomanry left ahead of the main advance with the difficult and exceedingly daring task of cutting the main telegraph wire between Gaza and Beersheba. Although the routes had been meticulously planned from aerial photographs, the total darkness necessitated complete reliance on compass bearings.

Leading the patrols were Lieutenants JH PARSONS and RMF HARVEY of D Squadron, each with five men from their squadron. Initially both parties, each taking a different course, made good progress, but suddenly Lieutenant Parsons' group was discovered. The enemy began firing into the party, which repeatedly tried to find a way forward but was blocked at every attempt. With the dawn beginning to break, all chance of reaching the still distant objective was gone and Lieutenant Parsons was forced to withdraw his patrol.

"Lieutenant Harvey's party met with no such mishap. The compass march was led by Sergeant H WOOD with extraordinary accuracy and skill and the Gaza-Beersheba Road was reached without the Turks becoming aware of their presence. The telegraph lines were destroyed about a mile south-east of Sihan and the party began their return march."

Record of the Worcestershire Yeomanry. Page 96

The discovery of one patrol had naturally alerted the Turks however, and general firing began along the line, although Lieutenant Harvey's party remained undetected until the increasing light eventually revealed them. Galloping back under a frantic enemy fire the patrol re-joined the squadron at 04.30, having sustained only one man wounded.

At 00.45 on 17th April the Warwickshire Yeomanry led the brigade down to cross the Wadi Ghuzze and then to Mendur. From here, the brigade moved south-east to take up a line from the right flank of the 3rd Light Horse Brigade at el Munkheileh to Khirbit Erk. Despite encountering isolated enemy parties, the new line was taken up before dawn on the 17th and was consolidated by 08.00, with the Worcestershire Yeomanry in the centre and flanked by the yeomanry's of Gloucester and Warwickshire to the left and right respectively.

There was much movement by the enemy throughout the morning and it became evident that the Gaza-Beersheba Road was well protected. The Turks must have realised that an attack was imminent, but apart from limited artillery fire they were content to await the advance. At 14.30 the brigade was relieved by the 6th Mounted Brigade and returned to Tel el Jemmi at 19.00.

The 18th April was spent in preparation for the main attack and apart from officer reconnaissance patrols, the brigade was not required. There were however the usual multitude of tasks to be carried out with the horses needing constant attention and care. The following quote, although referring to the journey out from England in 1915, illustrates the care and devotion of the men to their horses.

The main body of the Regiment rested in sheds for three days at Avonmouth, and then embarked on the S.S. Nile. My own troop, however, with one other, and details, walked straight from the train on to the S.S. Crispin or Crippen, as she was soon called, to take charge of about six hundred horses. She was a small boat, and had been used, so we were told, as a South American cattle boat. The whole of the top, first, second and third decks were fitted up with narrow stalls, 3ft 6in wide at the most; the passage-ways were very narrow, and the sloping gangways from one deck to another very deep. Each horse, fresh, frisky and frightened, on a head-stall only, had to be run up a gangway, along a deck passage and then down a gangway, along another narrow passage and then backed into a stall, which his hips would only just go through if you steered him carefully.

The officers were all arguing as to which horses should go on the bottom deck, and which should have the serener air of the top deck, but somehow or other with the help of brute force and b----y ignorance, those horses were soon all stalled, and with eighty souls to attend them the boat sailed early next morning.

There was of course no grooming to be done, as the horses were packed so tightly together; but every horse had to be watered separately, feeds had to be prepared and hay packed in hay-nets, like ladies hairnets, so that by the time the whole shipload had been watered, fed and hayed-up, it was time to start feeding again.

The bugle sounded almost continuously for something or other all day, and of course, among so few, the night guard duties were heavy indeed. Moreover, as the horse-boat of the Warwick Yeomanry had been torpedoed just behind us, we travelled without lights at night; which added immensely to our difficulties, for all the portholes had to be closed, and thus it became terribly hot and stuffy below decks after sundown.

At Gibraltar we were surrounded by fussy little naval boats enquiring into our credentials, but after an hour or so we were allowed to proceed. It had been a wonderful voyage for one who had never left England's shores before; and I shall never forget the magnificence of that first sunset in the Mediterranean. A slight mist had arisen on the water, and as the sun sank astern in a track of golden glitter, the mountains on the Spanish coast reflected ever deepening shades of red, orange, mauve and purple, which darkened further into indigo after the sun had gone down.

A day out from Gibraltar a curious illness was contracted by several of the horses. They went off their feed, and developed rapidly a kind of pneumonia, which in many cases prove fatal within twenty-four hours. It was pitiful to watch some of the best-loved horses in the Regiment taken suddenly with this disease. The symptoms were lack of appetite, a high temperature, glassy eye and gasping for breath. Very few horses thus afflicted recovered, and the veterinary staff and farriers were soon desperately over-worked in devotedly nursing their sick charges.

The cause of it was the foetid heat below decks, and the lack of a clear stream of fresh air through all parts of the vessel. Many of the horses had their heads very near the engine rooms, and it was in this part of the boat that the greatest fatalities occurred. Throughout the journey, owing to the narrow nature of the stalls, and the general crowding of the horses on the boat, no attempt had been made to clear any of the dung, and the gases from this, accentuated by the heat, may have been a decidedly contributory factor. Orders were thus given to clean out the stalls, and for two days we worked continually below decks, stripped to the waist, dripping with perspiration; breeches, puttees and boots soaked in dung-juice, shovelling horse-dung into baskets by the hundred-weights, hauling them up and emptying them overboard.

Each horse was stood out in a narrow passageway in turn, and his stall thoroughly cleansed, and disinfected.

A word of praise for the officers who realising the immensity of the task, readily gave a hand, not with the actual cleaning out, but with the disposal of "the golden balls". It was a sight to see some of them, heavily gloved, hauling up the dung-baskets and slinging the contents overboard. The remarks of the trooper who drew such an eloquent analogy between certain of the junior officers and the material they were handling, if relevant, were hardly in the best of taste.

Another difficult task, and a hateful one, as may very well be imagined, was the disposal of the bodies of the dead horses. There was hardly room for a horse to fall down in its stall as it died, and working in the cramped space it called for great strength to heave the carcasses into the passageways. If possible we turned the body onto its back, for the more easily manoeuvring along the gangway to the hatchways, through which the derrick chains could reach it for slinging overboard.

These frequent sea-burials were a melancholy sight, as men who understand know that horses have their characters as well as humans, and some of our very best pals were dumped into the waters of the Mediterranean. The sickness among the horses increased, and by the time we reached Alexandria no less than thirty-two had been thrown to Davy Jones."

Yarn of a Yeoman. SF Hatton. Pages 45-49

At 02.00 on 19th April, the brigade moved out from Tel el Jemmi and three hours later was assembled at el Munkheileh. Two squadrons of the Warwickshire Yeomanry moved forward and relieved the Buckinghamshire Yeomanry who then re-joined their own brigade. The rest of the Warwick's were detailed to guard the horses at el Munkheileh as the brigade was to make a dismounted attack against the area to the south-east of Atawineh Redoubt. The remaining two regiments of the brigade moved into the front-line at 06.00. The Worcester Yeomanry on the left was to maintain contact with the 3rd Light Horse Brigade, while the Gloucester Yeomanry was flanked to their right by the Australian and New Zealand Mounted Division; the Warwick's were reserve to the brigade.

The objective of the brigade was the right-hand flank of the Atawineh Redoubt, thus completing the attack of the 3rd Light Horse Brigade. The advance began at 0700, with the Worcester's and Gloucester's each having two squadrons in the front-line and supported by the third squadron. The Warwick's in reserve followed close behind, with B Squadron trailing the Worcester's and D Squadron behind the Gloucester's on the right. Heavy shellfire began at once, both shrapnel and high-explosive, but good progress was nevertheless made over the gradually rising ground which led to the redoubt. Although the 3rd Light Horse Brigade was initially ahead of the brigade, they held back until contact between the two was made at about 07.50.

Off to the right flank of the brigade, a ridge ran to the north-east and thus parallel to the Atawineh Ridge. This was known as SAUSAGE RIDGE. and was surmounted by the HAIRPIN REDOUBT. The protection of this flank was the responsibility of the Australian Mounted Division who engaged the enemy with fire from the Ayrshire Battery, Royal Field Artillery on the lower slopes of Sausage Ridge.

By 09.00 it had become evident that the enemy presence on Sausage Ridge and in the Hairpin Redoubt was far stronger than had been anticipated. Sniper fire against the Gloucester Yeomanry on the brigade's right continually harassed the advance and at 09.10 the Warwick Yeomanry sent C Squadron up to reinforce the right flank. The fire was nevertheless too heavy and further artillery was sent up to attempt to contain it, for the whole advance against the Atawineh position was now in jeopardy, and soon the artillery of both the mounted divisions was turned against Sausage Ridge. At 10.55, Brigadier-General EA WIGGIN, commanding the 5th Mounted Brigade, sent the following message to the commanding officers of the front-line units of the brigade;

> *"New Zealand Mounted Rifles Brigade coming up to take Sausage Hill on our right. When that is clear you will push on to the Gaza-Beersheba Road, turn left handed between road and telegraph wire and attack Rijm el Atawineh while the NZMR Brigade will attack Point 467. Do not advance until Sausage Hill is cleared.*
>
> Gloucester Yeomanry War Diary. PRO WO 95/4565

In accordance with this message, the Wellington Mounted Rifles attacked along the ridge at 11.30. On the way they picked up the 3rd Squadron, Auckland Mounted Rifles who had earlier acted as artillery escort and now took up position on the right of the firing line. Heavy enemy fire opened up at once, but the New Zealanders gallantly pressed on and within an hour were about halfway along the ridge. The enemy obviously had no intention of relinquishing its two redoubts in the Atawineh area and kept up a relentless pressure against the attackers throughout the morning. The strategically sited redoubts continued to support each other, any assault against one being enfiladed by fire from the other.

By midday it was obvious that a combined assault against one redoubt must be attempted to try and break the deadlock. In preparation for this attack, the 5th Mounted Brigade and the 3rd Light Horse Brigade swung their lines north to face Atawineh Redoubt. This caused the right flank of the brigade to become exposed and B Squadron, Gloucester Yeomanry was sent to fill the gap; it would also be able to engage and contain some of the enemy fire from Hairpin Redoubt.

Before the attack against Atawineh Redoubt could be launched however, the Turkish counter-attacks which were in progress against the 54th Division to the north-west, spread down the Gaza-Beersheba Road and at 12.30 fell against the left of the 4th Light Horse Brigade which was forced back thus leaving the left of the 3rd Light Horse Brigade exposed. Despite a spirited resistance by both brigades, the enemy was far too strong and the whole flank was withdrawn.

The situation on the left flank of the 5th Mounted Brigade was now critical and placed the whole flank in danger of collapse in the event of a sustained counter-attack. The only immediately available reserve was the Warwick Yeomanry's B Squadron who came into action at 12.45. So serious was the threat to the flank that D Squadron, from its position in rear of the Gloucester Yeomanry on the right, was withdrawn and rushed across to assist B Squadron. It seemed unlikely that the two extra squadrons could succeed in holding back a strong counter-attack and further reinforcements were requested from the 6th Mounted Brigade which was in reserve at el Munkheileh. Two squadrons of the Berkshire Yeomanry and one squadron, Buckinghamshire Yeomanry arrived at 14.30 and were immediately used to reinforce the left flank of the Worcester's.

IMPERIAL MOUNTED DIVISION
5TH MOUNTED BRIGADE
19 APRIL 1917

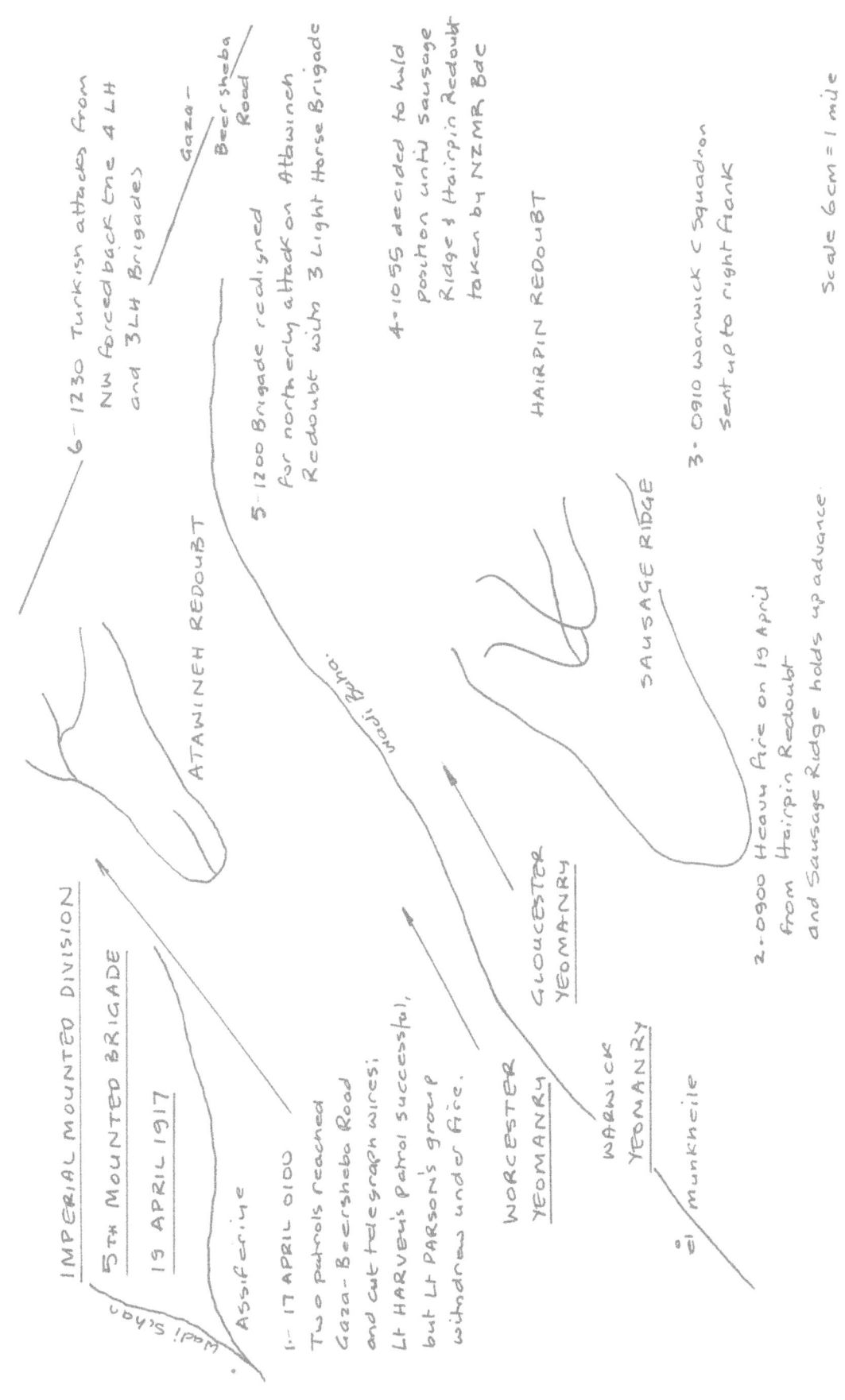

IMPERIAL MOUNTED DIVISION
5TH MOUNTED BRIGADE-SQUADRON DETAILS
19 APRIL 1917

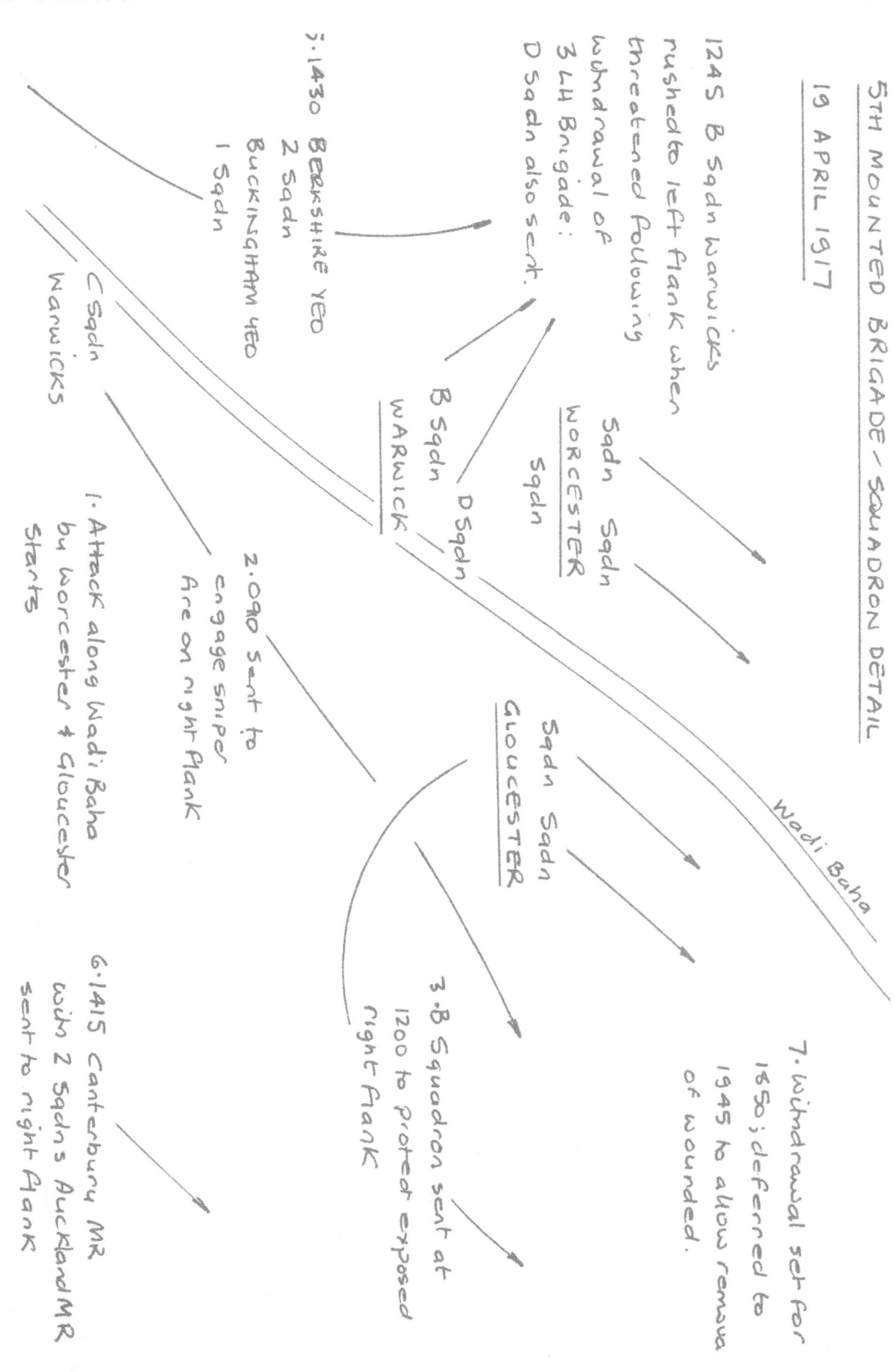

Problems had also been occurring simultaneously on the right flank.

Due to the failure of the Wellington Mounted Rifles to capture Hairpin Redoubt, the enfilade fire from there continued to pin down the Gloucester's. As already stated, B Squadron Gloucester Yeomanry had been sent up at around 12.00 to strengthen the right flank which had become exposed during preparations for the combined attack on Atawineh Redoubt. Initially this move was successful and the flank was secured. However, at 12.45 the Warwick Squadron which was in reserve was called off to the far left flank. When the Turks realised this, they re-doubled their fire against the Gloucester's and as the position became untenable, B Squadron was withdrawn to a covering position. Around this time -14.15- the Turks began massing for an advance along the Wadi Baha, astride which the brigade lay. With all brigade reserves committed and the 6th Mounted Brigade in action on the left flank, only the prompt arrival of the Canterbury Mounted Rifles and two squadrons of the Auckland Mounted Rifles saved the situation.

By a combination of timely reinforcement and gallant action the crisis had been recovered, although it could now be nothing more than a holding action. The enemy fire, particularly the artillery, continued to be heavy against all sections of the front late into the afternoon. The dismounted yeomen of the brigade lay on the baking slopes and desperately held their ground but with little prospect of continuing the attack. This fact was reluctantly recognised by the commanding officers of the Desert Column, who accordingly issued orders for a withdrawal to begin at 18.50. To allow time for evacuation of the wounded, which totalled about sixty for the brigade, this was deferred by an hour, and so at 19.45 the withdrawal began.

Passing through the 6th Mounted Brigade outpost line, the brigade picked up their horses which had been held at el Munkeileh. Tel el Jemmi was reached at 23.00 and after a short halt for water a bivouac was taken up at el Mendur so as to be able to support the outpost line if necessary.

The 20th April passed with the brigade in reserve and although the enemy heavily shelled the area, there were no serious counter-attacks. Late in the afternoon, the brigade relieved the 6th Mounted Brigade at el Munkeileh. The Gloucester Yeomanry held the left of the line from el Munkeileh in a southerly direction for about one mile from where it was continued by the Worcester Yeomanry along the Wadi Sheria as far as Khirbit Erk. The Warwick's were in reserve with brigade headquarters at Point 280 about two miles to the west.

Additional narrative 5th Mounted Brigade

Second Battle of Gaza April 16th
The 5th Mounted Brigade, on the following day, were ordered to take up a line some two miles east of El Mendur, its left under the Atawineh Ridge, its right at the junction of the Wadis Imleih and Sharia. This line it was to hold in order to keep in check any enemy forces from Sharia, threatening the flank of the infantry further north. On the right of the Imperial [Mounted] Division, the Anzac [Mounted] Division was to perform similar duties watching the enemy at Hareira from Shellal. Before moving from Tel el Jemmi two officers patrols were to set out at midnight to ride in the dark through the enemy lines with the object of cutting the enemy telegraph communications which ran along the Gaza-Beersheba Road, six miles distant from Tel el Jemmi and three and a half to four miles behind the known Turkish outpost line. Lieutenants JH Parsons and RMF Harvey of D Squadron, each with five picked and well-mounted men of the same squadron, were selected to carry out this enterprise.

In his fine cricket career for Warwickshire, Parsons had often met and overcome critical situations, but it is doubtful if any of them produced the intense emotions aroused by this expedition. Shortly after midnight the two little parties set out in the black darkness which alone made their ride possible, each on a different course, as it was felt that if one failed to get through the other might succeed. Of course the two routes to be followed had been mapped out with the utmost care beforehand. They had been drawn to avoid the known Turkish entrenchments as discovered by aeroplane photographs, and the impassable wadis, but every portion of the journey out and back had to be laid on a compass bearing. The smallest error in judgements of pace, the slightest deviation from the bearing to be followed would inevitably lead to discovery and failure.

For a time all went well with both parties, but suddenly a challenge rang out in front of Parsons' party. Had they made an error in their course or had the Turks taken up new posts which now made that course impossible? In the pitch darkness it was not possible to know. Parsons tried to slip quietly away and round by another way, but the enemy was now alarmed and started shooting. Everywhere where the horsemen tried to find a gap they met an alert enemy, and, as the first faint light of the dawn was showing in the east, Parsons had to give up the attempt and extricate his patrol as best he could.

Harvey's party met with no such mishap. The compass march was led by Sergeant H Wood with such extraordinary accuracy and skill that the Gaza-Beersheba road was reached without the Turks becoming aware of their presence. The telegraph lines were destroyed about a mile south-east of Sihan and the party began their return march. The firing at Parsons' patrol had probably set the enemy on the qui vive, but, whatever may have been the cause, the Turks were now thoroughly aroused. Promiscuous firing began everywhere, but as yet Harvey's patrol had not been discovered. The gathering light, however, at last disclosed their position and then it became a matter of pace and good luck to get out. The remainder of the journey homewards was made at full gallop under a hail of bullets and a little after 4.30 am both patrols were safely back with their squadron, having only had one man and one horse wounded. For sheer skill and daring, as distinguished from hammer and tongs fighting, this adventure stands as high as anything done by the Regiment in the war; it was a delightful piece of impertinence.

The Yeomanry Cavalry of Worcestershire 1914-1922. Pages 95-96.

6th Mounted/ 5th Mounted/ 3rd Light Horse Brigades

Casualties for the Second Battle of Gaza

"It was about 1.30 when Drake cantered up to where we were and told us that Valintine was badly wounded, my Troop Sergeant, Wheildon killed and others, besides many wounded including himself. Although suffering from a bad wound in the leg Drake managed to remain mounted and rode back to Belah where his wound was attended to, and a month later he was able to re-join the regiment. Wheildon had sat up to reload his rifle when he was shot in the head by a sniper."

Sergeant John WEILDON 310360 Warwickshire Yeomanry. 19 April 1917. Age 27. Son of John and Margaret Wheildon of Green Farm, Kineton Warwickshire. Jerusalem Memorial.

"Moving up nearer the firing line I met wounded officers and men tottering out of the danger zone, and familiar faces in the regiment passed me, including Valintine on a stretcher, Townsend with a smashed wrist, Sergeant Bateman with a mangled hand and Sergeant MacKenna hit in the body."

One of the senior officer casualties to the Worcester Yeomanry was Major St J L O'B FFRENCH-BLAKE who was on attachment from the 21st (Empress of India's) Lancers. Aged 28, he was the son of The Reverend R Ffrench Blake of Staple, Kent and was married. He had commanded A Squadron at the First Battle of Gaza and had operated against superior Turkish forces by short, sharp attacks without becoming heavily engaged.

Several men of the Worcester's were noted in the regimental history. Corporal Cameron Harris KERR 23 "a most promising NCO" was from Kidderminster, Worcester; Private F CRUTCHLEY 325956 sent out from Southampton in December 1916 and landed at Alexandria on Boxing Day. Private Joseph Henry MATTHEWS 325646 was one of the original yeomen from the start of the war, killed on the 19th April, 1917.

The 10/Light Horse Regiment started the day alongside the 9/LHR and suffered eight killed but some 10/122 wounded. Lance-Corporal Ralph Ernest DISHER. Age 31 from Bordertown, South Australia. Trooper Alfred Septimus BARTLETT died of his wounds on 21 April, aged 27 he was from Blackheath, London where his grieving parents continued to live at "Rosevean" Manor Way.

The 8/Light Horse Regiment started in reserve but was soon called to close a gap which developed on the left flank; many casualties were caused around 10.30. Two armoured cars came into the line but drew heavy fire into the area.

Lance-Corporal William WILLIAM 753 was from Warracknabeal, Victoria but lived in Marriners Reef Road, Maryborough, Victoria with his wife Charlotte;

Trooper William John WHITE No 851 was from Wallacedale, Victoria; Trooper William George DUGUID No 363, age 21, was the son of Charles and Jane Duguid of Magill, South Australia but had been born at Saltcoats, Ayrshire, Scotland. Men from familiar towns and areas fought and died alongside men from all over South Australia, from towns and areas unfamiliar to the author. Men with the same ideals and the same thoughts about home, wherever it was, and grieved for by parents and wives alike.

Finally, to highlight the often cruel irony of war, Trooper Leslie Harry CAREY No 1098 9/Light Horse Regiment. He fought through the actions described, came through unscathed when some eighty of his mates were killed or wounded and was sent to the coast for rest and recuperation. He was accidentally drowned on 1 May 1917.

Private Percy Howard BADCOCK Buckinghamshire Yeomanry was very possibly one of those killed as the regiment galloped across two miles of open plain. The left flank of the Imperial Mounted Division had been forced back by strong Turkish attacks; the 4th Light Horse Brigade withdrew at 12.30, the 3rd Light Horse Brigade shortly after. The Berkshire Yeomanry and C Squadron, Buckinghamshire Yeomanry's classic deployment saved the situation at Atawineh Ridge. Private Badcock was 29 years old and came from Woking, Surrey, where he lived with his parents John and Florence in Boundary Road. In the same action, Sergeant William Thomas Henry BARRY of the Berkshire Yeomanry was seriously wounded, dying later the same day. Aged 24, he was the eldest son, and lived with his parents in

Queen's Road, Windsor, working as an assistant in the Royal Library, Windsor Castle. Another Sergeant, with the Buckinghamshire Yeomanry, was Jesse JORDAN from Newport Pagnell, Buckinghamshire. He had been a policeman with the City of London Police before joining the yeomanry and was 26 years old when killed on the 19th April.

The fortunes of the 3rd Light Horse Brigade were varied through the day with an initial advance along the Atawineh Ridge, being held up under fire and counter-attack before they launched a final, unsuccessful attack in the late afternoon.

Of the 9/Light Horse Regiment:

Corporal Brian McKENNA, 22, of Peterborough, South Australia;
Trooper Richard George ROBINSON 31 of Meningie, South Australia.

Several men of the regiment died of their wounds at Deir el Belah;
Trooper Alfred LAWTON age 20, on the 22 April, originally from Suffolk, England;
Trooper Timothy LINEHAN on the 20 April, from Bunbartha, Victoria;
Trooper Kelvin ROACH also on the 20 April. Aged 24 he came from Kent Town, South Australia where he lived with his parents at 81, Kent Terrace.

IMPERIAL MOUNTED DIVISION
4ᵗʰ Light Horse Brigade
19 April 1917

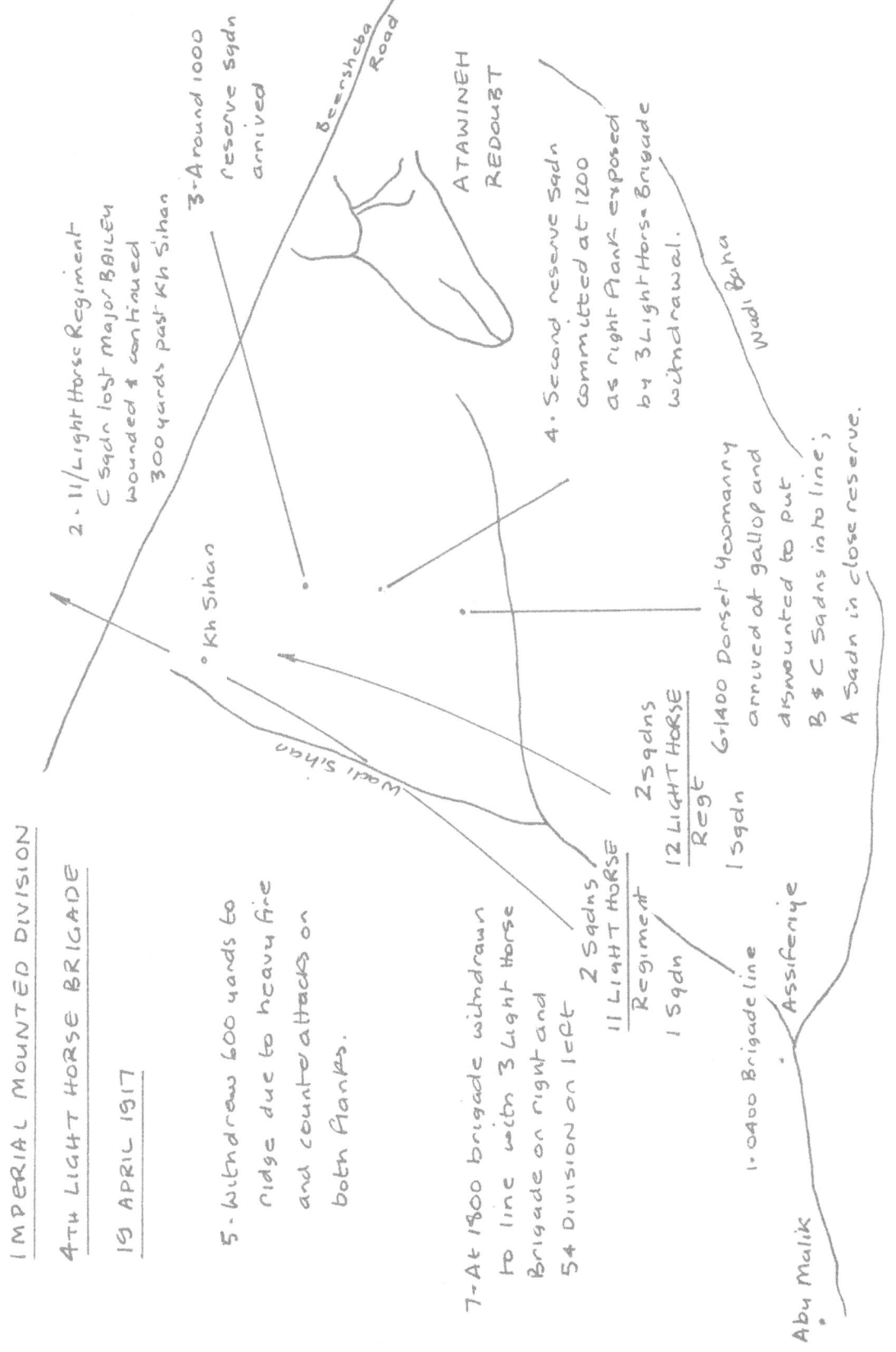

Second Battle of Gaza
4th Light Horse Brigade

ON THE EVENING OF THE 16th April, the 4th Light Horse Brigade was positioned about TEL EL JEMMI and in rear of the 3rd Light Horse Brigade. Only two regiments were present, as the 4/Light Horse Regiment had still to re-join from its duties at Lahfan.

The following morning at 04.00, there was a general "stand-to" as the First Phase of the advance began, although the brigade was not actively involved and remained in reserve. At 15.00 on the 17th April, the 12/Light Horse Regiment and one squadron of the 11/Light Horse Regiment, along with machine-gun support, moved to take over the outpost line from ASSIFERIYEH on the right, to the 54th Division on DUMBELL HILL on the left, currently held by the 3rd Light Horse Brigade. This line was held throughout the night and although due to be relieved the next day, this never took place, the brigade thus being responsible for this front until the start of the Second Phase. The line for the night of 18 April was detailed to the 11/Light Horse Regiment and one squadron 12/Light Horse Regiment, the remainder being kept in bivouac at El Mendur.

At 01.00 on the 19th April, the brigade began its final preparations for the battle by moving up to concentrate in rear of the outpost line, this being completed by about 03.30. Half-an-hour later the brigade dismounted and

> "deployed on a line from the southern branch of the Wadi Sihan at Assiferiyeh on the right, linking with the 3rd Light Horse Brigade, to a line drawn from Abu Malik to Khirbit Sihan on the left, to link up with the Imperial Camel Brigade."
>
> 4th Light Horse Brigade War Diary. PRO WO95/4562

Reconnaissance of the front had already been undertaken and small enemy posts in the upper reaches of the Wadi Sihan noted; these were cleared by mounted troops soon after deployment. As dawn approached at about 05.00, the link-up with troops to either flank was able to take place, and the whole line advanced a few hundred yards, the brigade continuing to straddle the Wadi Sihan. The brigade advanced at 07.30 with the 11/Light Horse Regiment on the left and the 12/Light Horse Regiment on the right; one squadron from each was held in reserve along with three machine-gun sections. There were about 4000 yards of completely open ground to be crossed to the brigade objective of Khirbit Sihan on the Gaza-Beersheba Road. After advancing several hundred yards, the 11/Light Horse Regiment crossed to the eastern bank of the Wadi Sihan so as to be able to attack Khirbit Sihan alongside the 12/Light Horse Regiment. Moving rapidly forward, a first ridge was taken against little close-contact opposition, although a heavy artillery fire from a north-westerly direction was kept up the whole time. With the Imperial Camel Brigade to the left, the 4th Light Horse Brigade continued the attack over successive ridges and by 09.30 had occupied Khirbit Sihan. Enfilade shell and machine-gun fire from both flanks assailed the position, which had now become a salient, as the 3rd Light Horse Brigade to the right was held up before Atawineh Redoubt, while to the left the advance from Sheikh Abbas was being decimated. There was a further complication at this point as C Squadron, 11/Light Horse Regiment had lost their Commanding Officer Major PJ BAILEY, wounded, and had thus not received the order to stop at Khirbit Sihan. They pushed on another 300 yards, which, although helping to protect the right flank of the Imperial Camel Brigade, further accentuated the salient. Shortly after 10.00 however, the former defenders of Khirbit Sihan were seen to be retiring to Atawineh Redoubt, and some measure of respite was obtained. One squadron was sent up from reserve to reinforce the right flank where a gap had occurred due to the disparity in the advances of the 3rd and 4th Light Horse Brigades. With the success of the overall attack dependant on similar advances by the adjacent troops, the brigade was forced to hold its tenuous position and await developments.

Not until midday was there a notable change in the situation, at which time the Turks launched a series of counter-attacks across the whole front. A major advance against the 54th Division to the north-west spread down the Gaza-Beersheba Road and, after brushing aside the Imperial Camel Brigade, threatened the left of the brigade. Unfortunately this coincided with the realignment of the 3rd Light Horse Brigade and the 5th Mounted Brigade to face Atawineh Redoubt; the planned withdrawal of the 8/Light Horse Regiment effectively isolated the 4th Light Horse Brigade. To support the now-exposed right flank of the 12/Light Horse Regiment, the second reserve squadron and one machine-gun section were sent up. Finding itself in such a vulnerable position and with its own reserves fully committed, as well as having suffered heavy casualties, the brigade had no option but to fall back 600 yards to a covering ridge. The timely arrival around 1400 of the Dorset Yeomanry of the 6th Mounted Brigade, from reserve at el Munkheileh, finally stabilised the situation, as they reinforced the right flank and closed the gap between the 12/Light Horse Regiment and the 3rd Light Horse Brigade.

It gradually became clear however that although continuity of the line had been maintained, there was little chance of continuing with the attack. Heavy casualties had occurred and all reserves had been deployed. The situation was the same across the whole front, and by late afternoon a withdrawal became inevitable. At 18.00 this was confirmed and the brigade took up a line from Asiferiyeh on the right, in contact with the 3rd Light Horse Brigade, across to the right flank of the 54th Division on Dumbell Hill.

Second Battle of Gaza
6th Mounted Brigade

THE 6TH MOUNTED BRIGADE WAS primarily Divisional Reserve for the operations from the 17th to the 19th April, but various squadrons played an active part in supporting the attacks. The brigade moved from IN SEIRAT after dusk on the 16 April and rode to Tel el Jemmi on the Wadi Ghuzze. Arriving at 01.00 the following day, the brigade was kept on standby until dawn The IMPERIAL MOUNTED DIVISION'S objectives were easily achieved and the only call upon the brigade was to march east to take up a line six miles away at KHIRBIT ERK, this being assigned to the Dorset Yeomanry at 14.30. There was little activity by the enemy in opposing this move, and during the evening the brigade was withdrawn to Tel el Jemmi leaving an outpost line in place.

The brigade remained at Tel el Jemmi throughout the 18th April, with limited reconnaissance patrols being sent out over the previous days ground. The enemy remained quiet, both sides preparing for the obviously impending assault. When the divisional orders were received late in the afternoon, it was learned that the brigade was to be in reserve, although ready to advance at once if needed. Accordingly, when the 5th Mounted Brigade left Tel el Jemmi at 02.00 on the 19th April, the brigade moved east and reached EL MUNKHEILEH two-and-a-half hours later. As the division was to attack dismounted, the horses were left in the charge of holders, while the remainder of the men awaited orders.

The Imperial Mounted Division's advance began at 06.30, midway through a two-hour bombardment by the divisional artillery. The Turkish artillery opened up at once with a heavy fire and the men of the brigade watched as their divisional comrades marched onto the open plain to meet it. The fortunes of this attack are described elsewhere, and as it was due to the siting and strength of the Turkish positions that it was brought to a halt by mid-morning, the brigade was therefore not required.

As noon passed, the Turks changed their stance from passive to offensive as they launched a series of counter-attacks, the strongest of which was against the left of the Imperial Mounted Division. Advancing in strength under cover of their continuing artillery bombardment, the force hit the 4th Light Horse Brigade at 12.30, causing it to fall back; the 3rd Light Horse Brigade was similarly affected soon afterwards. The whole flank was in danger of disintegration, when the holding force of the 5th Mounted Brigade sent an urgent message for the 6th Mounted Brigade to come up at once. The relief is best described by an eyewitness;

"Looking south-westwards from the Atawineh Ridge across two miles of level ground towards the Wadi Munkheileh, the writer could see the latter enveloped in clouds of smoke from the shells which were bursting over it. Suddenly he saw a sight which thrilled him; out of the wall of smoke which hid Munkheileh there emerged a mass of horsemen, which gradually opened out into extended order and filled the foreground. It was the Berkshire Yeomanry led by their Commanding Officer Lieutenant-Colonel JT Wigan DSO, and "C" Squadron Buckinghamshire Yeomanry. Disdaining to dismount, for they knew it was a matter of minutes, the Yeomanry galloped on, here and there a horse and rider coming down as they covered the two miles between Munkheileh and Atawineh Ridge. Dismounting, the Yeomanry came into action at once, and after driving in the first lines of the Turkish advance they effectively re-established the broken line. The situation was saved."

Major Oscar Teichman. Cavalry Journal No 100. April 1936. Page 171.
By permission of the Royal United Services Institute

As some measure of the bravery displayed in this small action, on a day of many other, unrecorded actions, the Buckinghamshire Yeomanry suffered twenty-four killed and wounded from the total of 48 men of C Squadron who went into action; eleven horses were also killed at this time. The Berkshire squadrons lost 1/3 killed.

The third regiment of the brigade had meanwhile been despatched to support the separated 4th Light Horse Brigade. Moving at 13.50 from reserve in the Wadi Munkheileh, the Dorset Yeomanry galloped across the plain to the right flank of the 12/Light Horse Regiment. Dismounting at once, B and C Squadrons struck out and met the enemy advance which was driving between the two Light Horse Brigades. The line was secured at this point and continuity restored without calling on A Squadron who were being held in close reserve.

It had become clear that although the valiant and desperate intervention of the brigade had succeeded in saving the situation, the line could not be advanced, only held. The enemy remained active late into the afternoon, until at 17.00 their artillery stopped as yet another series of counter-attacks began. One such attack was directed against the Buckingham and Berkshire men on the western flank of Atawineh Ridge, who held their ground and with bayonets fixed drove off the Turks. This was the last encounter with the enemy, for at 18.45 orders were received to retire to el Munkheileh, covering the 5th Mounted Brigade's withdrawal which was already under way. The Dorset's retired at 19.45 and rejoined the brigade at el Munkheileh

Second Battle of Gaza
New Zealand Mounted Rifles Brigade.

THE NEW ZEALAND MOUNTED RIFLES Brigade left DEIR EL BELAH early on the evening of the 16th April and took a south-easterly course via the Wadi SELKA. Picking up the Rafa-Beersheba Track, SHELLAL was reached at 03.00 the following morning. Advance parties were sent out and after receiving the all-clear, the brigade crossed the Wadi Ghuzze at 06.00 on the 17 April.

"The Wadi Ghuzzeh now formed the general line of the British position. It is much like one of our river beds, but carries water only two or three times a year. But the flow of water, such as it is, has cut deep down into the great Gaza-Beersheba plain, leaving perpendicular banks some 50 to 60 feet high. When our forces occupied this position there were four crossings of the wadi, leaving out the sea beach. The first was on the main road to Gaza; the next at Tel el Jemmi, which was used by the Division at the first battle of Gaza; the third was at Shellal on the Khan Yunis-Beersheba road. But many more were made by the troops until it became possible to cross almost anywhere. The Wadi Ghuzzeh in common with the Wadi el Arish comes down in spate at intervals during the rainy season, and it was in this condition when our patrols were examining it, prior to the first Gaza battle; for they found three or four feet of water running in it. By the time the wadi was occupied as our line of defence, however, there remained a few pools of water only and these were carefully conserved and used for horses and men. At Shellal there was a remarkable spring of clear water gushing forth from out of the eastern bank. And there were remains there of large Roman masonry cisterns. But it was highly impregnated with salts, tasting not unlike the "table waters" of commerce. The troops stationed at Shellal drank regularly of this spring, but continuance of the practice brought on stomach troubles.

Palestine abounds in "tels". The glossary...gives the meaning of the Arabic word as "mounds of earth", and as far as our experience goes they were always made by the hands of man. Usually they appear to be the remains of old cities such as Tel el Faruma (Pelusium) Tel el Saba (Beersheba). But there were two great tels on the Wadi Ghuzzeh about which nothing could be found. These were Tel el Jemmi, where the division crossed to make the first attack on Gaza, and Tel el Fara, seven miles further south on the wadi where the Rafa-Beersheba road crosses. These two tels stand up above the plain and can be seen for many miles on all sides. They are each flat on top with what were apparently once perpendicular sides. Both drop sheer down into the wadi bed, and Fara has been built up in ages gone by at the water line with huge masonry buttresses and courses of cut stone.

Just north of Tel el Jemmi is Um Jerrar, the ancient Gerar mentioned in Genesis. Abraham lived here and also Isaac and it was here that the trouble arose between Isaac and the men of Gerar over the wells of water which the former had dug. And it was rather remarkable that the only use made by us of this ancient site, for no buildings remain of any sort, was to clean out some seven or eight cisterns found there choked up with earth and many centuries old, and fill them with water carried on camel-back from Belah. This water was used by the troops holding the line. So again were the wells of Gerar made to be of use."

With the New Zealanders in Sinai and Palestine. Page 106

AUSTRALIAN AND NEW ZEALAND MONTED DIVISION
New Zealand Mounted Rifles Brigade
19 April 1917

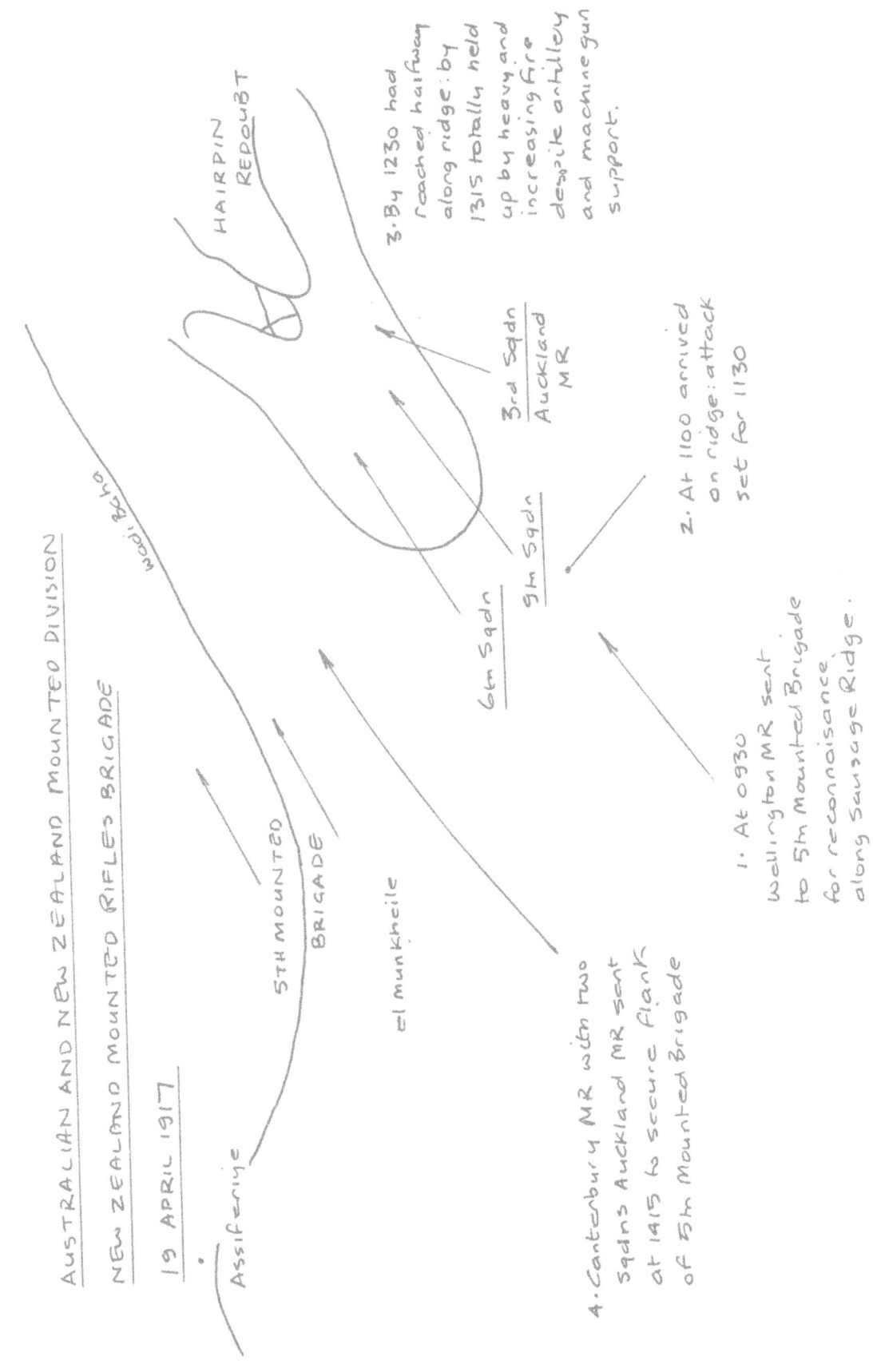

During the morning the brigade acted as flank guard to the AUSTRALIAN and NEW ZEALAND MOUNTED DIVISION. The Canterbury Mounted Rifles headed east towards GOZ EL BASAL and throughout the day reported the area quiet. To their left the Auckland Mounted Rifles reconnoitred towards HARIERA and SHERIA and noted much enemy movement on that front. One squadron reported a large cavalry force beyond Bir Ifteis, to the north-east, apparently moving to reinforce the Hariera-Atawineh sector. The rest of the day passed off without incident and at 19.00 the brigade was withdrawn to Shellal, along with the division and at 22.00 was able to get a few hours' sleep.

At 04.00 on the 18th April the brigade "stood-to", but as there was no action by the Turks, preparations for the days operations were able to be started. These consisted of the same observation parties as the previous day, and at 10.00 the brigade moved off. The Auckland Mounted Rifles led the brigade and by 11.45 were able to water at a well, as the screen was established at el Buggar and extended four miles to the north. Enemy patrols in this area were driven off, but hostile aircraft were able to operate freely, and dropped bombs as well as carrying out observation.

At 18.45 the brigade left the advanced line and moved back to Shellal. After resting for an hour-and-a-half, the march began to take up positions for the following day, the column moving out at 23.00. It was about nine miles from Shellal to the new position at EL MENDUR but the journey over the broken ground in the dark took the whole night. Moving to the east bank of the Wadi Ghuzze, the brigade formed up with the division and rode north, following the 1st and 2nd Light Horse Brigades. In the area of the Wadi Sheria there was a delay as the advance of the Imperial Mounted Division intersected the brigade's path, but once they were clear the wadi was crossed.

Mendur was reached at 06.00 on the 19th April, and the brigade took up position as divisional reserve; they were to operate as mounted troops so as to be able to rapidly reinforce any part of the line. The Imperial Mounted Division had begun its advance at 06.30 but had met with strong opposition from the outset. Accordingly, when they called for additional artillery, the Auckland Mounted Rifles were detailed to escort the Ayrshire Battery, Royal Field Artillery in support of the attack against Atawineh Redoubt. The 3rd Squadron carried out this duty, leaving camp at 09.00, but afterwards instead of re-joining the regiment as intended, they were put into the firing line. They remained detached from the regiment until the evening, working alongside the Wellington MR who arrived during the morning.

Despite the arrival of the artillery support, the enemy presence on Sausage Ridge continued to harry the attack against Atawineh Ridge. At 09.30 the Wellington Mounted Rifles was detailed to report to Brigadier-General EA WIGGIN, Commanding Officer of the 5th Mounted Brigade, who ordered a reconnaissance with a view to assaulting Hairpin Redoubt at the north-eastern end of Sausage Ridge to relieve the pressure.

Upon reaching the south-western end of the ridge at 1100, Colonel MELDRUM of the Wellington MR conferred with the commanding officer of the Inverness Battery, Royal Field Artillery and an immediate advance was decided upon. At 11.30 the 6th Squadron attacked along the ridge, closely followed by the 9th Squadron to their right, with the 2nd Squadron in reserve. The 3rd Squadron Auckland Mounted Rifles was picked up on route and prolonged the firing line to the right. The advance was immediately and heavily shelled from the enemy redoubt, although overhead covering fire by the Brigade Machine Gun Squadron helped to keep down rifle fire from entrenchment's along the ridge. After an hour of determined fighting, the firing line was halfway along the ridge, and at this time the Leicestershire Battery, Royal Field Artillery with two guns of the Ayrshire Battery, Royal Field Artillery arrived and was able to help control the increasing enemy shelling.

Even this concerted effort was not sufficient to carry the position however, and by 13.15 the attack was totally held up, which situation was reported to divisional headquarters. All the while, the redoubt was being rapidly strengthened and a staff officer on reconnaissance observed that about 600 Turks had reinforced the position. Colonel Meldrum's request for reinforcements was initially turned down, but at 14.15 the enemy began forming up in the Wadi BAHA. Realising that a complete brigade was needed to hold this sector, Desert Column immediately ordered up the two available regiments of the New Zealand Mounted Rifles Brigade as well as making provision for the replacement of the Wellington Mounted Rifles by a regiment of Brigadier-General RYRIE'S 2/Light Horse Brigade. Turkish occupation of the Wadi Baha gave particular cause for concern, as it not only threatened to split the 5th Mounted Brigade who were astride the wadi, but would also have enabled the Turks to attack the rear of several brigades. When the enemy launched just such an attack along the wadi at 14.30, immediate and decisive action was needed. Fortunately the Canterbury Mounted Rifles and two squadrons of the Auckland MR arrived at about the same time and, upon taking up the line to the left of the Wellington Mounted Rifles, the reinforced group confronted the counter-attack. Artillery fire was quickly brought to bear on the wadi and the Hairpin Redoubt which further helped to stop the enemy advance and bring the situation under control. By 15.00 the general position of the brigade was made more secure with the arrival of the 6th Light Horse Regiment who moved into support alongside the Canterbury Mounted Rifles.

Under these more favourable circumstances, the Wellington Mounted Rifles were able to renew their attack along Sausage Ridge, but were once again brought to a standstill by heavy shelling and increased rifle fire from the reinforced redoubt. The enemy response did not stop with merely preventing the advance however, for a counter-attack was then launched against the Canterbury's right flank. Their 2nd Squadron was sent up from reserve, along with the remainder of the Machine Gun Squadron, and this extra reinforcement was sufficient to repulse the Turks. In spite of this further rebuff, the enemy kept up a steady pressure and launched one counter-attack after another against many parts of the line.

"15.30: Two cars of the Light Armoured Motor Brigade were sent to report to the Officer Commanding the 5th Light Horse Regiment to deal with the enemy cavalry who were very numerous and active.

16.00: A body of this cavalry estimated at 2000 with some guns advanced from the direction of HAREIRA towards ABU SHAWISH. Their flank guard became engaged with the 1st Light Horse Brigade and machine-gun and rifle fire ensued.

17.00: A body of enemy hitherto opposing the 2nd Light Horse Brigade began to withdraw south-east towards BEIT ABU TAHA.

17.35: A large body of cavalry put at 2500 then began to attack the line held by the 22nd Mounted Brigade east and west of TEL EL FARA"

ANZAC Mounted Division Headquarters War Diary. PRO WO95/4521

With these advances the Turks brought artillery batteries which came into action against Hiseia, Shellal and Khirbit Erk, engaging the No7 Light Car patrol, a Field Squadron and the Leicester Battery RFA respectively.

The New Zealand Mounted Rifles Brigade was ordered to retire at 19.45, but to give cover until then for the 5th Mounted Brigade who had wounded to evacuate. Leaving their advanced positions first, the Wellington Mounted Rifles reached Tel el Jemmi at 01.00 on 20th April being followed in by the rest of the brigade. The 3rd Squadron of the Auckland Mounted Rifles was held in the outpost line and did not re-join the regiment until 09.00.

Second Battle of Gaza
22nd Mounted Brigade

THE TASK ALLOTTED TO THE 22nd Mounted Brigade for the 17th April was the reconnaissance of an area to the south and east of the Wadi Ghuzze at Shellal. Commanded by Brigadier-General FA FRYER, the brigade marched from DEIR EL BELAH on the evening of the 16th April, it's advance guard being provided by the Staffordshire Yeomanry, who arrived at Shellal at 04.30 the following morning. After a short halt to allow the Lincolnshire Yeomanry and East Riding Yeomanry to come up, the brigade moved over the Wadi Ghuzze and headed to the east. Securing GOZ EL GELEIB and Point 510, the Staffordshire's continued alone, with orders to establish and protect crossings over the Wadi IMLEIH, a large tributary of the Wadi Sheria running to the north-west. Upon reaching the wadi at 11.30, the Staffordshire's came under heavy rifle and machine-gun fire from entrenchments on high ground 800 yards east of, and parallel to, the wadi. One man was killed and a dozen wounded in the fire-fight which developed as the yeomen sought to progress from the cover of the wadi, but enemy fire was too great and the advance was halted. While attending to the wounded lying out in the open, Surgeon-Major AH PALMER of the Royal Army Medical Corps was seriously wounded by a shot to the back, subsequently dying of his wounds in Cairo on 2nd May.

To help the Staffordshire's in their task, at 13.20 the Inverness Battery, Royal Horse Artillery was sent up to assist and, upon its opening fire, the Turks immediately withdrew. At the same time the advanced line was established in the area just west of the Wadi Imleih. This was held until 19.00 when the outpost line was taken over by the 1st Light Horse Brigade and the brigade returned to Shellal for a short rest.

At 06.00 on 18th April the outpost line was again taken over by the brigade and was held throughout the day. When the operation orders for the following day were received during the afternoon, the Australian and New Zealand Mounted Division was required to move north to an assembly point on the Wadi SHERIA. At 18.45, to cover the division, the 22nd Mounted Brigade was moved to a new line, the right flank of the East Riding Yeomanry being set about TEL EL FARA on the Wadi Ghuzze on arrival at 22.15. Parties of Royal Engineers were due to establish wells at this point and would also be protected by the brigade.

At 05.40 on 19th April, the 2nd Light Horse Brigade was sent to form a series of strong-points, between the left flank of the brigade and Point 310 three miles to the north-west, thus completing the observation and defensive screen of the mounted troops.

During the morning there was little for the brigade to do, as the Turks were fully occupied by the frontal attacks of the Imperial Mounted Division and the advance of the Wellington Mounted Rifles just before noon. However, as the Turks realised they were containing the attacks at all points, they began to counter-attack the main assaults as well as trying to work around the flank and penetrate from the south-east. It was the latter move which affected the 22nd Mounted Brigade, which engaged enemy patrols from about 13.30 onwards.

By 14.15, when an order was received to send two regiments to reinforce the 2nd Light Horse Brigade, the 22nd Mounted Brigade was in action on a wide front. One regiment was sent at once, but an enemy advance forced General Fryer to retain the Lincoln and East Riding Yeomanry's to hold his own position. Further attacks during the afternoon were repulsed but a final advance by 2500 cavalry at 17.35 seriously threatened the line. Several batteries of mountain guns accompanied the Turkish troops and these were brought into action at 18.00 against the communication lines at Hiseia and Shellal. Turkish attacks at several places on the Australian Mounted Division line made the situation critical for a while, but they failed to press their advantage. At 18.45, the batteries of the division were withdrawn across the Wadi Sheria and were set to protect the new line. At the same time the 22nd Mounted Brigade was detailed to take up an outpost line from Point 310 on the Wadi Sheria - one mile south of el Magam - through el Dammath to Shellal on the Wadi Ghuzze and west to Weli Sheikh Nuran.

Second Battle of Gaza
2nd Light Horse Brigade

ON THE 16TH APRIL 1917, the 2nd Light Horse Brigade was in camp at DEIR EL BELAH along with two other brigades of the AUSTRALIAN and NEW ZEALAND MOUNTED DIVISION. During the evening they began the move to SHELLAL on the west bank of the Wadi Ghuzze, the fourteen-mile journey taking until 07.00 on the 17th April. The weary troops took the opportunity to rest and make tea, but even this was not without incident. At 08.30 an enemy plane attacked the brigade and dropped four bombs in its midst, killing an officer and six men and wounding a further twelve; over thirty horses were also killed or wounded. A heavy machine-gun and rifle fire was brought to bear on the plane but it managed to make its escape. Within two hours a further move was made, crossing the Wadi Ghuzze to take up a position two miles distant at EL IMARA as divisional reserve. However as there was no enemy opposition to the Desert Column's advance, the brigade was not called upon. At dusk, with its role of observation fulfilled, the division withdrew to Shellal, leaving a line of outposts from BIR QAMLE through el Imara to join the right flank of the IMPERIAL MOUNTED DIVISION.

As with all other units, the 2nd Light Horse Brigade spent the 18th April engaged on the establishment of advanced dumps of stores and the continued observation along their respective front. Of three troops sent out by the 7/Light Horse Regiment only one, patrolling south-east along the Gaza-Beersheba Road, had anything of note to report.

"The latter picked up three men of the Staffordshire Yeomanry who stated they had been on observation post on the previous day and received no orders to retire and had been attacked by Bedouins at 06.00. One man died and the other two were handed over to a Field Ambulance. According to statements the man who died was shot at close range after he had been wounded and stripped of his clothing and the two survivors were left as dead."

7th Light Horse Regiment War Diary. PRO WO95/4540

At 10.00 the brigade took up a position from Point 300 to Point 510 on the ABU SHAWISH Road and remained there until once again being withdrawn at 19.00. On this occasion the withdrawal was limited and the brigade formed up on the eastern side of the Wadi Ghuzze to await the arrival of the rest of the division.

For the operations on the 19th April the Australian and New Zealand Mounted division's role promised to be more active, for, in addition to protecting the south-eastern flank of the Imperial Mounted Division, it was to be ready to exploit any break in the enemy line. Moving off at 01.15 the brigade headed north and, after crossing the Wadi SHERIA one-and-a-half miles from el Mendur, rejoined the division.

Although initially in reserve, the brigade was soon called upon. At 05.40 the 5/Light Horse Regiment was sent off to establish a series of strong-points from el Dammath to Point 310 on the Wadi Sheria, in order to protect the south-eastern flank. To ensure sufficient cover for the digging of the thinly-spread posts, the 7/Light Horse Regiment was sent up at 07.00 for support. At the same time contact was made with other units in the protective screen, namely the 1st Light Horse Brigade to the north and the 22nd Mounted Brigade to the south. The third regiment of the brigade was placed at the disposal of Brigadier-General CHAYTOR, commanding the New Zealand Mounted Rifles Brigade. Accordingly, when at 14.15 that brigade, less the Wellington Mounted Rifles, was rapidly deployed to stem an enemy advance along the Wadi Baha, the 6/Light Horse Regiment was able to move off at once in support.

Around 10.45, enemy cavalry were spotted moving from the direction of Beersheba. The 7/Light Horse Regiment engaged them as they came within range and successfully checked the advance, the enemy remaining on a line from Goz el Geleib-Hill 510. From this line they brought four guns to bear on the Australian and New Zealand Mounted Division's right flank and the 7/LHR were forced to withdraw in the early afternoon, taking up a position on the left of the 5/ Light Horse Regiment. Enemy shelling continued into the early afternoon and at 15.20 a patrol of the 7/Light Horse Regiment reported a force of about two-thousand Turks moving along the Sheria-Beersheba Road just north of Abu Irgeig. Enemy cavalry soon became very active in this area and two cars of the Light Car Patrol were sent up to reinforce the 5/Light Horse Regiment's line. There was some engagement around this time and up until 17.00 when the Turks unexpectedly retired in a south-easterly direction.

The 5/ and 7/Light Horse Regiments held the line from Point 310 to Hiseia crossing during the night and all through the following day, the 20th April. A further move to Weli Sheikh Nuran finally allowed the brigade to go into reserve and rest.

Second Battle of Gaza
1st Light Horse Brigade

AT THE START OF THE First Phase on the 16th April, the 1st Light Horse Brigade was camped at KHAN YUNIS, about five miles south-west of the main AUSTRALIAN and NEW ZEALAND MOUNTED DIVISION camp at DEIR EL BELAH. Moving out at 20.30, the brigade rejoined the division near Sheikh Hammuda and continued with it to SHELLAL on the Wadi GHUZZE. Arriving at about 03.00 on the 17th April, the brigade took up position and snatched a few hours rest before the day's operations began.

At 06.00, the 3rd Light Horse Regiment was sent forward to take up a line of observation from Weli Sheikh Nuran - el Rueibia - Goz Mabruuk - Khirbit el Far. From here enemy activity to the south could be watched, and the few patrols that were encountered quickly returned to the south. The only engagement of the day came at 08.40, when the 3/Light Horse Regiment was attacked near el Rueibia, but this was successfully driven off and the day passed off quietly. The day's objective having been carried out, the division was withdrawn at 18.45, with the 1st Light Horse Brigade providing an outpost line using the 1/ and 2/Light Horse Regiments to take over from the 3/Light Horse Regiment, as well as that held by the 22nd Mounted Brigade north to the Wadi Sheria.

The following morning -18th April- the brigade was relieved and passed into reserve at Shellal. At 10.00 the rest of the AUSTRALIAN MOUNTED DIVISION took up a position for the day at Goz el Geleib, remaining there until the early evening. It was 18.30 when, with many miles of riding ahead of it, the brigade left Shellal to re-join the division. After forming up on the eastern bank of the Wadi Ghuzze at 20.00, the 1st and 2nd Light Horse Brigades prepared for the overnight ride; the New Zealand Mounted Rifles Brigade was to re-join en route, while cover to the south and south-east continued to be provided by the 22 Mounted Brigade.

At 01.00 on 19th April, the 1st Light Horse Brigade led the 2nd Light Horse Brigade, artillery and NZMR Brigade from the assembly point north-west towards the Wadi SHERIA. After about three miles, divisional headquarters was established, upon completion of which the brigade continued on to reach Khirbit Erk at 05.00. To accomplish the brigade's primary role of establishing an observation screen the 1/Light Horse Regiment advanced at once and within the hour had secured BAIKET EL SANA Ridge as well as the area south to the Wadi Sheria. The enemy opened up a heavy fire from their artillery positions at Hariera half-an-hour after this and maintained it throughout the day. As soon as this bombardment began, the brigade was ordered to push patrols forward to watch for any enemy advances which might be attempted under its cover. None of any consequence was made until the middle of the afternoon, when a large force estimated at two cavalry divisions and one infantry division was seen about 3000 yards to the north-east near the Gaza-Beersheba Road. Lieutenant-Colonel CF COX of the 1st Light Horse Brigade ordered up the Leicester Battery, Royal Field Artillery to counter this impending attack, as a successful enemy advance on this front would seriously threaten the troops already pinned down on Sausage Ridge.

> "The Leicester Battery came into action at a gallop and opened on the enemy infantry advancing from about Khirbit Um Adra. The enemy succeeded in getting within 400 yards of Baiket el Sana and here came under fire of the two squadrons from about Baiket el Sana itself and one squadron from the south and their advance stopped. Heavy shellfire was however opened on the Leicester Battery who were in the open. The teams were galloped up in turn and each gun taken out of action in turn without casualty and brought into action again in a position just west of Khirbit Erk."
>
> Australian and New Zealand Mounted Division Headquarters
> War Diary. PRO WO95/4521

To strengthen the line as well as give cover to the artillery at Khirbit Erk, the 1/Light Horse Regiment was relieved by the 2/ and 3/Light Horse Regiments. The line was also to be extended in a westerly direction along the Wadi Sheria to guard against an advance along the wadi. As they were moving out from Khirbit Erk, the relieving troops saw a large enemy force making just such an advance. One group of about 500 men was moving along the peninsula bounded by the Wadi Sheria and Wadi Imleih, while a second, similar sized force was approaching Khirbit Erk from the south. The 3/Light Horse Regiment immediately sent B Squadron to the bank of the Wadi Sheria and C Squadron was placed between the two wadis. As the dismounted attack developed, A Squadron was also committed and took up a position across the Wadi Imleih, until after an hours heavy fighting the enemy broke off and headed west towards EL DAMMATH. The brigade lines were concentrated along the Wadi Sheria and north to Baiket el Sana, holding this until ordered to retire to Tel el Jemmi at 19.00.

Second Battle of Gaza
162nd Brigade

At 22.00 on the 16th April 1917, C Company of the 1/5th Bedfordshire Regiment left the divisional bivouac area at IN SEIRAT. Commanded by Captain CR JAMES, its role was to establish an outpost line east of the WADI GHUZZE and thus protect the assembly of the brigade at DORSET HOUSE.

The brigade left In Seirat at 01.00 on the 17th, and by way of prepared crossings over the Wadi Ghuzze, reached the assembly point at 03.20. Brigade Headquarters was established here, with the 1/4th Northamptonshire Regiment being retained as brigade reserve. The other three battalions of the brigade advanced in a north-easterly direction up the smaller WADI NUKHABIR for about fifteen-hundred yards before deploying for the attack against the MANSURA RIDGE. Communication was established with 157th Brigade of the 52nd Division to the left, and the 163rd Brigade on the right.

At 04.45 the brigade advanced on a two-thousand yard front, divided between the 5/Bedford's with a section of the Brigade Machine Gun Company, and the 1/11th London Regiment on the right. Supported by the 1/10th London Regiment, the two battalions advanced against slight opposition and within an hour were on Mansura Ridge. Consolidation was started at once, and to ensure that control of, and communication with, the front line continued, at 06.50 Brigade Headquarters and brigade reserve were moved up from Dorset House to a hill twelve-hundred yards behind the advanced troops.

To assist with the consolidation, the 10/London's were put into the centre of the line and the number of machine-guns was increased to one section per battalion. The Turkish artillery response was mainly confined to sporadic shelling with shrapnel, which caused few casualties and did not impede consolidation. Early in the evening, rations and water arrived at the ridge, and the approaching darkness covered the increasing activity in the area. Three brigades of the Royal Field Artillery moved up into position ready to defend the 162nd and 163rd Brigades from both counter-attack as well as support them during the coming advance.

At 04.00 on the 18 April, the front-line troops stood-to but with no sign of the enemy apparent, an hour later the consolidation and preparations were re-started. Enemy shelling during the day was heavy at times and several casualties were sustained. A patrol of the 5/Bedford's daringly reconnoitred the WADI MUKKADEME in a north-westerly direction, nearly two miles beyond the front line and only a mile from the enemy strong-points at ALI EL MUNTAR and GREEN HILL. No enemy were encountered on the way however, and the patrol returned safely to report. Although the orders for the operations had been issued at 13.00 on the 18th April, the time of Zero Hour, that is the start of the artillery bombardment, still had to be set. At 05.00 on 19th April word was received by divisional headquarters that zero hour had been set for 05.30 and this information was immediately passed to the waiting company commanders.

Behind the Mansura and Sheikh Abbas Ridges the 162 and 163 Brigades assembled at 06.00. The position was comparatively safe as the artillery bombardment which had commenced at 05.30 kept enemy fire to a minimum. The 11/London and 5/Bedford's were currently holding the brigade front-line and would pass into support and reserve respectively when the rest of the brigade passed through them to the attack.

At 07.30 the 10/London on the left, alongside the 4/Northampton's went over the top of the ridge. Each was disposed in four lines at two-hundred yard intervals and had a frontage of 1000 yards. The objective was a ridge which overlooked the Gaza-Beersheba Road and lay between one-and-a-half and two miles distant.

All hopes for an easy advance before the enemy recovered from the artillery barrage immediately faded as the first wave cleared the crest of the ridge. Shrapnel and High-Explosive from the front was put down in lines of fire through which the troops had to pass, and casualties occurred straightaway. Even more serious was the heavy fire from around Ali el Muntar which continuously enfiladed the advance and inflicted further casualties.

54th (EAST ANGLIAN) DIVISION
162 BRIGADE
19 APRIL 1917

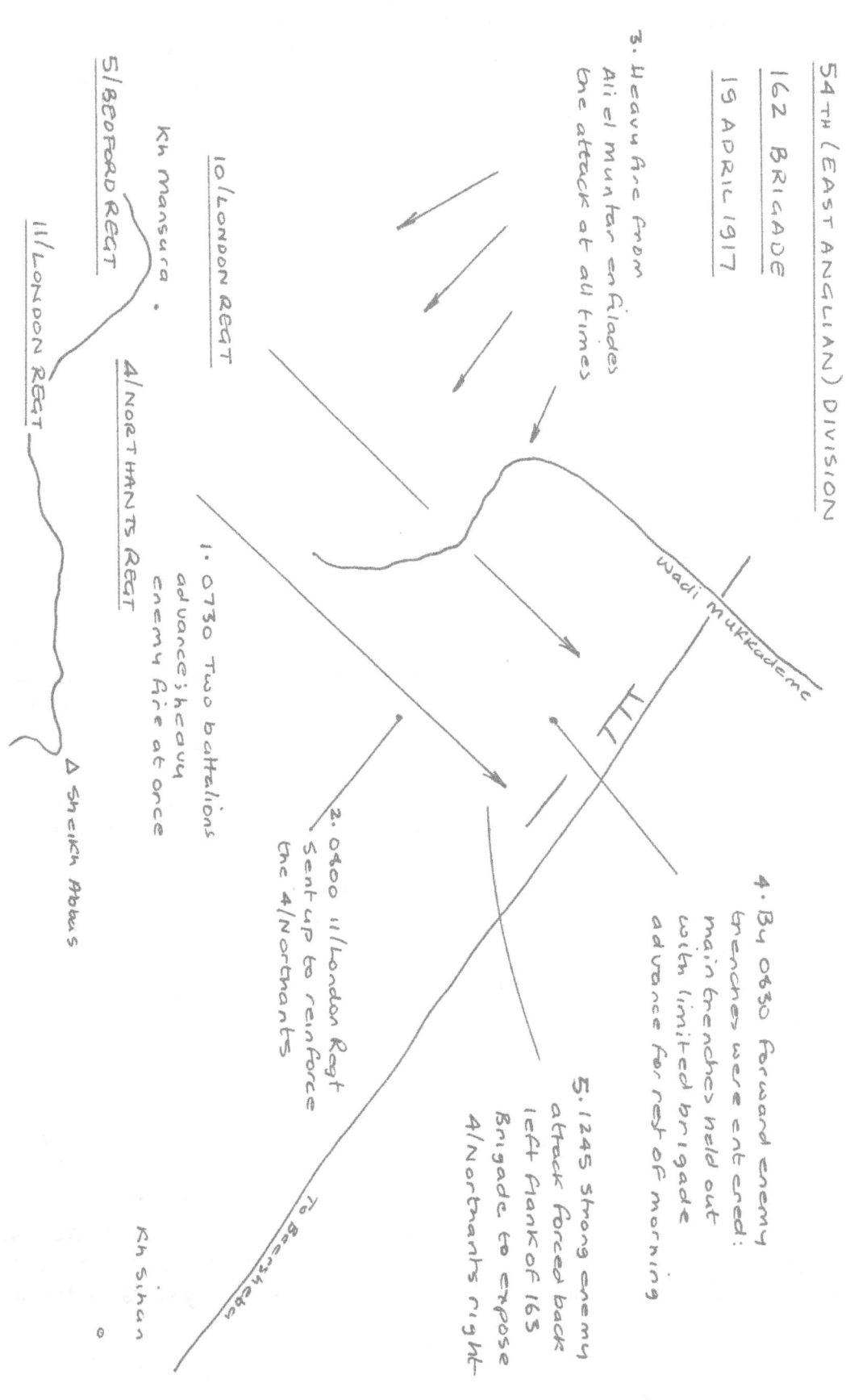

Just under an hour after the attack began, men of the 10/London's entered the first enemy trenches on the left of the brigade line. Due to a misunderstanding over the role of the 157th Brigade, [they were in fact 52nd Division Reserve] the left flank became exposed, the group's isolation was further pronounced as it had advanced more rapidly than the rest of the line. As the main body of the 10/London's and the 4/Northants became pinned down under an increasingly severe machine-gun and rifle fire, this group pushed even further forward. Under fire the whole time the small party of infantrymen and Lewis Gunners penetrated to within 120 yards of the main enemy trenches. From here they were able to enfilade several trenches and the Turks suffered heavily as they sought to engage the courageous group. However, this gallant and determined effort

"was not sufficient to allow the whole of the line to advance, unassisted as it was by artillery. Some men got right up to the enemy trenches but all were killed."

162 Brigade Headquarters War Diary. PRO WO95/4652

In the meantime, the 1/11 London's were sent up to reinforce the 4/Northants, and they succeeded in advancing the line a little, although they too were soon brought to a halt.

The intensity of fire had already caused serious problems of communication between the front line and headquarters of both brigade and the battalions. Telephone lines were repeatedly cut by shrapnel, and runners taking messages were either caught in the general fire or picked off by snipers. At 09.10 however a telephone line was established and brigade headquarters was able to halt the left flank while the situation was reviewed.

"The signal section showed great bravery in trying to keep this signal line in repair. Private SORE especially distinguished himself in his efforts to destroy the Gaza - Beersheba Telegraph line Though within 300 yards of large bodies of enemy troops he climbed a pole and cut one line and being then blown off the line, he got up and climbed it again and cut another and was in the act of cutting the third and last when he was again blown off by a field gun about 300 yards away and killed."

162 Brigade Headquarters War Diary. PRO WO95/4652

The enemy fire continued unabated in its severity for the rest of the morning and into the early afternoon. The three battalions held their positions as high-explosive and shrapnel burst all across the open plain and any movement was caught in the intense machine-gun and rifle cross-fire.

"The dead and wounded on this ridge remained as a line of skirmishers, the Turks sweeping them with machine-gun fire at intervals throughout the day. Consequently men wounded early in the day were killed and all were riddled by bullets."

1/11 London Regiment War Diary. PRO WO95/4654

Headquarters decided not to commit the 5/Bedford's from reserve, as there seemed little prospect of continuing with the attack, and although another section of machine-guns was sent up, they apparently failed to arrive.

Around midday, the enemy began to launch direct counter-attacks, as well as trying to exploit gaps in the line. But despite the lack of a continuous front-line, observation posts had been skilfully sited and all attempts against the 162nd Brigade were dispersed. However, at 12.45 a strong enemy force attacked across the front and directed itself against the left flank of the 163rd Brigade, which had suffered enormous casualties. Artillery support was immediately called for and although both the 270th and 271st Brigades Royal Field Artillery responded, it was not strong enough to prevent the flank being forced back. To close the gap which had now occurred on the right flank of the brigade, D Company of the 5/Bedford's was sent up, and with the arrival at 14.00 of 161st Brigade from divisional reserve to reinforce the 163rd Brigade, by 14.30 the retirement was stabilised. The last major attempt to break the 162 Brigade line came at 15.35 when

> "A strong counter-attack by the Turks was launched against the 10 London on the left from Ali Muntar and the Quarry [1100 yards north-east of Ali Muntar], but the 270th Brigade RFA being informed, opened a heavy and accurate fire, and within 10 minutes of opening only dead and wounded Turks remained on the forward slopes of the hill."
>
> 162 Brigade Headquarters War Diary. PRO WO95/4652

As the afternoon passed, the line remained much the same, and although very heavy rifle and machine-gun fire continued there was no movement by either side.

At 18.30 the 5/Bedford's were ordered to take up a line half-a-mile to the rear of the firing-line and dig in. The brigade then retired; the 10/London continued the new line in a north-westerly direction to join up with the 52nd Division, while the 1/11 London and 4/Northants passed into reserve below the ridge. These movements proved exceedingly difficult in the darkness and over the generally featureless plain, and were compounded further by the still heavy enemy fire. The situation of the 4/Northants serves as a tragic summary for the brigade.

> "Communication was established by telephone with Colonel John Brown, commanding the Northampton's, and information was asked for as to his position. He replied that he had no position, save for a line of dead men; and that he thought the best thing for the 5th Bedford's to do was to come to him along the telephone line, as this was their only hope of finding him in the open plain."
>
> History of the 1/5th Bedfordshire Regiment. Page 162.

During the evening, much-needed water and tools arrived and the line was strengthened overnight. These positions were held for the next two days with some wounded men being recovered from the battlefield. Incidents of dead and wounded being stripped of food and clothing were reported, but no actual "ill-treatment took place."

162 Brigade

Casualties for the Second Battle of Gaza

THE ATTACK OF THE 4/NORTHANT's on the 19th April was of an advance over open ground under artillery fire, which resulted in the establishment of a line a few hundred yards from the Turkish trenches, without cover and under heavy machine-gun fire. With this in mind it is not surprising that 8/130 were killed with a further 14 officers and 236 men wounded.

Private Alfred ADCOCK was 34 years old, Northamptonshire born and bred, when he was killed on the 19 April. In the main advance, C Company were on the right flank; three Northampton men killed were 17-year old Private Albert BATES of Adelaide Street, 28-year old Private William REDLEY who left a widow in Shakespeare Road and 22-year old Private Arthur HELMS of Turner Street. In the centre of the battalion's line was Private Frederick DAVEY with D Company. Born at Barnsley in Yorkshire he had lived in Leicester for many years and had originally enlisted in the Leicestershire Regiment; he was nineteen. B Company completed the battalion front on the left, two casualties being Private Robert PARKER from Higham Ferrers, Northants and Private Archibald BAILEY of Far Cotton, Northants. Also of Higham Ferrers was Private Horace Reginald BIRD. Although only 20 he was married and lived with his wife Lucy Jane in his parent's house at Westfield Street. Corporal William Benjamin Thomas PAYNE had originally enlisted in the Bedfordshire Regiment, ironically they were brigade support as he was killed in the devastating enemy fire of the 19th; aged 24 he left a widow Elsie Payne at East Street, Northampton.

The casualties to the officers of the 4/Northants were also very high, the following extract being an obituary to all, in the same melancholic vein as Colonel John Brown's comments.

> *"Six months later, when Gaza fell, Colonel John Brown and a few officers rode over to visit the old battlefield of April 19th. There they found one whole platoon lying in extended order right in front of the Turkish wire, with Lieutenant Stanley Marlow, son of Mr and Mrs AE Marlow of Preston Deanery Hall, at their head, his body being closest to the enemy lines. The visit cleared up the mystery of the many missing, for there six officers and many men lay as they fell six months earlier. They were merely clothed skeletons, but the Turks, because of their religious scruples, had respected the remains even to making a detour of their transport round the spot where a few bodies had fallen in the Beersheba Road. These bodies were reverently buried on the spot where they fell now known as "Northampton Mound".*

Northampton and the Great War. Pages 57-58.

Captain Robert Leslie MURRAY had been an undergraduate at Jesus College Cambridge when war broke out. He had already been Mentioned in Despatches for good work and on the 19th April led his company into action where he

> *"was badly wounded in the arm and kept on. He was hit in the leg and fell, yet rose again to lead his company until he was hit a third time and killed."*

Northampton and the Great War. Pages 58.

On the 19th April, the 5/Bedfordshire Regiment was initially in reserve but was called upon to provide one company to reinforce the right flank, D Company being sent. Twenty-two year old Private John EGAN was a member of that company, no trace of him ever being found. Born at Rugeley, Staffordshire he had lived in the town all his life and had enlisted in the South Staffordshire Regiment, subsequently being transferred to the Bedford's. Company Quarter Master Sergeant [CQMS] Albert TOPHAM was reported wounded and missing on the 19th, but although his body was reported by the Burial Officer of the 75th Division in January 1918, no record of his burial exists; he is commemorated on the Jerusalem Memorial. Several other bodies were reported at Northampton Mound but were not re-interred at the Gaza Cemetery and are likewise only shown on the Jerusalem Memorial. There were two officers wounded on the 19th, and as neither are recorded in the cemeteries at Gaza or Deir el Belah the immediate conclusion is that both survived. However, Second Lieutenant LL BRERETON is recorded in the War Diary of the battalion as being wounded, only to die of these wounds a full ten days later at Cairo.

The 1/10 London Regiment suffered 1/44 killed, with a further 7/134 wounded as they attacked on the left of the 162nd Brigade's front on the 19th April; a further three men died of their wounds.

Private Eustace Lovell BROHIER had been born in Colombo, South America and was still living there when the war broke out. He travelled to London and enlisted in the 28th Royal Fusiliers, later becoming a member of the 1/10 London Regiment. He was killed on the 19th April.

Private John Frederick HYDE was 32 years old when he was killed. He had lived at 183, High Street, Homerton, London with his father John before marrying Rosina Catherine Hyde and living next door at 181.

The majority of those killed with the 1/10 London Regiment were never recovered, one of them being 39 year old Private William NOLAN to leave a widow, Rosa Nolan at Vincent House, Old Street, London. The nickname of the 1/10 London Regiment being the "Hackney Gurkhas" meant many of the men were from the area and many died on the 19th April; Private Thomas LEWIS, 420380 Lance-Corporal William HAWES and 420212 Signaller Henry WEST. Thirty-four year old Private George WILLIAMS had been born at Leigh, Lancashire and had been English Master at Leigh Grammar School. After his death his widow Dora remarried and moved to Kyle Park, Uddington, Lanarkshire. One officer was killed, Captain Farmar, but there are few details available.

The 1/11 London Regiment lost 3/105 killed and 10/255 wounded with six more men who died of their wounds.

Rifleman George Charles POPE was 22 years old when killed on the 19th April. He had been born at Clerkenwell, London and had lived there all his life until enlisting. He was awarded the Serbian Silver Medal for Gallantry. One man with B Company was Rifleman Charles Leonard KOHN. He had been born in London and was married to Daisy Florence Kohn. D Company were also under heavy fire when the whole battalion was sent up at 08.00 to reinforce the 4/Northants; 21 year old Lance-Corporal Edmund James HOLLOWAY of Burges Road, East Ham, London was killed outright.

Many young men gave false ages when they enlisted. Two men of the battalion were only 17 when killed on 19th April; Lance-Corporal James Arnold Robert HEADING of Fetter Lane, London and Rifleman Thomas WALLER of Pretoria Avenue, Walthamstow, Essex. Finally, Rifleman John Arber CAREY from The Broadway, Leigh-on-Sea Essex was 19 years old when killed; he had enlisted in October 1914 and his only brother was also killed in the war.

Second Battle of Gaza
163rd Brigade

BEFORE THE INITIAL ADVANCE OF the First Phase is described, the following quote from one of the officers with the 1/5th Suffolk Regiment is of interest here, as it gives a little insight into the feelings of those who had been waiting for many days the attack to begin.

> "16th April
> We have been having another fairly black week, at least I have, as my slight wound festered and I have not been allowed to move about. However it has very nearly healed now, so I shall accompany the battalion into action when it next goes. I have been expecting the latter event every day to happen the next, but it has not come to pass yet. However I think tomorrow is "Der Tag". At 1am we move off and the position has to be captured by 5am. I do not think we shall encounter much opposition and I have every confidence in the result. My battalion is yet again leading the Brigade and C Company is again leading the Battalion. As I expect you know, Hubert is staying behind with several other officers and men, and will come up when required to replace casualties. He is very sorry at being left behind and feels like I did when I was left behind at Mudros when the Battalion left for Suvla.
>
> When I get anywhere near civilisation again I have promised to give C Company officers a big feed to celebrate the great occasion of my 21st birthday and your very kind present of a cheque will come in very handy then.
>
> I should think the situation here is unique in the history of the war. In fact it seems more like the Middle Ages. In every other theatre of war the rival armies have fought each other and then entrenched as close as possible to each other. Here the rival armies remain several miles from each other, each working like niggers completing their plans for the coming "trial of strength", hardly interfering with each other. Then when one of the armies has completed its arrangements, that army will sally forth into battle. I really believe we are at the beginning of the end. Most of the men are going into action with two water bottles this time so we ought not to suffer from the lack of water this time, next week I hope to tell you more interesting news."
>
> Captain ED Wolton 1/5th Suffolk Regiment. Papers in author's possession

At 11.30 on the 16 April 1917, the 1/5th Suffolk Regiment led the 163rd Brigade from their bivouac at IN SEIRAT. In common with the 162nd Brigade, one company of the leading battalion had already left to act as an advance guard east of the WADI GHUZZE. Followed by the 1/8th Hampshire, 1/4th Norfolk and 1/5th Norfolk Regiments, they marched to the Wadi Ghuzze and, after crossing by 01.25, took the track which ran to the south of the WADI SHARTA. The brigade assembly point at Sharta was not reached until 03.55, and immediate deployment by two battalions, the 8/Hants and 5/Suffolk's, for the advance against DUMBELL HILL was necessary. This initial objective was to be secured before the general advance began, for its height would afford good observation to the east and north-east. Little opposition had been anticipated at this stage, and accordingly the hill was secured on schedule at 04.45.

54th (EAST ANGLIAN) DIVISION
163 BRIGADE
19 APRIL 1917

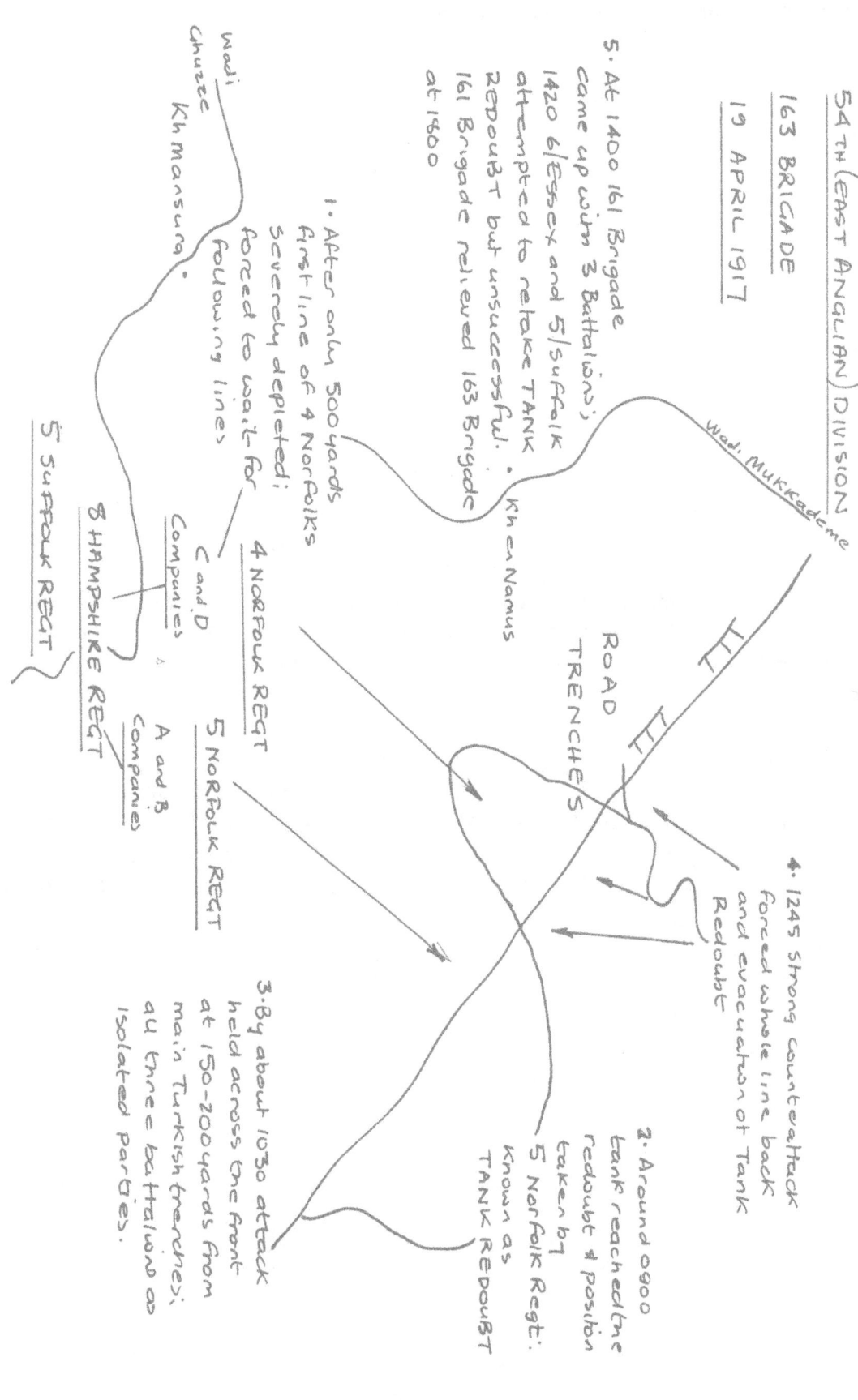

From here the brigade advanced against SHEIKH ABBAS Ridge; once again only two battalions formed the front line, each on a two-company front. The 8/Hants on the left had a little over a mile-and-a-half of broken ground to cross to the ridge, while the 5/Suffolk on the right had slightly less. The 5/Norfolk's followed as support, with the 4/Norfolk's being held as brigade reserve at Dumbell Hill. Small groups of Turks holding the ridge could be seen to retire as the British troops approached, the only casualties up to now being two men of the Hampshire's hit by snipers, and a few Norfolk's caught by long-range machine-gun fire. By 06.20, the Hampshire's were on Sheikh Abbas Ridge with the Suffolk's to their right. With little opposition having been encountered, the 5/Norfolk's were able to move straight from support and up into the line, thus prolonging the Suffolk's right and extending it to brigade headquarters on Dumbell Hill. Consolidation of the line began as soon as all troops were up, and continued, despite considerable harassment, well into the evening.

"The enemy shelled the area held by the brigade throughout the day with practically no effect, his ammunition appeared to be inferior and duds were frequent."

163 Brigade Headquarters War Diary. PRO WO95/4656

As there appeared to be no enemy counter-attacks forthcoming, each battalion was able to hold its section with only two companies, while the others moved back into reserve. At dusk the 161st Brigade was ordered to relieve the right flank of the brigade. This allowed the 5/Norfolk's to move to an assembly point in rear of the firing line preparatory to the forthcoming attack.

The situation during the night of the 17 April remained quiet. The positions held were unchanged during the following day, and the opportunity was taken to fully reconnoitre the ground ahead of the brigade line. Although intelligence reports had given estimates of the likely enemy strength and its main locations, the following message to 54th Division Headquarters presented a disturbingly ominous picture;

"163 Brigade report enemy to be still holding the trenches along the Beersheba Road in strength and to have constructed low wire entanglements in front of their trenches in W17 [near the redoubt].

162 Brigade reports from observation that enemy has done much work on positions SW of Beersheba Road during the night. Has constructed three large communication trenches across ridge in rear of trenches. Time 10.15 April 18."

54th Divisional General Staff War Diary. PRO WO95/4634

Nevertheless, trench digging continued in earnest, while reconnaissance of the foreground was made throughout the day. Although the Turks shelled the area, heavily at times, they appeared content to wait in their distant defensive positions for the inevitable attack. At 19.20 on the evening of 18 April, the Divisional Operation Order which detailed the forthcoming attack was received. The objective of the 163rd Brigade was a line of trenches which began one mile north-north-west of the present front line, and extended east-south-east to a redoubt nearly a mile away. As it was anticipated that the advance would begin early in the day, the 4/Norfolk's were moved up to join the 5/Norfolk's behind Sheikh Abbas. The time of the advance was not known at this stage, but a few minutes after five o'clock on the morning of the 19th April, word was received at 54th Division Headquarters that Zero Hour was set for 05.30. This information was quickly passed on to the company commanders, who were waiting with their battalions behind Sheikh Abbas ridge, and final preparations were made before the infantry advance began at Zero plus two hours.

The two-thousand yard front was divided equally between the 4/Norfolk's on the left and the 5/Norfolk's on the right. As soon as they mounted the ridge at 07.30, a devastating fire opened up. Previously light enemy artillery fire from the direction of FRYER HILL, four-miles to the north-west, increased to enfilade the advance with high-explosive and shrapnel; all along the front the enemy artillery got to work on the orderly lines of the Norfolk's.

"It soon became evident that the enemy artillery must have escaped serious dislocation during the preliminary bombardment and that his machine-guns were still in considerable strength. A heavy fire with both high-explosive and shrapnel was opened almost directly the advance commenced and long-range machine-gun fire was begun by the time the leading line was 300 yards from the Sheikh Abbas Ridge."

163 Brigade Headquarters War Diary. PRO WO95/4656

As soon as these troops had passed through the outpost line, the 8/Hampshire's followed them as support; A and B Companies moving as support to the 5/Norfolk's with C and D Companies supporting the 4/Norfolk's on the left. As if to deny their enemy even the slightest chance of reaching their objectives, the Turkish crescendo of artillery and machine-gun fire was rapidly supplemented by heavy rifle fire from the trenches along the Gaza-Beersheba Road. The left of the line was totally exposed to this storm of fire and suffered heavily from the outset. The 5/Norfolk's on the right had a minimal amount of cover as the ground dipped slightly, but would be likewise exposed when they reached the crest.

Yet with almost incomprehensible courage and determination the advance pressed on. Faced by an open plain of nearly two-thousand yards; assailed by high-explosive and shrapnel from the front and enfiladed from the left front; machine-gun bullets which peppered the sand at every yard; finally a heavy rifle fire cracked out from the trenches as the gallant Norfolk men led the daylight attack. As they fell, caught singly by a rifle shot or mown down wholesale by machine-guns, their places were taken by the men of the Isle of Wight Rifles - the 8/Hampshire's. They too met the same fate.

"The attack was pushed on with great dash, a first low ridge was crossed, and the second ridge, about 500 yards from the first Turkish trench was reached by 08.30."

163 Brigade Headquarters War Diary. PRO WO95/4656

TANK REDOUBT FROM SHEIKH ABBAS

This is the front on which the 163rd Brigade and the Imperial Camel Brigade advanced on the 19 April 1917. The vast distances which the troops were expected to cross to their objectives, as well as the featureless nature of the country, are clearly illustrated. By permission of IWM Copyright No Q47641

Although it was now only an hour since the attack had started, the picture of events at brigade headquarters had become very unclear. Not only was communication with the advancing troops very difficult, but with many officers having become casualties themselves, the information about the situation was often simply not available. Just before 09.00 the 5/Norfolk's were seen from brigade headquarters to be disappearing over the second ridge, and with the 8/Hants following them, control of the situation threatened to deteriorate even further. Consequently, a Staff Officer, Lieutenant MB BUXTON, was sent out at once to halt the 5/Norfolk's and obtain a clear picture of the front line.

"Soon after 09.00 the Tank was seen to reach the Redoubt in W23a and later to be on fire. At about 10.00 Sergeant Pearson 8/Hants reached Brigade Battle headquarters with twenty prisoners captured in "Tank Redoubt" which he said was in the hands of a small party of 5/Norfolk's and Imperial Camel Corps, the Tank having done great execution before being knocked out."

163 Brigade Headquarters War Diary. PRO WO95/4656

One of the men in this attack spoke in 1984 of his experiences.
"...on the 19th April we made an attack on the Turkish position. It was across a plain over a mile in distance and as flat as a pancake with not a bit of cover, it was the first time we had seen tanks, there was three, two got knocked out as soon as they started but one actually got to the target but caught fire and was known afterwards as burnt tank redoubt. We advanced in waves, by the way we didn't have steel helmets only sun helmets, a more perfect target could not have been provided for them and our casualties were very high. What was left of my lot got to within about a hundred yards where we laid down. How long we were there I don't know but I managed to fire 70 rounds off. The officer on my left was killed also the man on my right, then I saw an officer get up and wave his arm for us to charge, but just as I got up a bullet caught me in the leg. I managed to get back and into hospital but was back with the battalion in time for the next one".

Private Sidney William GASKIN. No 3119/240680.1/5th Norfolk Regiment.
Notes in author's possession.

On the left flank, three companies of the 4/Norfolk's had also suffered severely as they faced the withering fire. The first of two lines was so depleted that it was compelled to wait for reinforcement when only five-hundred yards from the starting point. Additional help was given as D Company was sent up from support and moved straight on to the right of the line. The battalion advance continued and by about 09.00 was within 150 yards of the Turkish positions. Unfortunately, the final impetus needed to assault the heavily defended positions was not available as all battalion supports were in the line; also, the 8/Hants had veered off to assist the 5/Norfolk's attack on the right against the redoubt. The survivors of the 4/Norfolk's were again brought to a halt to await reinforcement by the divisional reserve.

Back at Brigade Headquarters, progress had been made in getting an accurate situation report. A telephone line had been established to the 8/Hants who were on a ridge five-hundred yards from the objective; heavy casualties were confirmed. Further progress was being prevented by continued fire from machine-guns to the rear of the enemy front-line trenches, and although artillery support was called for, the range was too great for the eighteen-pounder batteries.

"By about 10.30 Lieutenant Buxton had returned to the 8/Hants telephone and reported the attack completely held up on the right. The 5/Norfolk's could be seen lying in considerable numbers on the lower part of the hill W16-W17 on which the enemy trenches were apparently all dead or wounded."

163 Brigade Headquarters War Diary. PRO WO95/4656

The attack was now held up at distances of between 150 and 200 yards from the enemy position. The firing-line had split into several sections, each against an enemy strongpoint, but none reached its objective despite suffering numerous casualties in the attempt. In the face of such opposition and with no reinforcements forthcoming, individual parts of the line were forced to withdraw a few hundred yards, in order to re-group and attempt consolidation of a line, however tenuous that might be.

At 12.45 a very strong counter-attack approached the brigade from a north-westerly direction, and, despite covering fire from both 162 Brigade and the artillery, the already weakened left flank was forced back. This in turn resulted in evacuation of the Tank Redoubt and a general retirement seemed inevitable. To try and stem this, the 5/Suffolk's were sent up with orders to halt the withdrawal, and to advance should an opportunity, and reinforcement, permit. At 14.00 161st Brigade, less one battalion, arrived and twenty minutes later a counter-attack to retake Tank Redoubt was launched. The 5/Suffolk and 6/Essex advanced to the second ridge previously held by the 5/Norfolk's, but in the face of a heavy fire were ordered to halt, as the chance of success seemed slim. Subsequently the 6/Essex was returned to Sheikh Abbas while the 5/Suffolk's held the position reached.

"Here, just down the reverse slope of a ridge, trenches were dug and a line on a wide front organised; A, B and C Companies were in the front line with D Company in support. At intervals throughout the day small parties of wounded Norfolk's came back through the line. The groans and calls of the wounded could be heard, but to send a party into the belt meant certain death and drew a heavy searching fire on those that were there."

History of the 1/5th Suffolk Regiment. Page 63

The 163rd Brigade had given the attack its utmost effort and determination, but was overwhelmed from the outset. The final line achieved was split into two main groups; the remnants of the 5/Norfolk's, including many of those who had entered and held Tank Redoubt against all the odds, now lay some 500 yards from that position. Remnant, too, describes the strength of the 8/Hampshire's who lay among them, reinforced by three companies of the 5/Suffolk's. On the left flank, the 4/Norfolk's, forced back from within 150 yards of the Turkish trenches, now held a line barely 500 yards from the enemy.

These positions were held until 18.00 when the brigade was relieved by the 161st Brigade and withdrew into reserve a mile behind Sheikh Abbas Ridge, 163rd Brigade Machine Gun Company being attached to the relieving force.

From the events described it was inevitable that casualties would be very high, but the final list for the brigade makes grim reading indeed. The War Diary gives the totals, and records;

"Lieutenant-Colonel BS Grissell DSO, Commanding Officer 1/5 Norfolk Regiment, wounded and missing; Lieutenant-Colonel WA Youden TD, Commanding Officer 1/4 Norfolk Regiment, wounded, and every Company Commander in the 4th and 5th Norfolk and 8th Hampshire Regiments wounded."

163 Brigade Headquarters War Diary. PRO WO95/4656

Wounded men of the brigade continued to return throughout the night, and covering parties were sent out to help them in. Due to the enormous casualties sustained by the 4th and 5th Norfolk's, the battalions were amalgamated the following day. Captain ED Wolton continues his account with a letter written home on the 24th April.

"You will be pleased to hear that I came out of the last battle alright. As I told you my Battalion was the first to attack [on the 17th] and we captured the first position [Dumbell Hill] with very few casualties. We immediately went on to the second position [Sheikh Abbas Ridge again] which was the most important. We went on as hard as we could go, as we knew that every minute which passed would give the Turks more time to recover from their surprise and reinforce their second position which was a hard one to capture. So we went on as hard as we could go, over the very broken ground, which was continually crossed by deep gulleys about 20 feet deep and about 50 yards distant from one another. When we arrived we saw the Turks disappearing in the distance. We at once consolidated the position and we had plenty of shells thrown at us, but as we worked hard we soon got underground and so were more or less safe. We worked in reliefs during the whole night and by the next morning we had made some quite respectable trenches. We continued digging during the day and most of the next night and it was lucky we did too, as we got heavily shelled. I can tell you that my battalion was in reserve the next day, but had to reinforce the front line under fairly heavy shell and machine-gun fire. We dug in under the fire of several snipers who seemed to increase as the day came to a

close. Here the narrative must end. I wonder what the papers have made about the Second Battle of Gaza. My Battalion was one of the very few lucky ones [for although] *we got shelled and machine-gunned pretty heavily we only had a very few casualties considering how far we advanced.*

Additional narrative 1/5th Norfolk Regiment

BEFORE THE WAR I WAS living at Reepham in Norfolk and on a visit to Norwich in October 1914, I saw the Kitchener Volunteers and thought "That's the life for me" and I decided to join up.

I went to East Dereham and joined up on October 5 1914, in the 2/5th Norfolk Regiment. We went to Peterborough for training and then to Bury St Edmunds and overnight we slept on Newmarket Heath. Later on we were doing rifle training at Thetford Heath which in those days was open land, a bit of woodland but no forest as it is now.

Well the1/5th Battalion had gone overseas and one day they called for volunteers to go out to Gallipoli. I volunteered and was sent to London to the Great Eastern Station, Liverpool Street, but no one knew anything about us and we were sent back to Bury St Edmunds!

Eventually however we did get sent out there but in the way we were diverted to Egypt as the Turks had crossed the Sinai and were threatening the Suez Canal.

At the First Battle of Gaza we were sent up on the flank of the attack and told to dig in. We had no water for 24 hours and I can tell you that the thirst in that part of the world was terrible.

For the Second Battle, I was in D Company, the attack was silly. We had over a mile of open plain to cross in broad daylight and there was no more cover than that floor there [pointed to the living room floor]. We had to pass through a gap in the ridge and then extend into three lines and we came under shellfire at once. The Turks couldn't have had better targets if they'd all been chalked out for them.

Only the officers knew the plan and I think that is a great failing of the British Army; I don't know if it is any better now but in those days there was hardly any communication between the Officers and men.

The day before the battle we began to assemble behind the ridge but we didn't know why we were gathering. Tanks had moved up the day before and although I had heard about them, that was the first time I had seen one. They were awkward looking things, much higher than the modern ones and we thought we would be able to walk up behind them (laughing) but instead they drew the fire and were knocked out anyway! All the officers were casualties. My CO [Commanding Officer] was St George and he was badly wounded and invalided home. A few years later I read in a Norfolk paper about a funeral director at Wells-next-the-Sea by the same name and I wrote to him. It was the same man and every year after that he sent me a postcard on the 19th April. One year when I didn't get one his wife wrote to me and said that he had died and that in all the years since he had been wounded he had never had a day without a headache.

The advance was silly as we were in three lines instead of single file. Anyway I didn't have wife or a girlfriend and so I thought here goes nothing. The idea behind military planning in those days was to advance a line and then by gaining superiority of fire you would be able to force them to keep their heads down!

Well, by the time we'd got to an advanced line we were so short of men that we could only lie there and keep *our* heads down. I fired off seventy rounds in one go and when I looked back to see if any reinforcements were coming up I couldn't see anyone. An Officer to the left of me was shot dead and a Lewis Gunner on my right was also killed. At that point I gave up all hope and waited for my turn. We didn't have steel helmets then, we only got those later for the third battle, we had the sun hats and they made a lovely target for the Turks.

An Officer on my left stood up and waved us forward but as I rose and moved forward I was hit in the leg by a bullet. I made my way back by crawling to the ADS [Advanced Dressing Station] just behind the ridge and when I reported in my shorts were covered in blood. I asked the orderly if I could have them and he asked me "What for?"

I said "For a souvenir" and he said "No you can't!"

I can't remember how I got back to the Forward Dressing Station [further back than the ADS]. I was trying to remember last night. Was it on a camel? No, was given the chance but said I'd rather crawl! The platform was right above the ground and the movement was like a rough sea.

I was given an injection against lockjaw and was in the hospital for a while. The hospital tents were shelled by the Turks but it was their own fault as the battery guns were just behind them.

My best pal was Jack SADLER but he was blown to pieces by a shell and that was the last I saw of him.

Another character in the battalion was a chap named PALMER He had this knack of always being able to find water no matter where you were. You'd be on a march and when you stopped for a ten-minute break he'd disappear off somewhere and come back with water.

One time we were camped on the edge of an orange grove and it was funny to think that at home there were none while we became very particular which we ate. We had "orange fights" with the ones we didn't want!

The flies were the worst. You'd be sitting eating your bread and jam and you'd have to scrape the flies off before taking a mouthful. We were lousy for three years. The rations we mainly had was Tickler's Marmalade and bully beef. Mind you, it wasn't like the corned beef you get here, no, because it was so hot that it came out all runny.

When the Armistice with Turkey was declared I was very ill with flu and it didn't mean much to me. My section had to march down to Beirut and by the time we got there were only four of us left. The M.O. [Medical Officer] was going to put me down as a "cot case" but I didn't want to be down in the bowels of a ship, I wanted to be up top and see what was going on. He put me down as "Walking" and the next day they came round and called "Cot-cases only" and so I had to stay behind-served me right. It did me a favour though because we landed at Taranto in Italy and marched up through the Alps and it was beautiful. We crossed the Channel and landed at Southampton on a Sunday and the only reception we got was from a load of dockers swearing and shouting because they had to work on a Sunday. We ended up at Purfleet [Essex] where we were demobilised and then it was up to us how we got home. We were given a rail warrant but I had a sister in London so I stayed with her.

It makes me cross when they talk about the Falklands Vets; what about the Palestine Vets? You never hear anything about us.

Private Sidney Gaskin
No 3119/240680
1/5th Norfolk Regiment

163 Brigade

Casualties for the Second Battle of Gaza

FOR THE 163RD BRIGADE, THE Second Battle of Gaza was an unmitigated catastrophe. The following obituaries must serve as a tribute to but a fragment of the total killed and nearly eight hundred wounded; figures comparable to, and in the case of the 5/Norfolk Regiment greater than, many battalions on the Somme for the 1st July 1916.

The 4/Norfolk Regiment lost 6/149 killed and 8/196 wounded; a further ten men died of wounds. Once again, many of those who died were younger than twenty years old, inevitably some only 17, such as Private Stanley John BOWES from Lenwade, Norfolk. But, most pronounced with this battalion, there were seemingly more than average numbers of men in their late thirties and early forties. A Lancashire man Private Willie BOOCOCK had been born at Nelson, probably lived there all his life and left a widow Hilda, at St Mary's Street; he was forty. Lance-Corporal George Alfred BALLS was 44, and lived at School Terrace, Lingwood, Norwich, not far from his birthplace at Strumpshaw; he had earlier been decorated for gallantry with the Distinguished Conduct Medal for. He was mortally wounded on 19th April and died of his wounds five days later at Deir el Belah. Sergeant Edward CAREY, son of Mr and Mrs Carey of Oak Street, Norwich aged 44 lost without trace; Private Alexander ELY, husband of Phoebe Alice Ely of Baldwin's Yard, Oak Street age 40; finally Private Edward TOOKE, a Norwich man of 24 years from Great Yard, Oak Street also lost without trace

Twenty-four year old Private Robert Reginald BARNARD was buried in the cemetery at Gaza reference XXIII.E.11. Born at Wymondham, Norfolk he enlisted in August 1914 and served during the Gallipoli Campaign of the following year. He was with D Company on the 19th April 1917, initially in reserve but soon called upon to support the right of the battalion's line, many casualties having been taken from the outset at 07.30 of the open-plain attack. One of those in that advance was 19-year old Private Albert FOX with C Company, severely wounded he died two days later at Deir el Belah; his widow eventually remarried and lived in Aylesham Road, Norwich. On such a scale, the recounting of personal details becomes at first depressing and then with lessening impact. To move away from the city and wonder at the isolation and tranquillity of those days of a tiny hamlet called Kelling, near Holt. What would have been behind the following details?

Corporal Robert John DEWING Age 30. Son of William and Sarah Dewing of The Street, Kelling, Norfolk.
Corporal Tom Stanley BRIGHTON. One of six brothers, four of whom fell.
Private Ernest Arthur BROWNE. Age 31 of Victoria Villas, Waltham Abbey, Essex
Private Leonard BROWN Age 19 of Friendly Terrace, Hatfield Heath, Harlow, Essex.
Twelve men from a total of 149.

The officer casualties for the brigade were summarised in the War Diary, the final line reading "every Company Commander in the 4 & 5 Norfolk's and 8 Hants wounded."

Parallel has been drawn between the casualties suffered by many battalions on the Somme in 1916 and those taken by the 5/Norfolk's. While such comparisons may seem contemptible, the purpose is to highlight the terrible losses of many East Anglian Regiments, for the most part virtually unrecognised.

Thus, for the 5/Norfolk's, nine officers and two-hundred and eleven men killed; seven officers and three-hundred and seventy-seven men wounded must say it all. Many of these casualties occurred in the first 500 yards, and only one hour into the attack. B Company had Private Sidney Herbert ENGLISH in its ranks. Twenty-five years old he came from Wootton Road, Gaywood, King's Lynn and had enlisted in the 5/Norfolk's at East Dereham in September 1914. He served at Gallipoli where the battalion lost heavily, a whole platoon having disappeared without trace, a mystery not cleared up until around 1985. Company Sergeant Major Charles BECKETT from Surrey had travelled to Dersingham, Norfolk to enlist.

He was killed on the 19th and is buried in Gaza Cemetery XXIII.B.9; a few rows along lies CSM Benjamin WELHAM. Lost without trace was 240473 Alexander OGILVEY, a Company Quarter Master Sergeant at only 22 years of age, his parents James Alexander and Jessie Morrison lived in Cromer Road, North Walsham, Norfolk. These were the men who held the companies together and with the loss of no less than thirteen sergeants, the whole fabric of the battalion was wiped out at a stroke. The men who would take over their places, their understudies if you like, were the less experienced but promising Corporals; eleven were killed on the 19th.

While the loss of a son or husband, neighbour or friend was devastating enough, there was another aspect of the casualty list for the 1/5th Norfolk Regiment, even more poignant. The appearance of the same surname does not necessarily mean they were related, however in one case it is confirmed. Lance-Corporal Thomas James CREASEY age 20 and Private Charles Robert CREASEY age 21 were brothers by the entry in the Jerusalem Memorial Register as both were sons of Henry and Barbara Creasey, of "Wembley" West Runton, Cromer, Norfolk. Many others can be inferred:

240310 Sergeant Edgar FISHER
240304 Sergeant Joseph FISHER
both born at East Tuddenham, both enlisted at East Dereham.

240038 Sergeant Archibald HASTINGS
240043 Private Bertie HASTINGS
born Cromer, enlisted Cromer, Norfolk.

240220 Private Austin George RUDRAM
240107 Private Charles James RUDRAM
born and enlisted at Mundesley, Norfolk.

Private Frank Basil SPURGEON was only 18 but had enlisted in 1914 at the age of 15! From High Street, Gorleston, Norfolk, his brother was also killed.

How could the battalion be the same after such losses? The bewilderment and shock to the survivors must have been an experience to have changed their lives forever. Only they, who had been there on Primrose Day 1917, could know its effects; only they suffered as they sought to retrieve some normality from the devastating experience. One such survivor spoke in 1984 of his Commanding Officer who had been badly wounded and invalided home. He sent a postcard each year on the 19th April; what thoughts were revived when writing it, one wonders? Then,

"One year when I didn't get one, his wife wrote to me and said that he had died and that in all the years since he had been wounded he had never had a day without a headache."

SW Gaskin. Notes in author's possession.

The 8/Hampshire Regiment had 8/190 killed and 5/165 wounded at the Second Battle of Gaza.

Rifleman Percy SHORT lived at Hamworthy, Dorset. From his address of Railway Cottages, Hamworthy Junction, Poole it can be reasonably deduced that his father, John, was a railwayman, perhaps his son having followed in his footsteps. However, a lifetime's work on the Great Western Railway was not to be, for he was severely wounded on the 19th April and died two days later. Rifleman William Harold SIMMONS was twenty-two. Enlisting at Newport, Isle of Wight, his address was given as Marlow, Buckinghamshire, his parents Walter and Lucy being publicans at The Jolly Cricketers, Bovingdon Green. After her husband Rifleman Albert VALE was killed, Alice Vale left Southwark, London, married and became landlady at The Crown Inn, Swindon, Wiltshire. Once again, the toll in Non-Commissioned Officers [NCOs] was great, with seven Sergeants being killed:

Bertie WEBSTER
Harold WAVELL
Charles SMITH
Arthur MARLOW
John MOREY
Arthur JAMES
Ernest CAWS

Five Corporals
Frank WOLFE, 27
Alfred TAYLOR
Arthur PRATT, 30
William LANE, 38
Stanley JEFFERY, 21

All perished on that day.

The 8/Hampshire's were initially in support on the 19th April, but as evident by now they were very soon involved in the battle. C and D Companies followed the 4/Norfolk's on the left flank; Rifleman Frederick RICKETTS of Wycombe Marsh, Buckinghamshire was killed with C Company aged 19, Rifleman Arthur James PARKINSON the same age. From Gosport, Hampshire, Rifleman Thomas CATLOW fell with D Company.

The 5/Norfolk's were supported by A and B Companies; Rifleman Leslie Leonard COOKE of Mayfield Villas, Aldershot, Surrey with the former and Sergeant Arthur JAMES from Yarmouth Road, Carisbrooke, Isle of Wight with the latter.

Finally, if one town sums up the maritime nature of Hampshire it must surely be Lymington, with its harbour moorings, shingle banks and widening channel which leads to spectacular views of the Island, a scene Rifleman Edwin ELLIOTT must have seen many times. He was wounded on the 19th April but did not die of his wounds until the 3 May.

The 5/Suffolk Regiment were in brigade reserve for the morning's operations. At 14.20 they co-operated in an unsuccessful attempt to retake Tank Redoubt, their final casualty total for the day being four men killed and 5/78 wounded.

Second Battle of Gaza
161st Brigade

ON THE 16 APRIL, THE 161st Brigade was in bivouac with the rest of the 54th DIVISION at IN SEIRAT. For the first phase of the coming operation, the brigade was to be Divisional Reserve, and so brought up the rear of the first column to leave, following the 163rd Brigade and Divisional Artillery. At 03.00 on the 17th April, after a two-hour march, the brigade reached the assembly point, a mile or so short, east of the WADI GHUZZE. In the shelter of the Wadi SHARTA the brigade was held in reserve, although its services were not needed for the First Phase, namely the capture of the Mansura and Sheikh Abbas Ridges.

During the 17 April, the brigade was employed in making and repairing roads in the el Kutshan area, except for two companies of the 1/7th Essex who were designated as artillery escort. At 18.45 the 1/5 Essex moved up to the southern end of the Sheikh Abbas Ridge, thereby allowing the 1/5 Norfolk's to withdraw in preparation for the Second Phase.

Early on the following day, the brigade, still less the two companies 7/Essex, was relieved by the 74th DIVISION and moved three miles to the north-east, concentrating just behind the Sheikh Abbas Ridge. Digging-in of the position was started, but being in the open proved hazardous as enemy shelling increased, and so a more sheltered spot, in the Wadi NUKHABIR off to the south-west, was adopted.

For the Second Phase of the battle, on the 19 April the brigade, once again in reserve, was sited so as to be able to readily support either of the two front-line brigades. However, although uncommitted as a brigade during the day, much marching was undertaken by two of its battalions. The first of these moves fell to the 7/Essex, who were detached from the brigade and placed under the command of the Imperial Camel Corps. The four companies regrouped at CHARING CROSS, a mile south of the brigade, at 06.15 and moved to the right flank of the Sheikh Abbas line. From here the battalion was under orders to closely support the Imperial Camel Corps attack on Khirbet Sihan, which, although not a primary objective, was thought to be an artillery strong-point and could thus enfilade and hinder the main attack.

The other three battalions of the brigade remained in reserve behind the ridge, and it was not until 13.00 that they were ordered up to support the 163 Brigade. Initially, the 4/Essex and 5/Essex dug in on the Sheikh Abbas Ridge, while the 6/Essex prepared to advance. Their role was to support the 5/Suffolk's who had moved up to stem the retirement from Tank Redoubt and were now on a forward ridge awaiting reinforcement.

At 14.20, the two battalions were ordered to retake Tank Redoubt, but were stopped by a heavy rifle fire. Orders were then received to seize the ridges which overlooked the position, the 5/Suffolk to consolidate them while the 6/Essex withdrew. By late afternoon, the 6/Essex were holding the right of the brigade line about Sheikh Abbas Ridge. The line was extended to the left by the 5/Essex, with the 4/Essex completing the line and joining up with the right of 162 Brigade which was held by the 5/Bedford's. This line was held without incident, apart from covering retiring troops, until the evening of 20 April.

Second Battle of Gaza
155th Brigade

On the evening of the 16th April the 155th Infantry Brigade left its bivouac at IN SEIRAT and marched to a crossing over the Wadi Ghuzze, one mile north of el Breij. From here the advance continued onto the EL SIRE Ridge and a position around KURD HILL was attained without opposition at 22.05. The success of the advance was primarily due to thorough reconnaissance and detailed preparation of the routes of approach. The area had been occupied earlier in the month by the 5/KOSB and this had given ample opportunity for such reconnaissance. Over the preceding months, many battalions had been in sight of "The Red House"; such was its topographical significance that it was marked on the early maps of Gaza and a poem had been written about it. The area was not without its hazards however.

> "April 1917
> Just across the valley was what had once been a charming country house and garden belonging to some rich inhabitant of Gaza.
> The "Red House" had the usual cactus enclosures, but was now derelict. The water-wheel had been broken up. The well, following the usual German custom, had been filled up with rubbish and befouled by the Turks, although such destruction is expressly forbidden in the Koran.
> This villa had its importance in the story of the 1/5th KOSB. For quite a long period it was held by a company of the battalion. They had orders to retire if they were attacked by the enemy in superior numbers. On the 4th April the company in the Red House was attacked by at least one or more (probably two) battalions.
> Captain AK Clark-Kennedy, who was in command, following his orders, withdrew.
> This difficult operation was conducted without haste and with extraordinary skill. The men retired in alternate platoons, keeping up a continual fire upon the enemy, who did not dare to follow across the open ground. He did not have a single casualty, and he succeeded in bringing back every horse, mule and camel, as well as everything else of the slightest value.
> His task was not made easier by an unfortunate incident.
> During the retreat one of the camels suddenly went mad or "magnoon." Now and then, for no known reason, a male camel will suddenly lose his head. He will run violently about and try to kill anybody that he can catch. His tail will be vertical and twisted like a corkscrew, and foam froths out through his long yellow and splayed teeth. <u>If this happens under ordinary circumstances, the correct procedure is to trip him up with ropes, tie him up, and them belabour him with sticks until he comes to his senses.</u> [Authors underlining]
> On this occasion the camel was promptly shot, and Clark-Kennedy's orderly retreat was not disturbed.
> The War History of the 1/5th King's Own Scottish Borderers. Pages 127-128.

52nd (LOWLAND) DIVISION
155 BRIGADE.
16-18 APRIL 1917

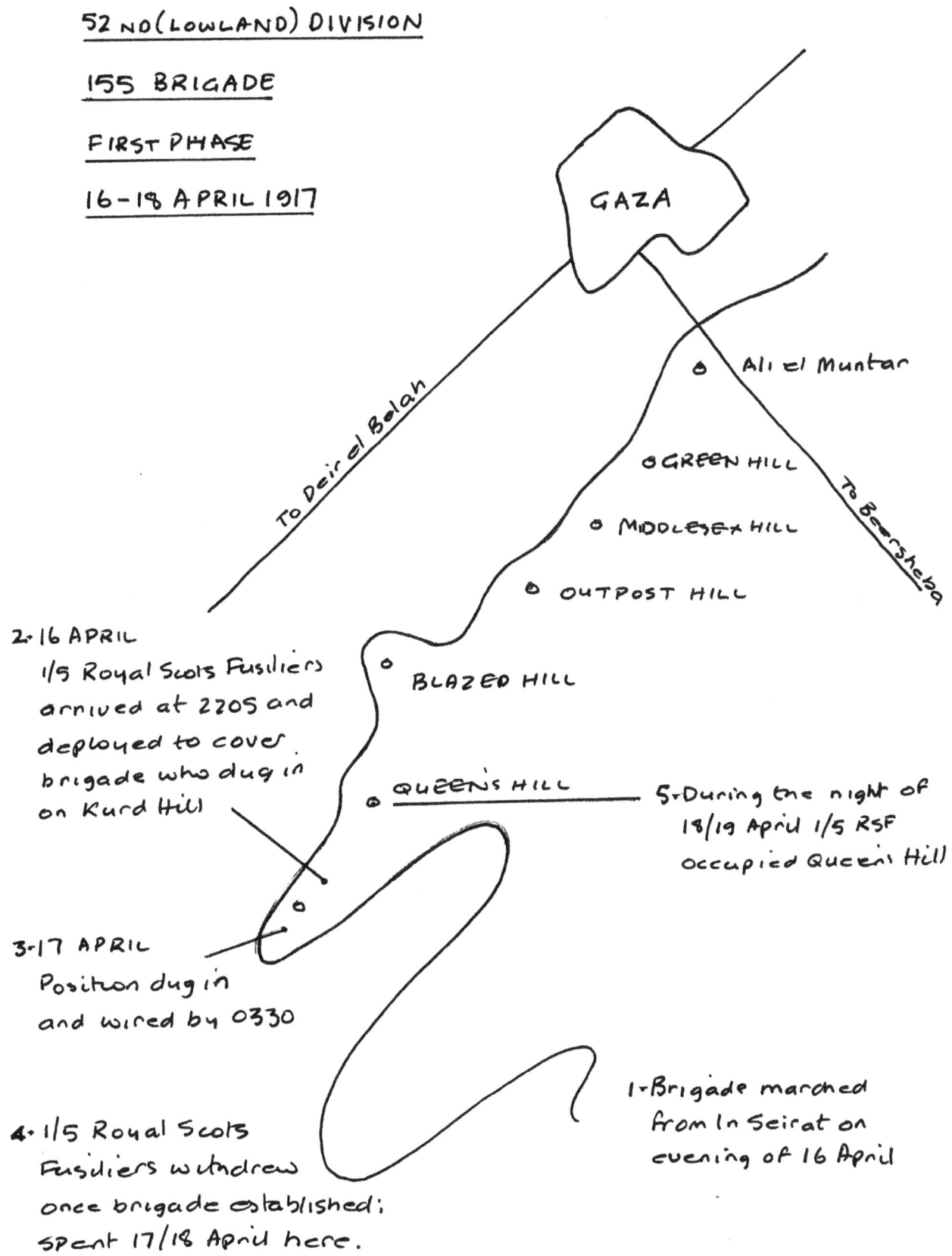

By 03.30 on the 17th April, wiring of the newly dug trenches was completed and as dawn approached, the men settled down to hold the line gained. The left of the position on Kurd Hill was held by the 1/4th King's Own Scottish Borderers, who were in two lines facing west. Their rear was protected by the 1/4th Royal Scots Fusiliers who held the right of the brigade line, while the 1/5th King's Own Scottish Borderers were in reserve.

During the entrenching of the position, the operation had been protected by the fourth battalion of the brigade. The 1/5th Royal Scots Fusiliers had been the first to arrive on Kurd Hill at 22.05, and deployed in the low ground forward of the position. Forming a protective screen, patrols pushed even further forward, some to within hearing distance of the Turks on QUEEN'S HILL. At 03.30 the battalion withdrew through the gaps in the wire on Kurd Hill, which were then closed, and then took up position to the south-west on WART HILL, one company digging a redoubt to cover the rear of the main position. As daylight broke on 17 April, the Turks realised the attack they had expected since the end of March was imminent. Accordingly, shell-fire was opened up on the positions all along the new front, causing several deaths and a number of wounded, some of whom were buried in their dug-outs. With the advanced line of the First Phase secured, preparations for the Second Phase could now be started. During the rest of the 17th and all throughout the 18 April, thousands of fanatis of water, as well as all the necessary stores, were brought up to advanced dumps just behind the line.

"Fantasse, plural fanatis, an Arabic word adopted by the Army. The fantasse was a small metal tank of which each camel carried two. It had a capacity of 12 gallons."

Official History. Volume One page 193

To protect this vital work, throughout the day the artillery with Naval assistance from the French Coast-Guard ship *Requin* and the Royal Navy Monitors M21 and M31, bombarded enemy positions across the front. Although this must have helped to suppress some enemy fire, it was not entirely successful for some thirteen men of the 4/King's Own Scottish Borderers were buried in their trenches by 4.2 Howitzer fire; all were safely extricated.

On the evening of the 18th April, the 5/Royal Scots Fusiliers moved out with orders to seize Queen's Hill. Occupied by the Turks during the day but deserted at night, the position was occupied and digging of trenches completed by dawn of the 19th April. At 05.30, bombardment of the enemy positions commenced with the woods to the north-west of OUTPOST HILL being subjected to forty minutes treatment with special shell [gas] from the start, then high explosive until 07.30. Five minutes after the start of the bombardment, the enemy opened up with an equally intense counter-bombardment, which caused many casualties among the waiting troops.

The infantry advance began at 07.30 on 19th April. The objectives of the brigade were the successive hills along the gradually rising line of the el Sire Ridge, ending with GREEN HILL and the mosque on ALI EL MUNTAR. The 155 Brigade advanced on a two-battalion front from Kurd Hill and was assisted by two tanks, part of a detachment which had arrived a few days before. The 5/King's Own Scottish Borderers were on the left and had two objectives. B Company on the right of the battalion front was to advance and assault MIDDLESEX HILL, being supported by A Company. The left of the battalion front was taken by D Company who would, with C Company following, engage the enemy on OUTPOST HILL.

The initial advance went smoothly, taking the form of eight waves with about 250 yards between each. LEES HILL was easily taken but even at this early stage -08.15- the were ominous casualties among the leading officers, Captain GIBSON, Lieutenant and Adjutant HOWIESON and 2nd Lieutenant GILMOUR all being wounded. The tank assigned to lead the battalion was named "OTAZEL" [Hot - as - Hell!] and itself became a casualty shortly after setting off. Attempting to cross a deep nullah, the obstacle proved too great and the tank nose-dived into it and remained stuck throughout the day. The following troops, ordered to stay behind her, held their position until a message from brigade headquarters quickly returned them to the offensive. BLAZED HILL to the north-west of Lees Hill was secured without serious loss and the success-emboldened men set off for the next objective. Descending in the hollow between the positions taken and Outpost Hill, opposition was still only minimal although moderate shelling continued unabated.

As the ground began to rise and the men's eyes lifted to their objective, now only five-hundred yards away, a hail of machine-gun fire tore into the orderly lines. Although facing directly into a heavy fire the enfilade fire from the left flank was even more devastating. Consequently, the line veered off to face that direction and a gap was created between the battalion and their front-line comrades to the right, the 4/Royal Scots Fusiliers. An order to try and remedy this situation by "inclining right" only divided the line further; two platoons struck a ridge to the east of Outpost Hill, while the main line continued to be drawn by the enfilading guns.

Pinned down by the withering machine-gun fire and further aggravated by shrapnel and high-explosive, the advance could only be continued in isolated rushes by short sections of the line. Rising up at the inspired command of one officer after another, the men valiantly progressed towards the summit of Outpost Hill. Under such conditions, heavy casualties were inevitable of course. Lieutenant DINWIDDIE fell seriously wounded in the early part of the attack, as did Captain T DUNN and 2nd Lieutenant HENERY, the latter mortally. All across the field, men fell dead and dying; the wounded could only look in vain for cover on the exposed rise and many were hit repeatedly. Lieutenant NICHOLSON was shot dead as he went to the aid of Captain Dunn who was himself shot again and killed. Despite continual depletion, the storming parties pressed on and at 10.18 the redoubt on Outpost Hill was captured.

As previously stated, the redoubt on Outpost Hill was only one of the brigade's two main objectives on that fateful April day. The 4/Royal Scots Fusiliers also moved off from Kurd Hill at 07.30 and, on the right of the front line, had GREEN HILL as their ultimate goal, but to assist the two companies of the 5/King's Own Scottish Borderers attack against Middlesex Hill on the way. They too had the support of a tank which was ordered to lead the battalion all the way to Green Hill. Moving off in a similar formation as their comrades, with A Company leading B Company on the right flank and C Company leading D Company on the left, the advance went forward in eight waves over a depth of two-thousand yards. The tank, this one was called "WAR BABY", led A Company but when "OTAZEL" ditched it was diverted across the front of the battalion to the revised destination of Outpost Hill.

At 08.30, the officer commanding the 4/Royal Scots Fusiliers, Lieutenant-Colonel H THOMPSON, shortly to be killed, reported that the front-line was still progressing steadily with few casualties. However, within a few minutes of this message a further part of the enemy line which had engaged the 5/King's Own Scottish Borderers opened up an equally intense fire on the battalion. From the front and left flank rifle and machine-gun fire dropped men wholesale in the lines as they advanced, while artillery positions from the right flank subjected the whole area to a heavy shrapnel bombardment.

The left of the battalion was now only about 200 yards from Outpost Hill and was gradually drawn into the fight for that position. Supporting platoons were sent up to maintain the left flank, but in the confusion many men lost their direction and ended up to the right of the line instead.

Just as the whole line threatened to be drawn into the fight for Outpost Hill, the right flank was ordered to push forward as planned. With their left flank open but with 156th Brigade to the right, the 4/Royal Scots Fusiliers resumed the attack across the ever-rising ground towards Middlesex Hill. The 156th Brigade Machine-Gun Company engaged some of the enemy on the eastern slopes of Outpost Hill which afforded a little relief, but from the range of hills to the front, frustrating as each was a little higher than its predecessor, the artillery, machine-gun and rifle fire took its unremitting toll. Even under such terrible conditions the ambulance wagons and stretcher-bearers of the Royal Army Medical Corps continued to work. Right up to the firing-line the wounded were tended, with the more serious cases being evacuated by the ambulances which were often hit themselves. The steadfast courage of the 4/Royal Scots Fusiliers eventually resulted in the capture of the outlying trenches of Middlesex Hill at 10.47. The troops further back could see the Turks retiring from their trenches and by 11.00 the whole position was taken.

A further example of the perseverance shown in the fight for the hill was that shown by a group of the 5/King's Own Scottish Borderers. The men of No2 Platoon, A Company under Lieutenant TURNER advanced for over a thousand yards, but of the original thirty men, only three or four actually reached their objective. Making contact with the 4/Royal Scots Fusiliers, the valiant group remained in a small trench and did not retire until 22.15, carrying their wounded out with them.

However, despite all the determination and gallantry displayed during the capture of Middlesex Hill, a precarious salient had been so formed. Although Outpost Hill had been taken at 10.18 the position had not been forsaken by the Turks and many men of the garrison now turned their fire to the south-western slopes of Middlesex Hill, thereby compounding the problems of the holding force. The right flank, too, was exposed as the 156 Brigade, doggedly supporting the right of the 4/Royal Scots Fusiliers, had advanced far ahead of the 54th DIVISION who were being annihilated off to the east near SHEIKH ABBAS. The hard-pressed troops could only hold the position against the odds in the hope that support would come from either or both flanks.

It was essential that the ground already won be consolidated as rapidly as possible and this was entrusted to the 5/Royal Scots Fusiliers; it will be remembered that they were at an advanced position on Queen's Hill when the main advance began at 07.30. As the 5/King's Own Scottish Borderers and 4/Royal Scots Fusiliers moved through the line on the hill, the battalion was to bring up the rear, detailing one company to hold each of the five main objectives as they were captured. Each of the four companies of the 5/Royal Scots Fusiliers, as well as the Cyclist Company which, was temporarily attached to the battalion, had one hill to consolidate, the following companies then passing over them to their own objective. In this way the whole El Sire Ridge would be captured and held, thereby threatening Ali el Muntar from the south-west and assisting the final assault by 156 Brigade from the south-east.

Initially, C Company under Captain AJ RODGER was left to hold Queen's Hill and as the forward troops advanced, Lees Hill was consolidated by Lieutenant RG COCHRANE with A Company. Although their main duty was that of consolidation, from their position on BLAZED HILL A Company was able to give much-needed covering fire to the attack on Outpost Hill.

The Cyclist Company under Captain Glendinning moved off at 08.25, through the troops on Lees Hill and advanced to the left of Outpost Hill. As the left flank of the main attack by the 5/KOSB was forced to a standstill, the Cyclist Company managed to continue until it was isolated. Under Capt Glendinning's instruction the men took cover in a wadi about 200 yards from Outpost Hill while he returned to the telephone station on Lees Hill to give a situation report, his own telephone communication having been disrupted by shellfire. He was told that a tank was moving up to assist and that he should follow it and seize the left defences of Outpost Hill in order to allow the 5/KOSB to complete their assault and capture of the whole position. Under Captain Glendinning the company attacked, only to be decimated by machine-gun and rifle fire from the redoubt itself and from the woods to the north; Captain Glendinning was killed and the survivors dropped back to the wadi.

When the first men of the 5/King's Own Scottish Borderers entered the redoubt on Outpost Hill at 10.18, instead of finding sanctuary they found hell. The redoubt was cleverly formed with its ends drawn back to enable the hill to be easily defended on three sides. The open rear was totally commanded from the trenches on the south-western slopes of Middlesex Hill and by artillery further up the ridge. The officers who arrived unwounded at the position must have quickly realised that its continued occupation would be untenable unless the heights which dominated it were also soon taken. The redoubt soon filled up and men of the following lines had to lie outside, taking what shelter they could from its walls. The intensity of the enemy fire which had been experienced during the advance soon paled by comparison as the exposed work was pounded by shrapnel, high-explosive shell and raked by incessant machine-gun fire. A heavy rifle fire continued to take its toll of those not hit in the overall carnage. Although Middlesex Hill was cleared around 11.00 the shelling alone proved too intense and at 11.10 the redoubt was abandoned.

52nd (LOWLAND) DIVISION
155 BRIGADE.
FIRST ASSAULT ON OUTPOST HILL
19 APRIL 1917

52ND (LOWLAND) DIVISION

155 BRIGADE

FIRST ASSAULT ON OUTPOST HILL

19 APRIL 1917

MIDDLESEX HILL o

Heavy fire from Turkish machine guns draws attack to left

5 - REDOUBT CAPTURED AT 10.18

o OUTPOST HILL

4 - Part of B Company take ridge to the east of hill

BLAZED HILL o

2. Two hills taken around 0815 for little loss.

o LEES HILL

3 1/4 Royal Scots Fusiliers left flank drawn by heavy fire from Outpost Hill

o QUEENS HILL

1/5 King's Own Scottish Borderers

1. Advance begins 0730

Brigade HQ at KURD HILL

Reinforcements began to arrive soon after this and a second assault was planned, with co-operation from 261 Brigade Royal Field Artillery who would bombard the hill from 12.00 to 12.30. The main reinforcement consisted of the 4/King's Own Scottish Borderers who had been ordered up from reserve at 10.30. Their Commanding Officer Major WT FORREST was given the task of organising the attack and decided upon two companies, with a third in support, of his own battalion along with the undaunted survivors from their sister battalion, the 5/King's Own Scottish Borderers. To the south-west of Outpost Hill there was a group of men of the Cyclist Company, 5/Royal Scots Fusiliers who had earlier vainly attacked the western defences of the hill, only to have lost their Company Commander killed and with many casualties. Captain J LEES and Captain WD Kennedy of B Company 5/Royal Scots Fusiliers had arrived by this time and after taking command, placed these survivors alongside their own B Company and part of D Company which formed the party now at the disposal of Major Forrest. The 155th Brigade Headquarters set the time for the assault at 12.30 but communications with the waiting troops proved very difficult. Consequently, just before midday and possibly unaware of the planned bombardment by 261 Brigade RFA, Major Forrest led the attack to recapture the redoubt.

52nd (LOWLAND) DIVISION
155 BRIGADE.
SITUATION AT OUTPOST HILL TO 1110
19 APRIL 1917

52ND (LOWLAND) DIVISION

155 BRIGADE

SITUATION AT OUTPOST HILL TO 11.10

19 APRIL 1917

EL SIRE RIDGE

1/5 Kings Own Scottish Borders No 2 Platoon A Company enters enemy trenches; 3 or 4 survive from original 30

MIDDLESEX HILL

3. At 11.10 Intense shelling forced withdrawal from redoubt

OUTPOST HILL

2. At 11.00 1/4 Royal Scots Fusiliers captured Middlesex Hill

BLAZED HILL

LEES HILL

1. 0915 Lees Hill consolidated by A Company 1/5 Royal Scots Fusiliers; C Co in reserve at Queens Hill. Rest of the battalion ready to advance to Outpost Hill and beyond.

QUEEN'S HILL

52nd (LOWLAND) DIVISION
155 BRIGADE.
SECOND ASSAULT ON OUTPOST HILL
19 APRIL 1917

52ND (LOWLAND) DIVISION

155 BRIGADE

SECOND ASSAULT ON OUTPOST HILL

19 APRIL 1917

REDOUBT RETAKEN 1210

MIDDLESEX HILL

OUTPOST HILL

BLAZED HILL

LEES HILL

Position held by 1/4 Royal Scots Fusiliers under constant, heavy fire.

Enemy driven from Outpost Hill engaged rear of 1/4 RSF

1- 1/5 Royal Scots Fusiliers Cyclist Company cut down while trying to work up western slopes of Outpost Hill.

3. 1/4 King's Own Scottish Borderers first assault repulsed.

2. Several assaults by 1/5 King's Own Scottish Borderers who had been driven out of redoubt at 11.10

Rallying point for final assault
1/4 KOSB (A B & D)
1/5 KOSB (A C & D)
1/5 RSF (C yc, B & D)

1/4 KOSB moved from Kurd Hill at 0930 and from Queen's Hill at 1100

The rising troops were the signal to the tense, waiting Turks. Machine-guns opened up with their impersonal, chilling rattle, the intersecting lines of fire cutting down many Scotsmen in the first few yards. Once again, even such daunting fire was not enough to stop the advance and steady progress was made up the hill-side. Natural pauses occurred as small areas of cover were reached, however, and from one of these Lieutenant JM POLLOCK of the 5/KOSB described the heart-rending scene:

"The fire from the enemy's machine-guns was terrific, spelling certain death to nearly all who were in the open. About 20 yards from the redoubt I obtained shelter in a small shell hole for a few minutes, and while lying there I saw Captain Cochrane rush forward and bend over the body of Captain Lumgair, who was lying wounded between the barbed wire and the redoubt trench. He appeared to be just on the point of lifting Captain Lumgair up, when a man near me said
"Look at Captain Cochrane; he'll be killed as sure as fate,"
and these words had scarcely been spoken before I saw Captain Cochrane stagger and fall to the ground. Captain Lumgair was a general favourite and Lieutenant WR Ovens and Sergeant Waugh made a desperate attempt to get him in. Sergeant Waugh lifted him up, when he was shot again, this time fatally."

52nd Division History. Page 324.

During the initial research for this book, the author wrote to many newspapers throughout the UK and the following reply, although not of any military importance, is a poignant illustration of the lasting effects of the events which seem so distant.

"11 November 1984
I was interested in your letter in the Border Telegraph. I don't think I can give you much information but my father, Captain WF COCHRANE was killed at The Second Battle of Gaza on 19th April 1917. It was said that he was trying to rescue his friend Captain RRM LUMGAIR who also died at that time. In about 1922 my mother and Mrs Lumgair went to Gaza to see The Cemetery there and they donated in memory of their husbands a ward in The Missionary Hospital - I would very much like to know what has happened to all that, with so much fighting can anything be left?"

By short rushes the line advanced to the edge of the redoubt and although some Turks fled as the Scotsmen approached, many fought desperately and bravely to hold the work. The eastern part of the redoubt was taken although the Turks continued to retain the western part, only about a hundred yards separating the opposing troops; the struggle continued even more desperately amid trenches which filled with wounded and dead. Time and time again men attacked the position in the wake of their comrades who had been cut down by the devastating fire. Captain Lees and Captain Kennedy were killed early on, with Lieutenant RP McKENZIE also being killed. Dozens of men of the 5/RSF were wounded but still the attack went on.

"One platoon and two Lewis Guns of B Company under Second Lieutenant GA FOOTE and about 20 men of the Cyclist Company under Second Lieutenant REDPATH lined the crest on the north where they were under the command of Lieutenant Colonel Simson of 5/KOSB until he was wounded. After that Second Lieutenant Foote took charge until relieved by Major Crombie 5/KOSB in the evening."

5/RSF Diary WO95/4607

The 155 Brigade Machine-Gun Company tried valiantly to assist and a machine-gun was actually carried into the redoubt by Captain PIRIE, Lieutenant STEWART and two men. As they got into action however, the group was struck by a shell, its leader and one man being killed outright and the others being wounded. Desperately needed Lewis Guns were destroyed by the intense shell-fire being rained down on the position and the struggle to drive the enemy off the hill continued with rifles, bayonets and bombs.

As the force of about four-hundred men was whittled down by the continued efforts of the enemy, several moves were made to try and relieve the situation. Second Lieutenant GIBB of the 5/King's Own Scottish Borderers led a small party of men out onto the left flank to try and locate some of the enemy machine-guns. They got as far as the cactus hedges but were driven back and 2nd Lieutenant Gibb was later killed. Officers in the redoubt were prime targets, for as they openly encouraged and organised the assorted units they were picked off by snipers. At one point Major CROMBIE of the 5/King's Own Scottish Borderers ordered his group to fix bayonets, but as the first wave mounted the parapet all were knocked back, killed or wounded. Further waves at the ready were stood down. The supply of ammunition to this fire-ridden area was a well-nigh impossible task, but somehow enough was taken right into the firing-line, the following quote being a good example of the respect won under such conditions.

19 April 1917
"Most of the camels carrying the reserve ammunition had become casualties soon after the advance started, so that boxes of small arms ammunition had to be man-handled forward along the fire-swept ridge. On this, as on many another occasion, the Egyptian camel men behaved with striking bravery and coolness, and earned the respect of the British fighting men."

The 52nd Lowland Division. Page 321.

Command of the garrison became increasingly difficult as officers continued to become casualties and communication with headquarters was well-nigh impossible. Of the two battalions primarily engaged about Outpost Hill, seventeen officers of the 4/ and 5/King's Own Scottish Borderers were killed. Numbered among this total were five captains, which meant that command of companies fell to Lieutenants and Second-Lieutenants. By mid-afternoon Lieutenant RB ANDERSON of the 4/KOSB was the most senior officer in the redoubt who was still unwounded.

Telephone communication between the redoubt and the brigade headquarters at Kurd Hill was never fully established, despite the untiring efforts of the brigade and divisional signallers. Lieutenant Anderson personally sent a dozen runners with the message that the garrison was continually taking heavy casualties and that artillery support was urgently needed. One runner alone was successful and although the desired artillery support was called for, it seems that the message was not received by the 261 Brigade Royal Field Artillery. Lieutenant LOGAN of the 4/Royal Scots Fusiliers had been sent forward with the fourth wave of the 5/King's Own Scottish Borderers attack, his role being to act as Forward Observation Officer for the artillery and to establish a telephone line when the redoubt was taken. In the heavy shelling of the advance his signal equipment was destroyed and although he continued on alone while his men went back for replacements, he was not heard of again. Corporal LINDSAY of the 4/King's Own Scottish Borderers eventually succeeded in running a line from brigade headquarters to a forward position. It was assumed that this was in the redoubt itself as when a situation report was requested from this position, Lieutenant FOOTE, of the 5/Royal Scots Fusiliers replied that he was in the redoubt and that despite heavy opposition, he could hold on. Once again, the similarity of the area deceived those in command, for he was not in the redoubt but in a trench about 150 yards before it.

"Of the party who went into the Redoubt not much is known. Only one Officer, 2Lt H GILLIES of this battalion survived and he was wounded but was able to come away. He left the work about 15.00 but owing to the shock and effects of his wound was unable to give a clear account of his movements.

5/RSF War Diary. PRO WO95/4607

The true situation in the redoubt remained critical however. In the apparent absence of any reinforcements or supplies and in the face of such severe pressure, which was not merely sustained but which had actually increased in the last two hours, by 17.30 the garrison was withdrawn. Holes were made in the cactus hedging to the rear of the position and the wounded were gradually evacuated, although many were hit again while doing so and killed. The Turks continued to press in on the redoubt and by 18.45 the last of the garrison had been withdrawn.

155 Brigade

Casualties for the Second Battle of Gaza

THE 155TH BRIGADE PLAYED THE major role in the 52nd Division's operations on the 19th April, attacking along the successive hills of the el Sire Ridge, the highest and most distant of which was Ali el Muntar.

The 4/Royal Scots Fusiliers had 2 officers and 58 men killed with a further 12/169 wounded; a further 3/8 Died of their Wounds. C Company was on the battalion's left flank as they made their way towards Green Hill and heavy fire from the flank caused many of their casualties, twenty-year old Lance-Corporal William LIGHT being one of them. Born and raised at Newmills, Ayrshire he was buried in the cemetery at Gaza. One of his comrades in C Company was Private Robert DRUMMOND from Hamilton Place, Darvel, Ayrshire; he was also twenty but his body was not found. To complete the two-company front, A Company advanced on the right flank. Private Thomas Arnott MILLAR was with them as they followed the Tank "War Baby" this being soon diverted to the ever-intensifying fight for Outpost Hill. He was killed as they advanced, or perhaps as they captured, at 11.00, Middlesex Hill, yet another twenty-year old to die. Other than the fact that he came from Burnley, Lancashire the record of 203177 Arthur JACKSON is minimal; his rank however is unusual in that it is given as DRUMMER.

The casualties to the officers of the 4/Royal Scots Fusiliers were proportionately as high as those suffered by the men; Lieutenant LOGAN has been detailed in the text. As the battalion achieved its objective of Middlesex Hill at about 11.00, it is easy to imagine an attendant lull in the fighting. This was not the case however, as the battalion was on a salient, far forward of the troops on either flank. The Divisional History continues;

"A gap had now developed between the troops on either side of the ridge. Many officers had fallen and Lieutenant-Colonel H Thompson set to work to fill it up with any men he could get. Whilst doing so, he fell mortally wounded, shot through the throat. His second in command, Major HR Young was helping him, and about the same time fell mortally wounded in the head."

Major Hugh Roxburgh YOUNG died of wounds on 21st April 1917

Lieutenant-Colonel Harold THOMPSON died of his wounds in Cairo on 22 April 1917. Served with the 5/Argyll & Sutherland Highlanders during the Gallipoli campaign, was awarded the DSO for Dueidar on 22 April 1916 as a Major and subsequently promoted to Lieutenant-Colonel.

The 5/Royal Scots Fusiliers also lost heavily in the actions along the el Sire Ridge on 19th April 1917. 4/26 were killed with another three men dying of their wounds; 4/133 were wounded. These figures are the more surprising as the battalion was designated to follow the main attack and consolidate each of the five hills as they were captured; the intense and protracted battle enveloped all troops however.

Captain John LEES aged 29 was killed sometime after 12.00. He had arrived with B Company to the south-west of Outpost Hill and took charge of the shocked survivors of the Cyclist Company. In a combined attack, many casualties were taken from the intense machine-gun fire, Captain Lees being one of them. The 155 Brigade Machine Gun Company fought determinedly at this time, a machine-gun being carried into the eastern part of the redoubt to assist the attack. Captain William Sherwan PIRIE, in charge of this company, was killed by a shell at this time; he had previously been awarded the Distinguished Conduct Medal.

In the 5/RSF there were a good number of men from Derbyshire; from their regimental numbers and enlistment areas it would appear they had joined the battalion direct rather than being transferred from other units. Private Robert GRANBY, born and enlisted in Chesterfield; the town is famous for the twisted spire on its church. From nearby Mansfield, twenty-one year old Private Charles Thomas HARDY was the son of Charles and Harriet Hardy of Blackball Road, Huthwaite; killed on the 19th April without trace. A third Derbyshire man was Private Ernest HODGKINSON. From the quaint-sounding village of Irentonwood, he moved to nearby Idridgehay; the third name evocative of the county of his enlistment was his enlistment office at Wirksworth. All these areas were great mining communities, coal the more recently and lead for hundreds of years previously.

Two men from the same street in Ayr served with the battalion at the Second Battle of Gaza. Private John McMORLAND was 23 and lived at 69 Green Street and although he survived the day, he was to die of wounds on the 8 June. Private Andrew DICK was from 99 Green Street and he died of his wounds on 24th April at Deir el Belah. Finally, Lance-Corporal William FAULDS. The son of Alexander and Mary Faulds, he was married to Mary Dunlop Faulds and he lived at New Bridge Street, Ayr. He was thirty years old when he went into action with B Company, perhaps being part of Captain Lees' final attack on Outpost Hill, perhaps part of the group which held the eastern portions of the hill during the late morning. He was never to be seen again-another name on the Jerusalem Memorial.

The casualties to the 4 King's Own Scottish Borderers were 6/37 killed with eight officers and 133 men wounded. Captain Walter Francis COCHRANE was the Officer Commanding D Company and was originally from Kirklands, Galashiels. His counter-part in A Company was twenty-six year old Captain Robert Robertson Morrison LUMGAIR, who hailed from Hawick, Roxburghshire, his widow Gladys being left at "Rosalee". Their death in action has been vividly described by Lieutenant JM POLLOCK and is quoted in the text, the footnote being that the two men died together and were buried in adjacent graves XXVI.D.7 and XXVI.D.8 Gaza Cemetery. The most senior casualty to the battalion was Major Walter Torrie FORREST, being the second-in-command. Thirty seven years old he was the son of George and Margaret Forrest and came from Kelso, Roxburghshire. He had been a rugby player with the Scottish International side and was nick-named Wattie Forrest, presumably a phonetic expansion of the initials W.T. He was wounded as he led the second assault on Outpost Hill, but lay all day in a trench until dark. Lieutenant Pollock once again takes up the story.

"These men left and I was about to follow them when I recognised the voice of Major Forrest, who was calling for water. I crawled along the trench to where he was lying and gave him all the water that remained in my bottle. Although I could not see him owing to the darkness, he had evidently been very badly wounded, and I propped him up on the side of the trench for the purpose of carrying him back, but I realised the task was hapless, as his condition was such that he could not be moved. The Turks had evidently seen my movements, and they fired at me from not more than 20 yards. I was quite alone at that time and as it was my duty to avoid being taken prisoner I felt obliged to leave the trench." Major Forrest's body was eventually recovered and he was buried in the Gaza cemetery.

The 4/KOSB had been originally part of the South Scottish Infantry Brigade, only later changed to the 155th Brigade. The towns which formed its main catchment area were grouped around Galashiels on the River Tweed, and included Melrose and Selkirk. Before the days of boundary changes, these all lay in the county of Selkirkshire with men also enlisting from the neighbouring counties of Berwick, Roxburgh and Peebles. From Coldstream, Berwick came Private Charles Nelson DUNN; twenty-nine years old he was the son of John Dunn. The town is now well-known to get information on the nearby battlefield of Flodden Field, where on the 9 September 1513 English archers from Piper's Hill wreaked havoc on the Scottish pikemen below. Although not a casualty at Outpost Hill, Sergeant Andrew DUNCAN was almost certainly present. Aged 33 he came from Wilton, Roxburghshire and later lived at 1, Glebe Mill Street, Hawick with his father John Duncan. Upon marrying, he lived with his wife Catherine Gordon Duncan at 2, Glebe Mill Street. He died of wounds [without date of incident given] on 25 October 1917 and lies in Gaza VII.A.1

This then is the area from which men joined the battalion, and fought at Outpost Hill; many people visit the area nowadays for the small town of Kirk Yetholm is the end, or start, of the Pennine Way.

Private William BELL from Lauder, Berwick was killed on 18 April along with 34 year old Private Robert FRIER of Stow, Midlothian. Both were lost without trace, probably due to 4.2 inch Howitzer fire as the First Phase line was held during the day. The diary notes 13 men of the battalion were at one time safely extricated after being buried by artillery fire.

The final battalion of the brigade to be covered is the 5th King's Own Scottish Borderers who had 12/86 killed and 7/196 wounded.

One man who had seen war before 1914 was Private John BAIN. At 44 years of age he had served in the South African Campaign, or Boer War, which had ended in 1901, being originally from West Hartlepool, Durham. His widow Margaret Bain lived at Chapel Street, Berwick, the most northerly English town. He was killed on the 19th April as he advanced with B Company against Middlesex Hill, perhaps caught in the hell of Outpost Hill into which much of the company was drawn or perhaps among those few men of the two platoons who managed to run the gauntlet of enfilade fire from Outpost Hill and surmount a ridge to the east His body was never found. Private John WILSON was also to leave a widow, Margaret Jane Wilson, at home in Braehead, Crossmichael, Kirkcudbrightshire; he too was 44 years old.

Private Arthur Evans RICHARDSON was but 19 years old. Born in Dumfries, he lived and enlisted there; he was the son of John and Jessie Richardson of Church Lodge, Bank End Road. He served with D Company, the objective of which was Outpost Hill itself, taken with a frontal assault at 10.18. Whether or not he was one of those killed during the assault; whether he endured the indescribable shrapnel, high-explosive and machine-gun fire as the battalion held on to the redoubt; whether he was forced to lay outside the already packed work can never be known. Another enigma of death held by the name on a town's war memorial.

Second Battle of Gaza
156th Brigade

On the 16th April the 155th Infantry Brigade was in bivouac at IN SEIRAT with a total strength of 134 officers and 3434 men. For the operations of the next two days it was detailed as divisional reserve in readiness for that role. At 21.00 the first of two columns marched out of camp, the 1/7th Scottish Rifles leading the 1/4th Royal Scots. Ninety minutes later, the 1/7th Royal Scots followed the 1/8th Scottish Rifles along the track to a crossing over the Wadi Ghuzze. As they were in reserve, the brigade took a different route to that of the 155th brigade, and crossed further south near the junction with the Wadi NUKHABIR. While the brigade dug in at this position, two companies of the 8/Scottish Rifles under Major CARSON, were sent to rendezvous with 261st and 262nd Brigades, Royal Field Artillery near SHEIKH NEBHAN and to escort them as and when required.

The 52nd DIVISION's initial objective of a line from MANSURA to KURD HILL was achieved without difficulty by 06.45 on 17 April. The brigade remained in its position by the two wadis throughout a generally uneventful day until, at 17.50, the field batteries were escorted to a new position two-and-a-half miles away near TEL EL AHMAR.

On the following day, the brigade was called upon to supply working parties to help improve the roads leading to Mansura Ridge, for they would be heavily used during the impending operations, and were little more than tracks at present. At 18.00 on the 18 April orders for the Second Phase were received, in which the brigade was to take a full and active part. The 52nd Division was to seize the whole El Sire Ridge leading to, and culminating with, Ali el Muntar. The 54th Division would operate to the right, taking the trenches along the Gaza-Beersheba Road before wheeling left towards ANZAC RIDGE to the north-east of Ali el Muntar.

The 156 Brigade was charged with taking two difficult positions; The WARREN on the left of the advance and, to the right, ALI EL MUNTAR itself. Three battalions began moving up from their reserve positions shortly after the receipt of these orders, being led by the 8/Scottish Rifles. Working parties of the 7/Royal Scots were still on fatigues at this time and so the battalion did not reach the new position around Tel el Ahmar until 05.30 the next morning.

At 07.30 on the 19th April the artillery bombardment stopped and the attack began. The 155 Brigade advanced along the el Sire Ridge and the 156 Brigade had to wait for them to come into line on the left before advancing themselves. By 08.15 the 155 Brigade had taken LEES HILL and were advancing alongside the brigade, which was then able to advance.

The brigade frontage of 1200 yards was divided equally between three front-line battalions, the 7/Scottish Rifles being in brigade reserve. The pattern of advance was much the same as 155 Brigade, that is, eight half-company waves with 200 yards between each. Contact with the right of 155 Brigade was to be maintained by the 8/Scottish Rifles who would direct themselves on the centre of GREEN HILL. On their right was the 4/Royal Scots and completing the brigade front was the 7/Royal Scots, directed on Ali el Muntar. Because the advance was so reliant on steady progress by the brigade on the left, any hold-up there would be reflected across the front. Consequently, the early advance of the two brigades was stopped when Outpost Hill was approached.

By 09.30, the 7/Royal Scots on the right flank were astride the Muntar-Sheikh Abbas Road due east of Outpost Hill and about 2000 yards short of Ali el Muntar. At this time, an intense struggle for Outpost Hill had developed, so a halt was ordered until its outcome had been determined. By 10.30, with the hill tenuously held by the 155 Brigade, as the advance was restarted, enemy troops ahead were spotted leaving their trenches on MIDDLESEX HILL. Along with the 4/Royal Scots Fusiliers of the 155 Brigade to the left, the brigade pushed forward and just after midday the left of the 8/Scottish Rifles was about 300 yards short Middlesex Hill. However, as already seen, the fight for Outpost Hill had become more intense and bitter throughout the morning and early afternoon. Consequently, further progress by the 156 Brigade was very limited and for the rest of the day the men of the three battalions were forced to lie out on the open plain.

52nd (LOWLAND) DIVISION
156 BRIGADE.
SITUATION TO 1140
19 APRIL 1917

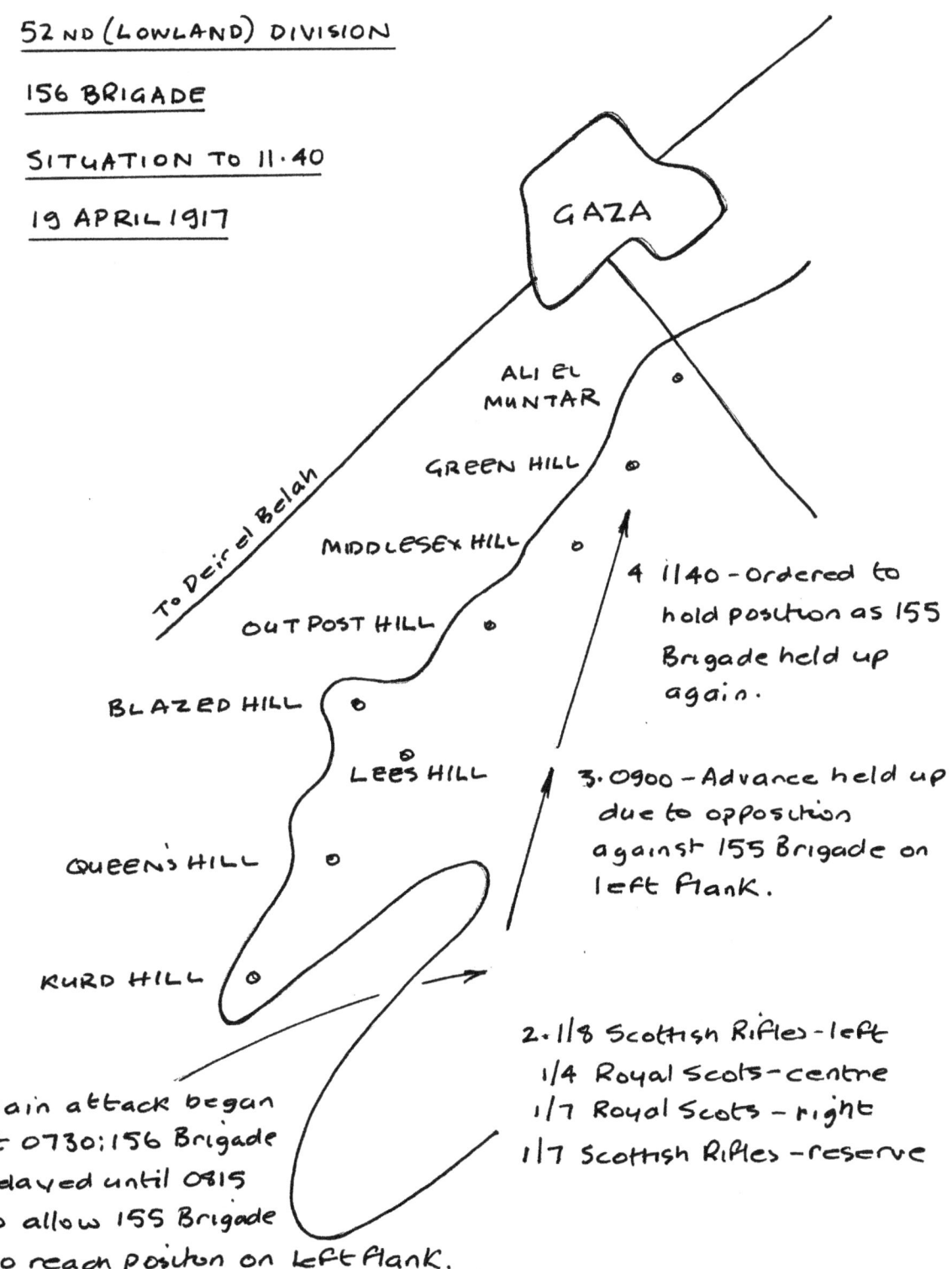

52nd (LOWLAND) DIVISION
156 BRIGADE.
EVENTS FROM 1200 ONWARDS
19 APRIL 1917

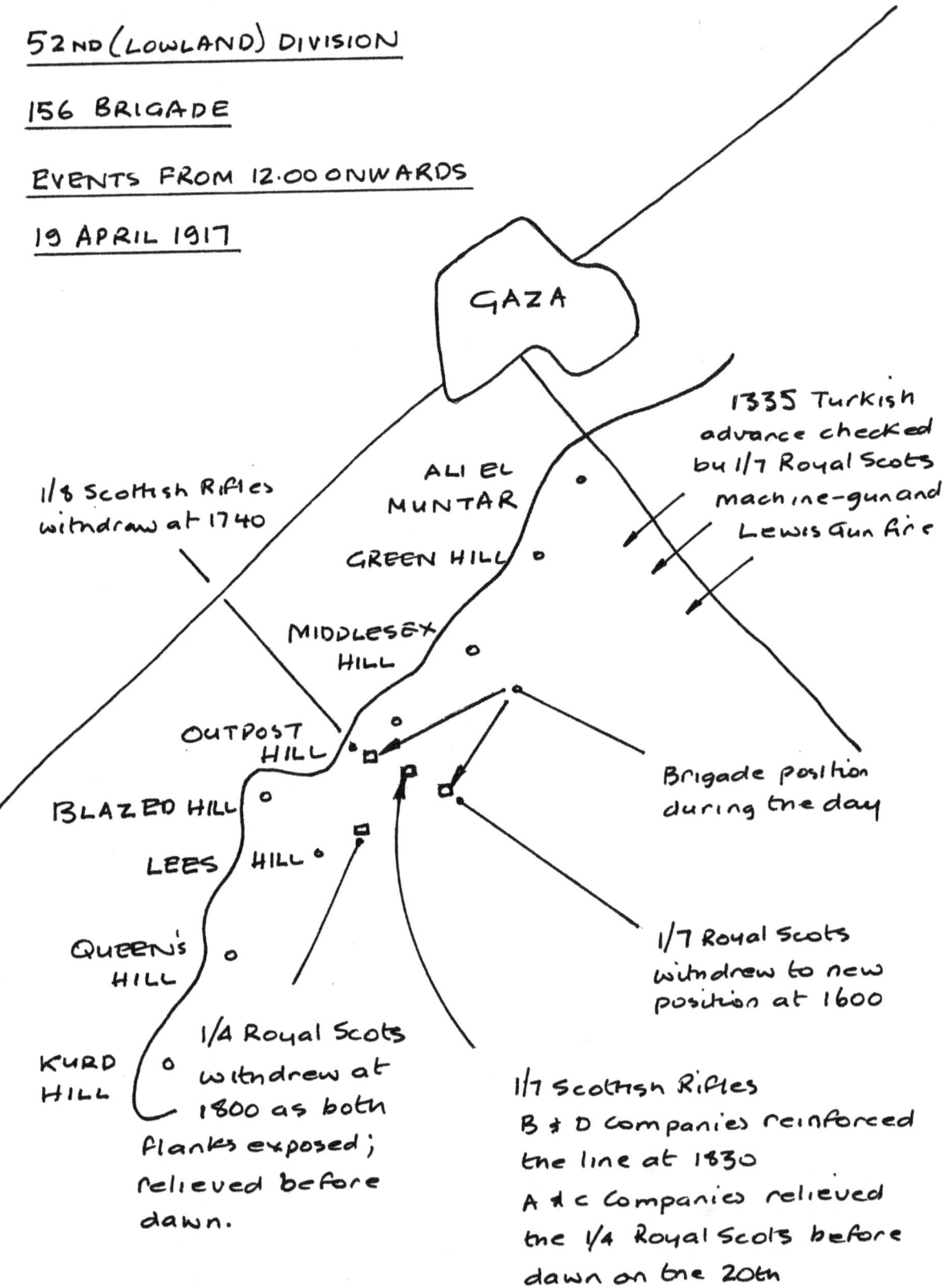

At 13.35 a large force believed to be the Turkish 54th Division, appeared to be moving round the east of Gaza to reinforce the line. Although pinned down by the constant rifle and machine-gun fired from positions to the north-west, the 7/Royal Scots managed to bring a heavy fire to bear and halt the advance from the north-east. Shortly after this advance was repulsed, the 7/Royal Scots were forced to withdraw when a heavy shrapnel fire was directed upon them. Four-hundred yards were sufficient to relieve the pressure and the battalion dug in, ready to face counter-attacks while waiting for the 155 Brigade to come up.

If the situation of 155 Brigade on Outpost Hill was dire, that of 156 Brigade was hardly less desperate. The encouraging ease with which the early morning advance had been achieved was long-forgotten as the men lay out on the open plain. Unlike their comrades about Outpost Hill, who were at least engaging the enemy, the men of the Royal Scots and Scottish Rifles were forced to hold their positions, all the while under heavy fire. From Middlesex Hill and Green Hill came the continual rattle of the machine-guns, a heavy rifle fire adding to their deadly effect; even when Middlesex Hill was taken by the 4/ Royal Scots Fusiliers at 11.00 there was little appreciable diminution of the fire. As already stated, shrapnel fire opened up during the afternoon, increasing the already numerous casualty list. Compounding the tragedy was the fact that all the casualties of the 156 Brigade were sustained not in assaulting their objectives but while waiting, in totally exposed positions, for the 155 Brigade to accomplish their almost impossible task.

From their positions above Middlesex Hill the Turks realised that they had halted the enemy attack on Outpost Hill to their right. Long lines of stationary troops lying out on the open plain to their left bore witness that the attack there, too had failed. Small parties worked their way down the eastern side of the hill and successfully separated the 4/Royal Scots Fusiliers from the left of the 156 Brigade. This was doubly critical for not only were the 4/Royal Scots Fusiliers totally isolated, but the 8/Scottish Rifles were now threatened on their immediate left flank. Increased pressure from this new development continued until at 17.30 the 8/Scottish Rifles were forced to withdraw several hundred yards. This left the 4/Royal Scots Fusiliers as the only advanced battalion, themselves being withdrawn to the division's new line later in the evening.

At 18.30 there was a great concentration of Turkish troops in the direction of Middlesex Hill and reinforcements from brigade reserve on Mansura Ridge were sent up. Under Captain R BLAIR, B and D Companies 7/Scottish Rifles arrived in the line but the expected counter-attack failed to develop into anything more than intermittent skirmishes. During the night the line was dug in as much as possible but the work proved long and hard. The ground was sun-baked, stony and was being worked by men weary and shocked at the end of a gruelling day. Dawn on the 20 April showed the brigade to be holding the most advanced line of the division. The 8/Scottish Rifles were about 400 yards south-east of Outpost Hill and had been reinforced by B and D Companies, 7/Scottish Rifles. To their right were A and C Companies who had relieved the 4/Royal Scots at midnight. The line was completed by the 7/Royal Scots who, in position near Khirbit en Namus, were in touch with the extreme left of the 54th Division. As soon as it was light enough to see, the Turks began raking the whole line with machine-gun and rifle fire, the meagre fruits of the nights work proving their worth.

This line was held throughout the 20 and 21 April. However, it was too far forward to be held indefinitely and so a second line some 1500 yards back was started. This ran in front of both Blazed and Lees Hills then across to Mansura, being dug deeply and wired more thoroughly than its predecessor. While this line was under construction, the advanced troops of the 156 Brigade was kept supplied with water, rations and ammunition as required, night being the safest time for such operations.

At midnight on the 21 April all outposts were withdrawn to the new line which was then closed. Trench warfare had arrived in Palestine, for both sides were now in strongly wired positions with no possibility of an offensive being attempted without meticulous planning and adequate forces.

156 Brigade

Casualties for the Second Battle of Gaza

THE BRIGADE HAD A TOTAL of 2/36 killed at the Second Battle of Gaza, with a further 1/17 who died of wounds.

The 4/Royal Scots was an Edinburgh battalion which was in the centre of the brigade advance on 19 April against Green Hill and Ali el Muntar. With few casualties early on in the day, there may well have been a feeling of confidence among the men. Outpost Hill changed that however as with an exposed left flank the battalion slowed and then halted. On the open plain without any cover the casualties increased the total wounded being 6/106.

Company Quarter Master Sergeant James KEMP killed; Private John Morton PRESTON killed; Private Francis James ANGUS killed; all Edinburgh men.

The 7 Royal Scots had 8/120 wounded as the brigade's right flank battalion. Caught in the same fire, without hope of cover or respite, men such as Private James BELLINGHAM were mortally wounded. Some more men from Edinburgh were killed;

Private Francis Buchan Murray CAMPBELL
Corporal Thomas Redpath Graham DEWAR 21
Private John Walker GOULD 41.

It is difficult to tell if any of these men were survivors of an earlier disaster to the battalion which took place on home ground. On 22 May 1915 A and D Companies boarded Train No18 at Larbert, Stirlingshire and began the journey south to embark for Gallipoli. At 06.45 the troop-train hit a projecting local train at Quentin's Hill Junction, near Gretna, this disaster being compounded seconds later as the London express ploughed into the wreckage. Fires began throughout the tangled wreck and 3/207 were killed in the inferno, with another 5/219 being injured, this from a total complement of 15/483.

The third battalion of the brigade front was the 8/Scottish Rifles on the left flank. Held up as described, they were under enfilade sniper fire from Outpost Hill as well as machine-gunfire during the periods when the hill was lost by the Turks. The wounded amounted to 9/144 at the end of the day with the killed being an additional 1/16.

Second Battle of Gaza
157th Brigade

Before describing the part played by the brigade in the operations at the Second Battle of Gaza, several quotes bear reading as a general background to the area in which all the troops were operating.

Bir el Abd was much the same as any other bit of desert, save that the higher sand hills were lacking, the country consisting of rolling slopes of no great elevation well spotted with scrub. It boasted a fine breed of chameleon, and we also found a number of little tortoises, which were pressed into service to give a bit of sport! Tortoise racing was a slow business, but eminently sporting, because the tortoise is so splendidly unreliable. On one occasion one of the competitors in a big sweepstake was discovered to consist of a shell only-the tortoise who had once dwelt therein having died and turned to dust. In consideration of this it was given a start of six inches, but long odds were offered against it. However, at the end of the time limit-eight minutes-no competitor had moved at all, so the tortoiseless one was adjudged the winner amid great applause.

Page 113

The nights were now extremely chilly, but the flies had not yet succumbed. They swarmed everywhere, and the discovery of a dead camel an inch or two under the sand in A Company's bivouac rejoiced their pestilential hearts. It is the immemorial custom of the desert not to bury dead camels or horses but to let them lie. Then you know where you are and the sun cooks the carcasses till they become inoffensive. This is, however, repugnant to the tidy minds of European sanitary experts, who give orders for burial of the deceased. The wiser Egyptian is overruled and has to do the burying. Now it takes a simply monstrous hole to hold a camel, and the result of the clash of English and Egyptian ideas is a very imperfectly buried carcass, just covered from the beneficent influence of the sun, but filling the surrounding air with its disgusting aroma.

Page 116.

El Arish, the ancient Rhinocolura, lies near the mouth of the Wadi el Arish, which runs away southward into the heart of Sinai and is believed to have been the River of Egypt, the southern boundary of biblical Palestine. The wadi hardly deserved the name of river today, but during the winter months it is sometimes covered with water to the depth of a few inches, flowing slowly down to the sea. Along its banks the inhabitants plant their crops among the palm trees, watering them assiduously from wells, with the assistance of tiny donkeys, about the size of goats, each carrying two enormous water jars. The town is the capital of the Mudirieh of Sinai, and boasted a British resident and a force of Beduin police, but was abandoned with the rest of the province when Turkey declared war. The country round the town is almost completely bare of scrub, a mass of tumbled hills of sand, rounded slopes and razor-like crests, alternating with deep valleys between almost sheer cliffs. Here and there are palm trees or other evergreen trees, and in the low ground round the wadi are numerous fig trees. The town itself was a disappointment to the men, who could not but expect some of the amenities of civilisation in a place of whose military importance they had heard so much. At the western end was an ancient fort, now in ruins from bombardment by our monitors, one or two more pretentious houses with plaster fronts, and the mosque whose white minaret, though not of any great height, we had seen through a gap in the sand hills from so many miles to westward. But most of the buildings were single-roomed, flat-roofed huts, with tiny slits for windows. The troops were not allowed into the town but a glimpse could be obtained from without of the few streets, paved only with the desert sand. From a little distance, however, el Arish was surprisingly beautiful. It matched exactly with the grey yellow of the sand, which swept up to it and rose behind it unrelieved by the distraction of scrub, while the white dome of a little tomb, the faded plaster of the mosque and the occasional dark green of a low tree among the buildings, gave just the right contrast in colour. Seen in the clear light of dawn, in the evening glow, it had a haunting beauty which all who knew it will remember.

We lay in el Arish for a couple of months, with changes of camp every week or so, and we learnt afterwards that this was a period of special training to fit us for the fighting which was expected in Palestine. It must be admitted that we had not recognised it as such at the time, outposts, guards and fatigues of every kind did not seem to leave us overmuch time for training. Still we did manage to fit in a good deal of work with the smaller formations, and one or two days of Brigade and Divisional training to boot. Two night operations, yes, we will say it now, a most detestable form of exercise, linger specially in the memory. Night work in this sort of country is always difficult because there are so few landmarks. A Brigade can be moved on a compass bearing with every chance of success if the mover has the necessary elementary knowledge. But the commander of a smaller unit, say a platoon, going to or returning from a certain place in the dark, rarely has any knowledge of the right bearing to work on and if the night is cloudy, he is surrounded by a Stygian darkness in which he soon feels a little doubtful of his uncharted way. He begins to zigzag a bit, peering through the gloom for some familiar landmark. The men, who for the most part would be completely lost in three minutes on their own, are critical and unsympathetic, and rightly, for this is what an officer is paid extra for. They whisper caustic comments in the rear. All sense of direction seems to suddenly fail the unhappy man, and he sinks into the depths of a misery which few others can equal. At last a light shines out ahead. Making towards it with a wild hope he sees the darker marks of bivouacs against the sand, and suddenly recognises his own company lines. With a heart full of thankfulness he halts and dismisses his men, and retires to his own hole fondly believing that no one but himself knows what had happened.

Pages 130-131
The 1/5th Highland Light Infantry 1914-1918

ON THE 16th April 1917, the 157th Infantry Brigade was camped with the rest of the 52nd DIVISION at IN SEIRAT. When divisional orders were issued, the brigade learned that it had been given the task of establishing the right half of the initial line from which the main attack would ultimately take place. The brigade staff had anticipated operating on this front and with remarkable foresight had contrived a ruse to protect the brigade's advance. Through prior reconnaissance it had been learned that the hamlet of EL BURJALIYE contained a Turkish advanced post. Situated in the cactus-walled orchard the small garrison had a good field of fire and would have no doubt inflicted heavy casualties. However, on the 9th April one company of the 1/7th Highland Light Infantry advanced and captured the post, held it until dusk and then returned to camp. The following morning the Turks re-occupied the deserted garden but were doubtless puzzled when the same force drove them out the afternoon. This continued daily and apart from much rifle-fire and noise appeared totally pointless; its true worth and originality were still to be revealed. On the 16 April Major JB NEILSON led A Company, 1/5th Highland Light Infantry forward to occupy el Burjaliye. He withdrew as was now normal, but after dark re-occupied the orchard and placed an outpost line to the north and north-east of the hamlet. The Turks were unaware of this second move and would therefore be prevented from using the position during the early morning advance of the 17th April.

While 157 Brigade operated on the right of the line, close contact was to be maintained with 155 Brigade on the left. To ensure this took place right from the start, one platoon of C Company 1/5th Highland Light Infantry was sent at 19.45 to midway between the brigades to meet a similarly detailed platoon from the 1/4 Royal Scots Fusiliers. At 20.30 the brigade, along with two sections of 413th Field, Royal Engineers, crossed the Wadi Ghuzze twelve-hundred yards north-west of SHEIKH NEBHAN. Once assembly on the eastern bank was completed, the march resumed until the brigade reached a point just over a mile before el Burjaliye. Water bottles were refilled for a final time and extra ammunition issued, the pack animals which had carried the loads being sent back. The brigade separated before the three front-line battalions moved to their allotted parts of the line, the 1/5th Argyll and Sutherland Highlanders being in reserve.

"The companies slept in position wearing all equipment and with each man's rifle lying beside him. The night was very dewy and bitterly cold."

1/5 HLI War Diary. PRO WO95/4611

52nd (Lowland) Division
157 Brigade.
19 April 1917

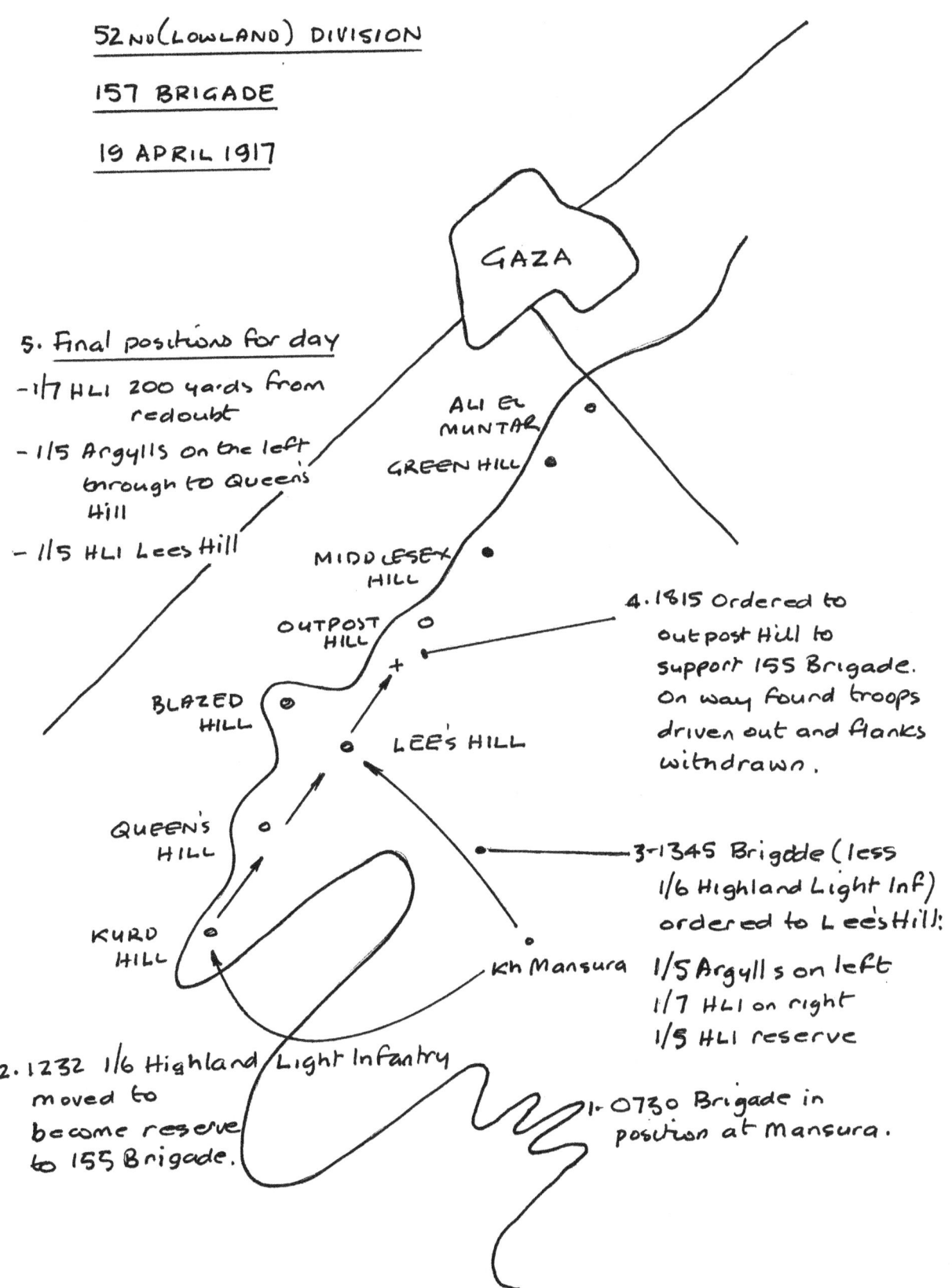

The line was held by the 5/Highland Light Infantry on the left with the 7/Highland Light Infantry in the centre and prolonged by the 6/Highland Light Infantry, each being on a two-company front with the remainder in support. Being on the right flank, the 6/HLI were further supported by the extreme left flank of the 54th Division which was held by the 1/5 Bedfordshire Regiment.

The 52 Division attack began on time at 04.45 on the 17th April, there having been barely two hours sleep for most of the men. The first task for the brigade was to establish itself on a position from where the accompanying artillery could directly view MANSURA RIDGE and thus cover the next stage of the advance more effectively. A mile to the north-east, HILL 230 was an ideal spot from which to achieve this, and moving rapidly in the early half-light the 6/Highland Light Infantry occupied it within thirty minutes. The centre and left battalions moved on TEL EL AHMAR and by 05.15 the brigade held a line facing in a north-easterly direction between Tel el Ahmar and Hill 230. While the artillery registered on their new target, patrols were pushed forward to within 150 yards of the base of Mansura Ridge.

Shortly before 06.00 the 162nd Brigade could be seen pushing up the slopes of Sheikh Abbas Ridge off to the right. Observing this from brigade headquarters at el Burjaliye, Brigadier-General JB POLLOCK-M'CALL decided at once to halt the artillery bombardment and advance on Khirbit Mansura and Mansura Ridge, thereby preventing any possible enfilading of Sheikh Abbas and protecting the rear of 162 Brigade.

The order to advance was received by the three front-line battalions at 06.15 and they began to move straight away. The 6/Highland Light Infantry had slightly more ground to cover and so they were allowed to bear round before the whole brigade attack developed. Overhead covering fire was given by the 157th Brigade Machine Gun Company who would also watch for, and deal with, any counter-attack on the left flank. Mansura Ridge was not strongly held however, and despite some sniping fire was quickly scaled. From the crest the men of the three highland battalions could see its defenders disappearing across the plain towards Ali el Muntar. By 06.45 the whole ridge had been taken, but as consolidation began, the enemy fire opened up. The Turkish artillery was accurately ranged on their former positions and the whole area was soon being heavily shelled. From Outpost Hill and Lee's Hill, to the north and north-west, machine-guns raked the front and digging-in of a line 800 yards from the crest was hazardous. Even so, it was not sufficient to stop the determined attackers from establishing themselves on the site, and during the afternoon the enemy fire abated. By dusk, as the trenches were completed, the front was put on standby for expected counter-attacks, although they failed to materialise.

"At 22.00 C Company knocked off wiring and took over night trenches from D Company which came back into support after 17 hours under continuous fire, the last 14 of which had been strenuous digging."

1/5 HLI War Diary. PRO WO95/4611

The night passed quietly, and on the 18th April further consolidation and preparation began. The Turks obviously realised that a major attack was now imminent and the whole front was heavily shelled at intervals throughout the day. Stores which had been brought up to el Burjaliye were now carried to the final dump at the base of Mansura Ridge and the brigade was detailed as divisional reserve behind the ridge. Once in place the brigade was to be on constant alert in order to attack FRYER HILL, to the north-east of Ali el Muntar, when circumstances permitted. As the 54th Division would be assisting at this stage, the brigade's role was completely dependent on success by them, as well upon the 155th and 156th Brigade's progress along the el Sire Ridge. The orders were passed down through the chain of command and at 20.30 the plan was discussed at company level. Battalion orders were issued at 22.30 and after the final task of taking down the wire in front of the trenches, there was the chance for a brief rest before the early morning start to the main attack. During the evening a patrol of three men under Second Lieutenant JCR WATSON of C Company the 6/Highland Light Infantry reconnoitred towards the Gaza-Beersheba Road and returned at midnight to report;

"We left the centre of our trenches at 19.05 marching on a bearing of 36 degrees magnetic. About 200 to

300 yards out we crossed a line of trenches evidently dug by our people at some previous date. From there onwards the ground is smooth and slightly undulating and offers no obstruction of troops wheeled traffic. The area seemed to be mostly covered with barley and caution had to be taken as this rustled a good deal. Little was heard and practically nothing could be seen as it was very dark. Firing was heard from the direction of the 54th Division (machine-gun) but no sign of any patrol was seen. The point reached was Gaza 1.40,000 W21.5 [barely 400 yards from the Gaza-Beersheba Road]. This was at 21.15 and at 21.25 we started to return. Wheeled traffic was heard moving in a north-easterly direction in the Ali Muntar direction but there did not seem to be sufficient of it to raise any suspicions. On our left and right flanks sounds were heard as if wooden stakes were being driven into the ground. I assumed that our wiring parties were at work, a good way on within [our] flanks. We passed through the 1/5 Highland Light Infantry outpost line at 22.50, our orders being to be back by 23.00. The party returned complete and without mishap."

6/HLI War Diary. PRO WO95/4612

On the 19th April the two-hour artillery bombardment began 05.30 and the 5/Highland Light Infantry moved off to take up a position, in a sheltered nullah south of Kurd Hill, as reserve to the 155th Brigade. On arrival at 07.20, the battalion was placed in readiness to support the left flank of the brigade, on the northern slopes of QUEEN'S HILL, should it be threatened. By 09.50, the 155th Brigade had advanced over Lee's Hill and was assaulting the redoubt on Outpost Hill. It was therefore considered unnecessary to retain the 5/HLI and they were despatched to re-join their own brigade near Mansura. Ironically, as they arrived back at 11.40, Brigadier-General JB Pollock-M-Call, commanding the 155 Brigade, requested that a battalion be sent over for support as the situation had deteriorated; as already recounted, Outpost Hill had been captured and lost and was now the scene of a bloody and protracted struggle.

The 5/Highland Light Infantry settled down after their winding march to a mug of tea and had their water-bottles refilled. The 6/Highland Light Infantry was ordered across to support 155th Brigade instead, but it was not until 12.30 that they were ready to move; two companies had been on outpost-line duties and had to re-join the battalion first. Initially destined for Lee's Hill the battalion was redirected instead to Kurd Hill, while the commanding officer and adjutant moved forward to report to the 4/King's Own Scottish Borderers on Lee's Hill at 14.00. Shortly after this, the battalion was ordered forward to a holding position on Queen's Hill and moved off at 14.45.

At 13.30, possession of Outpost Hill was still being fiercely contested and reconnaissance by the Royal Flying Corps indicated a strong build up in the woods to the north of the position. In order to strengthen the 155th Brigade further against the impending counter-attack, the remainder of 157th Brigade was ordered by telephone at 13.55 to move to Lee's Hill. The 5/Argyll and Sutherland Highlanders moved off a few minutes later and were followed by the 7/ and 5/Highland Light Infantry with the 157 Brigade Machine Gun Company bringing up the rear.

As the fight for Outpost Hill had demanded so much attention, consequently there had been much mixing of the units in the area. The confusion was further compounded by the heavy casualties among the officers in charge of directing the operations. To try and get an accurate assessment of the situation therefore, a 157 Brigade Staff Captain was sent ahead of the brigade. On arrival at 155th Brigade Headquarters on Kurd Hill, although the threatened counter-attack had not materialised, the picture which emerged was grim.

"There were then about 100 to 200 men of the 155th Brigade in or around the Turkish redoubt on Outpost Hill, and these men were lying in a precarious position as they were under severe shell, rifle and machine-gun fire particularly the last. The remainder of the 155th Brigade were unable to get up to the redoubt."

157 Brigade Headquarters War Diary. PRO WO 95/4611

So, even though there appeared to be enough troops available to reinforce the redoubt, the situation was one of stalemate. The 157th Brigade took up position between Queen's Hill and Lee's Hill while further operations were discussed. An advance against the southern slopes of Outpost Hill, even by the fresh troops of the 157 Brigade, was out of the question. An advance from the east would be more likely to succeed, but would take about an hour to initiate; it was now already 15.00. It was therefore concluded that no further advance would be possible that day and the brigade was ordered to dig in and consolidate the position held.

At 17.00 Major-General WE SMITH, General Officer Commanding the 52nd Division, arrived on Kurd Hill and ordered the 157th Brigade to relieve the 155th Brigade who would then become divisional reserve. As the details for the take-over were being explained however, developments took a turn for the worse. At 18.20 a large Turkish force was reported to be preparing to counter-attack and a battalion was urgently needed by 155 Brigade. The 7/Highland Light Infantry was sent off at once with orders to reinforce the redoubt or retake it if already lost. The relief of the line was taken up with the 7/HLI on the redoubt and in contact with the left flank of 156 Brigade. The 5/Argyll and Sutherland Highlanders prolonged the line in a south-westerly direction to Blazed Hill and thence to Queen's Hill, while the 5/Highland Light Infantry were in reserve on the southern slope of Lee's Hill. Inexplicably, the 6/Highland Light Infantry who were earlier detailed to support the 155 Brigade remained at Queen's Hill, well to the rear, all afternoon. As the relieving force tentatively made its way up to Outpost Hill they met the withdrawing survivors evacuating their many wounded. Whilst at first it would appear that victory had been cruelly denied once again and a heavy casualty list incurred in the process, the strength of the enemy re-occupying force which was subsequently ascertained by strong officer patrols made it very unlikely that the position could have been held against such odds. One patrol under Second Lieutenant AW PHILIP and Second Lieutenant GR LAMB itself came under heavy fire in the process, and the latter officer, reported as wounded and missing, was subsequently confirmed killed.

It was therefore decided to adjust the outpost line to allow Outpost Hill to form a salient into the line, thus minimising the ground abandoned. The final line for the night was from the left of 156 Brigade to 200 yards south-west of the redoubt, through a point by the cactus hedge-Blazed Hill-Queen's Hill. Patrols kept contact with the 53rd Division who held the left from around Heart Hill.

157 Brigade

Casualties for the Second Battle of Gaza

THE BRIGADE HAD **7/25** KILLED and died of wounds, with 6/202 wounded.

On the 18 April Private James CHRISTIE of B Company 6/Highland Light Infantry was killed as the battalion established itself on the Mansura Ridge. This preparatory move was necessary to allow stores to be stockpiled closer to the main objectives for the 19 April. Aged 23 he was from High Street, Irvine, Ayrshire. Another casualty during these moves was 26 year old Private John OUTTERSIDE from Bradford, Yorkshire. His widow Edith was left at Stanley Street, Bradford Road, Idle near Bradford while his parents John and Emma lived in the town itself at Howarth Lane.

The other battalions suffered a few such casualties; a herald of the losses soon to be borne.

Private Joseph McELROY 7/HLI
Private Charles LEITCH 7/HLI
Private Alexander FERRIE 5/HLI
Private Samuel BUSTARD 5/HLI

Captain John Rankin BROWN was 31 years old and was a native of Bellahouston, Glasgow. His father was the Reverend John Brown DD and together with his wife Margaret was left at Ainsley Place, Edinburgh. Of the five officer casualties to the 1/7th Highland Light Infantry Second Lieutenant William Gordon GRANT was the first to die, on the 17 April, once again in the 52nd Division's preparations for the main attack. His parents lived at 10, Buchanan Street, Glasgow and he was buried at Gaza Cemetery XXXI.E.13. Upon checking through the Deir el Belah Cemetery Register, the name of Second Lieutenant Alexander GRANT 1/7th Highland Light Infantry was noted. Age 21 he died of wounds on 24th April, but as the names William and Ada Grant 10, Buchanan Street were then recorded, the realisation dawned that the two were brothers. Not one telegram, but two were delivered in quick succession to the tragic household.

Second Battle of Gaza
159th Brigade

ON THE 16TH APRIL, THE 159th Brigade was in bivouac at TEL EL NUJEID, a mile or so north-east of its sister brigade at Sheikh Rashid. In the forthcoming operations, it too was to make a demonstration in a north-easterly direction, its area for observation being SHEIKH AJLIN on the coast. For the First Phase of the battle, the brigade was to fully reconnoitre the foreground but was not to seriously engage the enemy.

At 03.30 on the 17th April, the reconnaissance parties moved out and advanced to their designated positions. D Company of the 1/7th Cheshire Regiment crossed the WADI GHUZZE and took up a position on the coast, about half-a-mile short of the enemy post at Sheikh Ajlin. One company of the 1/4th Welsh Regiment also moved out and took up a position half-a-mile south-west of Samson Ridge and both parties extended onto a 400 yard front to observe the enemy's activity.

By 05.30 the first reports from the advanced troops had reached 159 Brigade Headquarters. At first, Samson Ridge was seen to be strongly held, but, as the divisional artillery opened up, the defenders disappeared from view. On the coast, the 1/7th Cheshire's reported only small patrols near Sheikh Ajlin, and the position did not appear to be heavily defended. As news that the 52nd and 54th DIVISIONS had gained their objectives, the reconnaissance parties were withdrawn at 09.50 to the outpost line about MONEY HILL. The rest of the day passed off quietly for the brigade. During the evening, the 158th and 160th Brigades took up a line from the coast to Kurd Hill, and thus forward of the brigade's own line. This was consolidated during the night and was to be the reserve line for the Second Phase.

At 11.00 on 18 April, Major-General DALLAS, Commanding Officer of the 53rd Division, met the brigadiers to discuss the plan for the following day. An hour later, the 159th Brigade headquarters was moved in a north-easterly direction from Tel el Nujeid to an advanced position half-a-mile past Money Hill, where a conference was called to detail battalion responsibilities. The 7/Cheshire's were placed on the left flank along the coast, with Sheikh Ajlin as their objective. The 4/Welsh were on the right flank and directed against Samson Ridge, with the 4/Cheshire's in the centre, primarily to support them but in a position to divert left if required. Brigade reserve was the 5/Welsh and each battalion had one section of the 159th Brigade Machine Gun Company attached to it. Little else happened during the day, until that night when all batteries of both 265th and 266th Brigades, Royal Field Artillery were moved up to new positions and were ready at 04.00. Notification that Zero Hour was set at 05.30 on the 19th April was received at 53rd Division Headquarters at 05.05, and this information was passed on to the waiting company commanders. On the 17 April, Tanks had been used for the first time in Palestine and their presence would prove invaluable during the Second Phase. Now, in the opening minutes of the battle, a second new weapon was introduced - special shell or gas.

At 05.30 on the 19th April the bombardment commenced. The initial target for the two artillery brigades was the extensive trench network to the east and north-east of Samson Ridge, where reinforcements were probably being held.

53rd (WELSH) DIVISION
159 Brigade.
19 April 1917

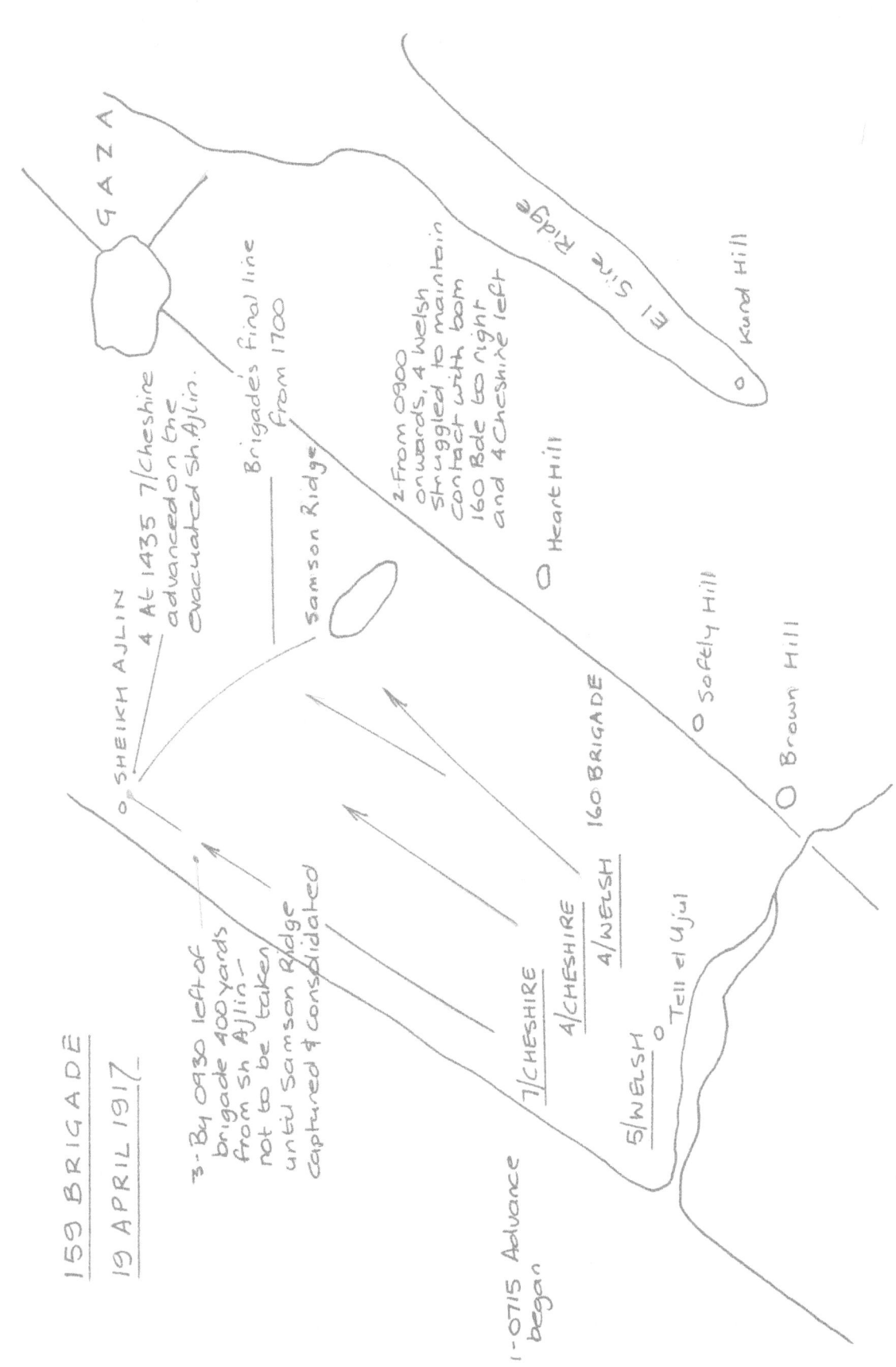

The 265th Brigade Royal Field Artillery engaged three areas with gas shell until 07.06; these were known as Romani Trench, el Burj Trench and el Arish Redoubt, from which both Sheikh Ajlin and Samson Ridge could have been reinforced. To the east of Samson Ridge, two areas known as Kantara Trench and Dueidar Trench were engaged by 266th Brigade Royal Field Artillery, as they could have supported either Samson Ridge or any of the objectives on the 52nd Division front. When the firing of special shell had finished, at varying times for the different targets, the artillery began registering on Samson Ridge. During the night, an alteration to the plan of attack had been made, in that Sheikh Ajlin would not now be assaulted until Samson Ridge had been taken, so the artillery was now instructed to concentrate on that position.

At 07.15, the 53rd Division attack began as the 159th and 160th Brigades left their trenches and stepped out onto the sand dunes. As stated, the Ajlin position was no longer a primary objective, so the 159 Brigade was now charged with advancing to within assaulting distance and ascertaining the strength of the defending force. Three battalions formed the front line, while the 5/Welsh remained as Brigade Reserve. On the left nearest the sea, were the 7/Cheshire's, with the 4/Cheshire's to their right. The 4/Welsh took the right flank to complete the front, and were in contact with the left of 160 Brigade.

The advancing troops passed through the outpost line held by the 158th Brigade, and by 08.00 the 4/Cheshire's were 400 yards in front of it, having encountered no opposition as they advanced on a two-company front. On the left however, the 7/Cheshire's were much more restricted. Thorough prior reconnaissance had revealed that only on a narrow band, away from the steep slope to the beach, was the ground negotiable, and therefore they were forced to adopt a narrow half-platoon front.

At first, the 4/Welsh managed to maintain contact with the 160th Brigade as well as continuing to provide an effective right flank for the 159th Brigade. However, as the 160 Brigade advance was slowed down, and then around 09.00 stopped, the 4/Welsh line became drawn out as it struggled to fulfil its dual role. The two Cheshire battalions continued to advance as ordered in an effort to determine the strength of the Ajlin defences; by 08.30 they were both under strong fire, snipers being particularly active. an hour later, the left of the brigade line was 400 yards from Sheikh Ajlin and it halted to maintain observation until ordered to attack. The line filtered in a south-easterly direction and then almost due south to connect with the left of 160 Brigade who were totally held up before Samson Ridge. Any advance by the 4/Welsh would have created a salient, stretched their already sparsely held line and weakened the position of the 4/Cheshire's who were slightly ahead of the main line. The brigade was therefore compelled to wait, for the most part totally exposed to enemy fire, for the assault and capture of the strongly held Samson Ridge by the 160 Brigade.

That task in itself continued to be a slow and costly one however. At 11.30, the 160th Brigade was ordered to assault at once, but despite pushing the line forward a few hundred yards, they were forced to halt. Further progress by the brigade was observed and reported by the 4/Welsh who still held the right flank of 159th Brigade, but were not empowered to assist with the assault. It was not until around 13.20 when repairs to the tank were effected that the outlook became more optimistic. The ridge was assaulted at this time and captured by 13.55, but came under heavy shell-fire almost immediately, and strong counter-attacks were expected. This situation probably prompted the reiteration, at 14.00, of the earlier order not to assault Sheikh Ajlin until the ridge was consolidated. However, thirty-five minutes later the need for decisive action was avoided, as the Turks were reported to have evacuated Sheikh Ajlin. The 7/Cheshire's cautiously advanced with two companies, and 265th Brigade Royal Field Artillery was ordered not to fire on the position. Brigadier-General TRAVERS, Commanding Officer of the 159th Brigade, reported this development to 53rd Division Headquarters, and at 14.45 the rest of the battalion entered and began consolidating the position. An outpost line was sent forward, and established itself on a ridge which they named CHESHIRE RIDGE.

At 15.15, instructions to prepare for further attacks by the brigade were received from Division Headquarters, but no advance was to be made until sufficient artillery support had moved up. To this end, A Battery/267 Brigade Royal Field Artillery was ordered up to a position one-mile south of Sheikh Ajlin in order to be able to bombard the area between the 159 Brigade and el Arish Redoubt. Unfortunately, although Samson Ridge and Sheikh Ajlin had both been strongly held, it had now become apparent that the Turks had not considered them to be their main defence to the south-west of Gaza. Taking the two positions had cost the two brigades over 500 casualties; the 53rd Division was now faced with a resumption of the attack against the primary Turkish defences which were centred around el Arish Redoubt. In the light of this, and combined with news from the 52nd and 54th Divisions, it was decided by East Force Headquarters to postpone the attack until the following morning. 159th Brigade was charged with holding the line from the left of 160th Brigade on Samson Ridge, to the sea at Sheikh Ajlin. The line was taken up by all four battalions, the 5/ Welsh coming up from reserve between the two Cheshire's battalions at 17.02. The positions were consolidated and artillery fire was kept up in order to reduce the likelihood of sniping and counter-attack. During the night, orders were received that all further operations had been postponed and the present positions were to be held.

159 Brigade

Casualties for the Second Battle of Gaza

THE 159 BRIGADE HAD ONLY 1/11 killed, but still enough for a football team. 1/1 died of wounds and 1/66 were wounded.

With few to research, the following must necessarily serve as both an obituary to the dead and an insight to the feelings of many on the eve of battle.

Private Albert Edward CHATFIELD was the son of Albert Edward Chatfield of Grove Cottage, Old Charlton, London although he and his sisters were brought up by his aunt at Mill Green, Macclesfield. Showing an aptitude for art, he studied at Oldham Polytechnic and then at Macclesfield School of Art, his work being incorporated in a design at his old school of St George's. Aged 34 he fought at the First Battle of Gaza on 26 March and was uninjured, only to be killed as the battalion advanced on the left flank of the 160 Brigade on the 19th April.

The extract is by Sergeant WH WILLIAMS R.E. and describes the Easter Day Service behind the front line.

We had a Church service yesterday in the evening after dark. We could not hold it in the day because the Turks would shell us. After the service we had the Communion. It was a most impressive sight. We were all kneeling out in the open and the clergyman was carrying on the service with the aid of a lantern and a candle. We were singing the hymn "Lead, kindly light" when the moon was just rising over the adjoining hills. It is a thing which I shall never forget. We are expecting an attack tonight and it is a strange thing how everyone looks forward to this kind of thing because no one knows whether he will come out of it alive or not. It is hard on the people here, they all have to clear out and leave their crops and homes, such as they are, get pulled down. War is a terrible waste, and on one cannot properly realise it unless they are actually amongst it."

Carmarthen Journal. June 8 1917.

Second Battle of Gaza
160th Brigade

On 16 April 1917, the 160th Brigade was in position at SHEIKH RASHID, and, upon receipt of Divisional Order No 32 early in the morning [04.00 in fact] spent the day preparing for the forthcoming operations. During the morning, Brigadier-General WJ BUTLER conferred with his counter-part from 159 Brigade and the two agreed their objectives. The 160 Brigade was to advance in a north-easterly direction and ascertain the strength and disposition of the enemy about HEART HILL. This lay at the extreme south-east end of the SAMSON RIDGE trench system, and its engagement would divert attention from the 52nd DIVISION's advance along the el Sire Ridge.

At midnight on 16th April, two companies of the 2/4th Queen's (Royal West Surrey) Regiment moved out and took up observation in the vicinity of AWAKE HILL. Officers of the same battalion simultaneously carried out a reconnaissance of the ground to the north-east of the observation position.

By 08.15 news was received that the 52nd and 54th Divisions had gained their objectives, on the el Sire Ridge and Mansura/Sheikh Abbas Ridges respectively, and consequently at 09.50 the brigade withdrew its reconnaissance parties. The two companies concerned took up position at the RED HOUSE, on the Wadi Ghuzze at its junction with Kurd Valley. The day passed quietly, with orders being received late in the afternoon [17.45] which detailed an advanced line to be taken up after dark the same day. The brigade was to hold a line from the left of 155th Brigade on Kurd Hill, and extending nearly two miles in a north-westerly direction. From the edge of the sand-dunes, the line would be prolonged to the coast by 158th Brigade who were scheduled to move up simultaneously. The 160 Brigade sector was allotted to the former reconnaissance party, which moved up and held the line until 06.40 the following morning -18th April- at which time one company returned to the Red House, while the other company established an observation post on Softly Hill. During the 18 April, consolidation of the new line continued until 18.30, when details of moves preparatory to the following day's operations were received. Brigade battle headquarters advanced to the caves at TEL EL UJUL and over the next hour-and-a-half the rest of the brigade moved up.

The two remaining companies of the 2/4 Queen's were accompanied by one-and-a-half sections of the 160 Brigade Machine Gun Company and moved to Red House. The 2/4th Royal West Kent Regiment with No.4 Section Machine Gun Company moved to Money Hill, as did the 2/10th Middlesex Regiment with No.2 Section. Finally, the remaining half of No.1 Section was attached to the 1/4th Royal Sussex Regiment who moved to GARDEN POST, next to Red House. Artillery support for the brigade was to be supplied by the 266th Brigade, Royal Field Artillery, which moved to the rear of the divisional outpost line during the night. Further orders were received which now stated that the position Sheikh Ajlin was not to be assaulted until Samson Ridge and the adjacent high ground had been secured; all the 53rd Division's hopes now depended on the successful attack of the 160 Brigade.

53rd (WELSH) DIVISION
160 BRIGADE.
19 APRIL 1917

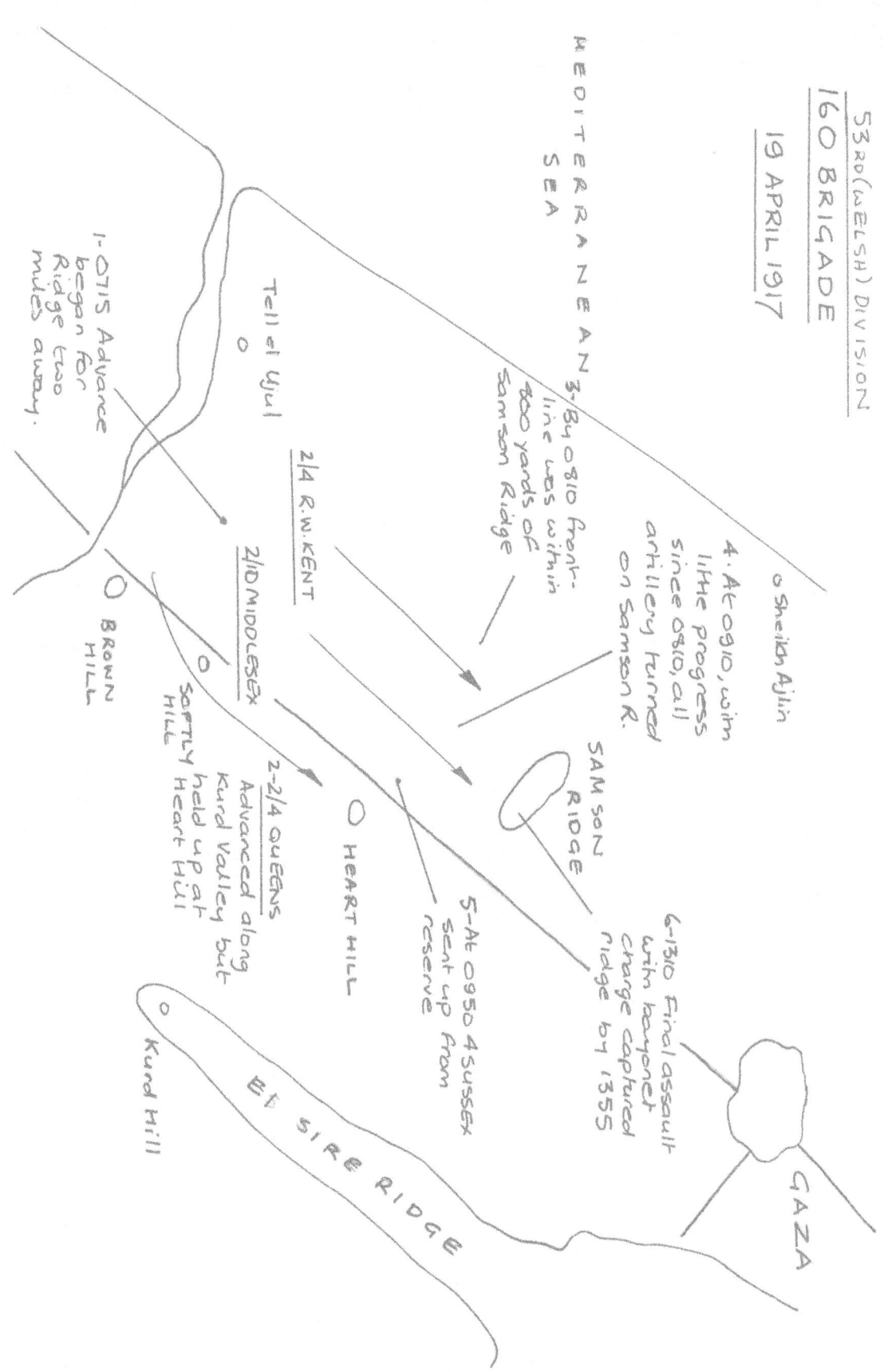

DUNES SOUTH-WEST OF GAZA, FROM SAMSON RIDGE

After the costly and protracted struggle for Samson Ridge, this is the view which met the 160 Brigade. Looking north-east, it shows the heavy sand-dunes which separated the 159 and 160 Brigades from the primary Turkish defences centred around the great el Arish Redoubt. By permission of IWM Copyright No Q47643

At 07.15 on 19 April the brigade left its positions and struck out for the ridge nearly two miles away. On the left of the two-battalion front was the 2/4 West Kent's with the 2/10 Middlesex to their right; each had a frontage of 500 yards, and allotted it to two companies with the other two in support. The 53rd Division advance was fifteen minutes earlier than the rest of the infantry, as progress over the heavy, drifting sand was likely to be consequently slower. The brigade passed through the outpost line and the initial advance met with little opposition. By 08.10 the forward troops of the 2/4 West Kent's were within eight-hundred yards of Samson Ridge, with the 2/10 Middlesex, to their right, similarly placed fifteen minutes later.

At this point the defenders of Samson Ridge made their presence felt as they opened up with heavy rifle- and machine-gun fire. First, the 2/4 West Kent's were held up, and then as the 2/10 Middlesex came alongside they too were pinned down. For nearly an hour there was hardly any progress, and at 09.10 the General Officer Commanding the 53rd Division, aware that overall success hinged on the capture of the ridge, ordered the 160th Brigade to move forward to the assault. Artillery across the whole front was turned onto this target, and although the line was able to edge forward a few hundred yards, the enemy fire still prevented a general advance.

The 2/4 Queen's had also advanced at 07.15, but had followed the course of a wadi up the KURD VALLEY so as to be able to maintain contact with the 52 Division on the el Sire ridge. They too passed the outpost line at 08.30 and after picking up the company on Softly Hill, took up position half-a-mile further on. At 09.43 they were ordered up to support the right flank on the front, by engaging the heavy machine-gun fire from woods to the south-east of Samson Ridge. However, as they moved up, they came under heavy fire from the woods, and were obliged to halt around HEART HILL, and engage the enemy from there. As necessary as this local action was, in the greater context of the attack on Samson Ridge it now meant that the right flank of the 2/10 Middlesex was unsupported. This necessitated the 4/Sussex being committed from reserve at 09.50, and by 11.00 A and C Companies were alongside the Middlesex, with B and D Companies close behind. About this time, the 2/4 West Kent's attempted to assault the left of the ridge, but were once again repulsed.

At 11.30 Major-General Dallas repeated his earlier order to take Samson Ridge as soon as possible. Reports that troops and guns were being withdrawn from the position gave some encouragement, and the 2/4 Queen's attempted to advance against the eastern end of the ridge. However, the enemy fire from the woods continued unabated in its intensity, and they were again compelled to devote their attentions to engaging that flank. This proved a task in itself, and the battalion was unable to take any part in the actual assault of the ridge.

The critical stage of the battle had now been reached. Some of the enemy force had retired from the ridge, and although still strongly held, the three battalions of the brigade were able to edge their way forward. By 12.45, barely 200 yards separated the opposing lines, and

> "160 Brigade was ordered to put an Officer in command of Sampson Ridge [sic] and to hold it at all costs when captured."
>
> 53rd Division General Staff War Diary. PRO WO 95/4614

The final assault on the ridge came at 13.10. From the laboriously taken and desperately held lines, now only 60 to 100 yards from the objective, the 2/4 West Kent's, 2/10 Middlesex and 4/Sussex rose from the fire-swept ground to which they had clung to for nearly five hours and charged. With bayonets fixed, they entered the trenches of an enemy who continued to resist stubbornly and bravely, despite the fact that many of their comrades had already been withdrawn.

On the left of the line, the 2/4 West Kent's captured part of the ridge, and at 13.20 a small group pushed forward nearly 200 yards towards the great el Arish Redoubt. Parties from the rear of the line extended to the left to contact the 159 Brigade which would soon be able to attack Sheikh Ajlin. In the centre of the line the 2/10 Middlesex, with a few men of A Company, 4/Sussex, entered the redoubt on Samson Ridge, and for forty minutes bitter hand-to-hand fighting took place. As they used bombs to clear dug-outs and strong-points within the redoubt, the whole ridge came under heavy shell-fire as the Turks attempted to regain control of the position.

Lieutenant-Colonel Pearson of the 2/10 Middlesex took command of the assaulting troops and at 13.55 was able to report that the whole ridge was taken, although he found himself with a deteriorating situation. First, the capture of Samson Ridge had cost the brigade about 540 casualties, chiefly among the 2/10 Middlesex and 2/4 West Kent's. Secondly, in trying to gain contact with the 159 Brigade on the left, the 2/4 West Kent's had extended their front by 200 yards, thereby spreading their already depleted ranks. Finally, the right flank remained totally exposed as the 2/4 Queen's were still in action around Heart Hill to the south.

Readily appraising the situation, Lieutenant-Colonel Pearson immediately requested two battalions to help consolidate the position and continue the attack. The 1/1 Herefordshire Regiment were detailed from 158th Brigade to support the troops of Samson Ridge, and ammunition, water, tools and Stokes-Guns were sent forward with them. At 14.20, an advanced line was established on the forward slopes of the ridge, and dug in with the assistance of the 439th Field Company, Royal Engineers. Plans were then drawn up to hold the line with a series of strong-points across the front. The left flank of the brigade remained in the hands of the West Kent's, who would also maintain contact with 159 Brigade. The Middlesex were on the forward slopes of Samson Ridge and thus in advance of the redoubt they had so gallantly captured. The Sussex were somewhat intermingled at this point, but were reinforced by the 1/Herefords who had come up at 15.30, and the two battalions prolonged the line towards Heart Hill. The Queen's brought up the right flank and provided contact with the 52nd Division. Consolidation of this line was a long and tedious one, especially after the event so the day, and was still in progress when the 1/5th and 1/7th Royal Welsh Fusiliers arrived at 01.00 on the 20th April. Shortly afterwards the brigade was relieved, except for the Queen's who remained in their now-familiar location and were assigned to Brigadier-General Mott, commanding the 158th Brigade. The 2/4 West Kent's, 2/10 Middlesex and 4/Sussex marched out and became Divisional Reserve, bivouacing halfway between Money Hill and Samson Ridge.

160 Brigade

Casualties for the Second Battle of Gaza

IN ANALYSING OF THE CASUALTIES of the Gaza actions large numbers, like so many other actions of the Great War, become the norm. Details of those killed tabulated by the hundred; died of wounds a further dozen or so; wounded two hundred or more per battalion to show a brigade total perhaps 50% of the nominal thousand men. Against this background, it is all too easy to then say a brigade had only 83 killed, or even less difficult when a battalion had fourteen killed. A reminder is needed that each name was a man whose death had far-reaching consequences both to his soldier comrades and friends as well as his family at home.

The 160 Brigade lost 5/83 killed with another 0/13 who died of wounds; the wounded totalled 20/342. Of the officers, three were aged 21, 22, 24; another 21 year old who took part in the battle was Second Lieutenant Gerald Horsley MAPLESON who was killed by a sniper on the 26th April.

Second Lieutenant Stanley Grant HARE of the 15/Middlesex was attached to the 2/10 Middlesex and was killed in the battalion's right-flank advance against Samson Ridge. Second Lieutenant Alan Herbert GREGSON of the 2/4th Royal West Kent Regiment was the 22 year old, having moved from his home at Pinner in Middlesex to become a student at Selwyn College Cambridge. The battalion was alongside the 2/10 Middlesex, the attack being held up just after 08.00. Forced to lay out in the open for some five hours, there is no record whether these two officers were killed during this period or in the final determined assault which captured the ridge at 13.10. The third officer to be covered here is Lieutenant Norman Harden EVANS, 24, of the Royal West Kent's. He was severely wounded in the attack on Samson Ridge and died later the same day, being buried in Gaza Cemetery XVIII.G.16. From Ashburnham Road, Tonbridge, Kent he was a pupil at Tonbridge School from 1907-1910, being a member of the Officer Training Corps [O.T.C] He was working as a solicitor when the war broke out and after being commissioned was sent to Suvla Bay, Gallipoli in October 1915. Upon the peninsula being evacuated, he was sent to Egypt and in October 1916 was on his way home for when his ship, *The Arabia*, was torpedoed but which he survived. After three weeks leave in England from November 19th he left for Egypt, never to return. He was engaged to be married to Miss Reynolds, sister of Captain EJ Reynolds, MC, of the West Yorkshire Regiment. His mother having already been widowed was to move to Norbury, London after the death of her only son; the true result of a minimal casualty list.

Of the men, the 4/Sussex had fourteen killed and two died of wounds. Sergeant William Robertson CLEMMENTS was 38 and lived at Abercrombie Cottage, Queen Street, Arundel, Sussex with his wife Sarah. He was a member of C Company which was sent up from brigade reserve at 09.50, going into the line alongside the Middlesex. The position of Samson Ridge was assaulted at 13.10 with a bayonet charge over 60/100 yards, bitter hand-to-hand fighting continuing for over 40 minutes. In the same attack, although not necessarily same company was Company Sergeant Major Harry QUESTED from Chilwell Terrace, Horsham, Sussex. Aged 39, he had been a member of the Territorial Force for several years and had been awarded the Territorial Force Efficiency Medal for service. He was fatally wounded and died at Deir el Belah on 22 April.

The 2/10 Middlesex had 2/30 killed, another 6 Died of Wounds and 7/131 wounded as they were in the centre of the brigade attack on Samson Ridge.

Private Albert Edward BURLAND was killed with C Company, his father having been decorated for gallantry with the DCM. Lance-Corporal Rowland LEEKS was 34 and lived with his parents at 78, Shaftesbury Road, Hammersmith while 23 year old Private Charles Ernest WINTER lived a few doors away at No 66. Both were killed in action on the 19th April.

From Lincolnshire came Private William PEEL. Born at Skegness he moved to Highbury, London with his parents before the war and enlisted in August 1914 aged 18. He served in France and was another of those to be killed in the attack on Samson Ridge

Finally, the 2/4th Royal West Kent's had 3/44 killed and 11/139 wounded. As there are few details to hand, the names alone must suffice.
Company Sergeant Major Askew William PALMER 29

Sergeant Graham BARFIELD 27
Sergeant John LIPSCOMBE 34
Corporal George DAWSON 21
Corporal Samuel WEST
Lance Corporal George Thomas GORDON 25
Private Luigi CASCARINO formerly Somerset Light Infantry
Private John HOWARD 41 formerly The Buffs
Private Harry Werner HULL formerly Middlesex Regt

All killed at Samson Ridge, Gaza 19 April 1917

Finally, the record of one officer who was wounded is of interest. Lieutenant GL GOULD was a student at Tonbridge School and joined the Inns of Court Officer Training Corps in March 1915 before being commissioned into the 3/5 Royal West Kent with whom he served at home until July 1916. Sent to Palestine attached to the 2/4 RWK, he was appointed Grenade Officer, then took part in the Battle of Romani in August 1916 and the First Battle of Gaza on 26 March 1917. On 17 April 1917 during the build-up operations for Second Gaza he was wounded by a gunshot to the left arm, the fractured bone necessitating hospitalisation. He subsequently transferred to the Royal Flying Corps as Flying Officer Observer and with 113 Squadron/ 5th Wing took part in operations north of Jaffa and at Amman, Jericho. He relinquished his commission in September 1921.

Second Battle of Gaza
158th Brigade

THE 158TH BRIGADE COMPLETED THE establishment of the 53rd Division, but was not required during the preliminary moves on the 17th April. Brigade Headquarters remained at DEIR EL BELAH, two battalions being stationed there, while the other two were placed at an area called ST. JAMES'S PARK, about three miles to the north-east. From the latter place, the brigade provided working parties for road construction up to the Wadi Ghuzze. At about 17.00 on the 17 April, details of a new, advanced line to be taken up after dusk were received. This was allotted to two battalions only, while brigade headquarters and the 1/5th and 1/7th Royal Welch Fusiliers remained at Deir el Belah. Because of the length of the line, over two miles from the edge of the sand-dunes on the right to MARINE VIEW on the coast, it was not possible for it to be continuously held, and so a series of strong-points was established instead. Consequently, at 18.00 the 1/1st Herefordshire Regiment left St. James's Park, crossed the Wadi Ghuzze and, after passing Tel el Ujul, took up the right half of the line. An hour passed before the 1/6th Royal Welch Fusiliers followed them and took up their station on the left of the line.

During the 18th April, stores and ammunition were placed at dumps in the Wadi Ghuzze, and although the area was shelled intermittently there were no casualties in the brigade. At 17.00 the 5/Royal Welch Fusiliers were sent up in order to reduce the frontage of the two battalions; upon arrival the line was to be advanced 300 yards in order to give the artillery more room to operate. This new line was dug-in during the evening and into the night, not being completed until 03.00 on the 19 April. One company of each battalion was withdrawn to Tel el Ujul as reserve, thus leaving nine companies to hold the 1200 yard front.

At 07.15 on 19th April, the 53rd Division's advance began, and as the men of the 158th Brigade watched them disappear into the distance, they waited, ready to move at a moment's notice in support if needed. The 7/Royal Welch Fusiliers and the 158 Brigade Machine Gun Company moved from Tel el Nujeid to Regent's Park at 08.20, thus completing the brigade strength. The morning passed with the attack brigades being stalemated before Samson Ridge and the 158th Brigade therefore remained in reserve. At 11.24 however the 5/Royal Welch Fusiliers were placed at the disposal of Brigadier-General Travers, Commanding Officer of 159th Brigade, and were to be ready to support the attack against Sheikh Ajlin at short notice; the 6/Royal Welch Fusiliers were similarly disposed thirty minutes later.

Samson Ridge continued to be the obstacle, and it was not until it was captured that the 158th Brigade was called upon. At 14.00 the 1/Herefords, who were also on standby, were ordered to advance to the right flank of the ridge to support the 2/10 Middlesex Regiment of 160 Brigade who were in danger of being counter-attacked. Under the command of Major GREEN, A and B Companies, right and left respectively, arrived in the firing line thirty minutes later. The enemy fire against the battalion was not heavy, but was accurate and about twenty men were wounded at this time.

Because the 2/4th Queen's [160 Brigade] were held at Heart Hill, the open right flank of the 2/10 Middlesex was now taken over by the 1/Herefords, who now found themselves with the same problem of an open right flank. As no further reinforcements were likely to be sent up before dusk, the commanding officer of the 1/Herefords had no option but to commit his two reserve companies; D Company was sent to the left of the battalion on Samson Ridge, while C Company reinforced the right of A Company.

53rd (WELSH) DIVISION
158 Brigade.
19 April 1917

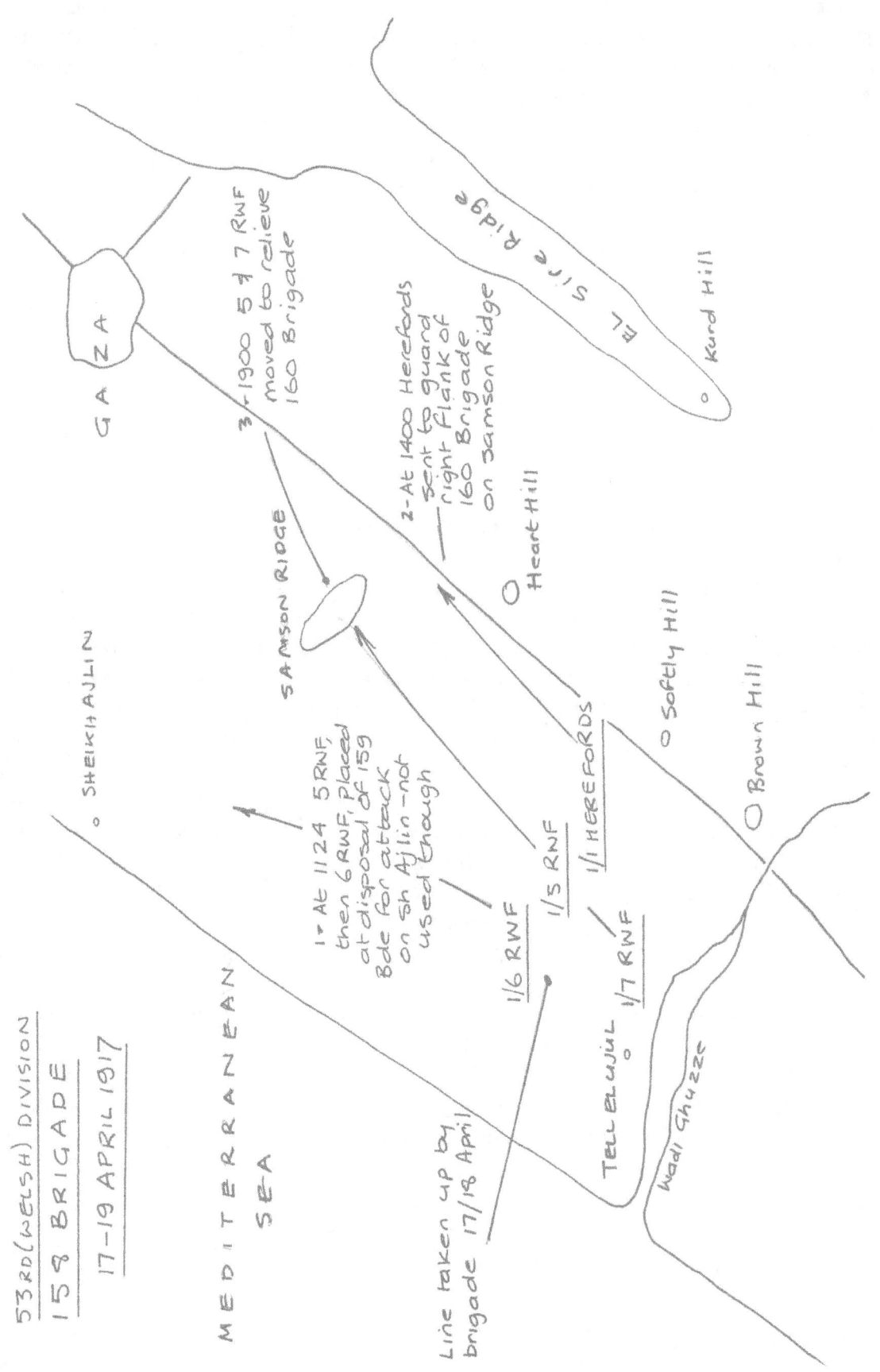

The situation remained unchanged until the evening, and at 19.00 it was decided to relieve the battered 160th Brigade with the 5/ and 7/Royal Welch Fusiliers. The two battalions arrived at 01.00 on the 20 April and took over the line held by, from the left, the 2/4 Royal West Kent, 2/10 Middlesex and 4/Sussex.

"There the Brigadier-General Commanding met the commanding officers of the Herefords, 2/4 West Kent, 1/4 Sussex and 2/10 Middlesex and discussed the position. Guides were obtained and battalions taken into the line. The relief was a matter of very great difficulty. The night was very dark and the sniping considerable, but the main difficulty lay in the way in which the trenches were held."

158 Brigade Headquarters War Diary. PRO WO95/4625

The 1/Herefords concentrated on the right of the new brigade line, their position being called HEREFORD RIDGE. From here they dug trenches across the open ground towards the 2/4th Queen's who continued to hold their previously held positions on SNIPERS RIDGE and HEART HILL. On the evening of the 20th April, the 6/Royal Welch Fusiliers returned to the brigade from attachment as reserve to 159th Brigade. They were sent up as reserve to the right flank, but as all further operations were postponed, the brigade line remained the same until the end of the month.

Second Battle of Gaza

Conclusion

WITH THE REALISATION THAT THE town of Gaza could not be taken, the many hard-won positions were to be held until further notice. Relief battalions were sent up for this role and the exhausted, battle-shocked troops were marched back to rest areas, leaving behind hundreds of their dead comrades. Some battalions had suffered so many casualties that they ceased to be effective fighting units and had to be amalgamated with other such battalions.

While it may appear that the strategy for the Second Battle was largely similar to the First Battle, the reasoning had been sound. Fresh troops were used for the attack, with more time being taken to establish the starting line for the final assault. While the element of surprise had been lost, any further delay for a second attack could have resulted in very large reinforcements being sent from Beersheba away to the east. This would have made the prospect of taking Gaza an even more daunting one, hence the decision to continue so soon after the March attack. An innovation of the use of tanks was incorporated and although there were mechanical failures, they did force the Turkish artillery and troops to concentrate on them. One downside to this was that the advancing troops also tended to follow them and casualties were inevitably sustained.

Lieutenant General Sir Archibald Murray had originally asked for four Divisions even for the First Battle, but as has been noted one Division was withdrawn just before the attack. The Second Battle was fought with the same depleted numbers and, as will be seen, the final capture was accomplished by no less than seven Divisions later in the year.

As with earlier statements, it is not the intention of the author to analyse the reasons for the failure of the Second Battle to capture the town of Gaza. It is once again intended that the account of the battle be a tribute, and memorial, to the men who fought it.

Trooper Arthur Henry NOAKES
No 270380
Royal East Kent Yeomanry/10th Battalion Buffs
Born 16 June 1897 at Tonbridge, Kent
Enlisted 17 May 1915 at Ashford, Kent
Demobilised 16 April 1919.

Trooper Noakes at Cairo, early 1917.

"I was always hungry. When not fighting most of the time we were marching 20 miles a day. This caused a cloud of dust which settled on perspiring faces making rivulets, then when the rainy season started it washed away wooden bridges cutting railway supplies. I don't think there was such a thing as a typical day. The coastal strip was flat, sandy and dusty. The Judean Hills were rocky and craggy. The slightest scratch caused desert sores. I never experienced trench warfare as there was not a continuous front line. After taking an objective, observation posts were set up, listening posts at night. After one long march I was obliged to report sick with a blistered heel. Marked light duty I was supposed to be resting for a few days, but next day the orders were changed! With some others I was taken by camel to a RAMC camp. That night was moon-lit and we were bombed by enemy aircraft but they dropped in the sand and did not explode. Next day we travelled by sand-cart to Ramleh Junction, a large store dump. Here we were machine-gunned from the air with one camel killed and one Egyptian Labour Corp man wounded. Next day we went by rail to base hospital at Kantara. A week to get there and the blister was healed by then. Two weeks at base then back up the line."

Corporal John COMMON
No 200235
1/4th King's Own Scottish Borderers
Enlisted 31 March 1908 in the 2nd Volunteer Battalion KOSB
Demobilised 17 March 1919

4th KOSB El Arish 1916. John Common on the left

4th KOSB crossing the Egypt/Palestine border

Private John Henry BOSSINGHAM went through the Gallipoli and Palestine Campaigns until he died of wounds on 17 December 1917 at Junction Station, near Jerusalem. He was nineteen years old. From the Fenland town of March in Cambridgeshire, he lived in Creek Road with his parents and enlisted in the 1/5th Suffolk Regiment with the number 9767.

There the story may have ended but for the correspondence between the author and his sister in 1984/5. At the time she was living in Lincoln and from the first letter in response to a newspaper appeal it was clear that after over sixty-five years he was still held in the greatest affection. The fact that his death was at last being highlighted was of great comfort to her; instead of one-way thanks from the author, it was almost a complete reversal with every little bit of information and help being so gratefully received to make it most-humbling. Two photographs and the following condolence letters give a poignant conclusion.

Dear Friend

I am writing on behalf of myself and the rest of the signalling section of A Company which poor Jack Bossingham was a member to thank you for the lovely parcel which arrived today as I daresay you know he was hit on the 15th of December and died of wounds. We thought it the best thing to do with it was to divide it out amongst the section as of course we were all chums together and otherwise it would have been knocking about up and down the lines and ultimately lost. I cannot express to you how sorry we were to lose him. He was such a bright and cheery lad and good comrade. However he died doing his duty taking a message and it will be some small consolation to give his friends to know that his death was painless. He never recovered consciousness after being hit. I will be very pleased to supply any further details you can assure his people that he received every attention and was taken away as soon as possible. I thank you for all your kindness especially the lady who knitted the socks. Hoping our action will meet with your approval

Yours sincerely
L/C H Winstanley
240382
A Company

A member of the Casualty Clearing Station to which John Bossingham was taken was compelled to write the following letter to try and soften the blow of his death.

Dear Mr Bossingham

I am very sorry to have to convey to you some sad news viz the loss of your dear boy Pte J H Bossingham. He was bought into our Casualty Clearing Station on Sunday last the 16th inst with a gunshot wound in the head. He was immediately examined by our surgical specialist but it was found unfortunately that an operation would be quite futile. Your son was unconscious all the time he was with us the bullet having lodged in his brain.

But we could not save him and he slowly sank and passed away very gently at 6/45 pm on Monday the 17th [December]. I buried him the following afternoon in our Cemetery here and the no of his grave is 60. A cross will be erected over him shewing name and particulars. I wish I could convey to you a full idea of where he lies. If you take a map of Palestine and trace the railway running from Jaffa to Jerusalem you will see it passes through a junction. It is near the Junction Station that the cemetery is situated. I feel great sympathy with you all

With best regards and wishes
Believe me to be
Ever yours sincerely
JH Parsons

A letter was also received by Mr Bossingham from one of his son's friends from his home town of March in Cambridgeshire.

26-12-17
Dear Mr Bossingham,
Being a native of March and knowing your son Jack, I must send you a letter expressing my sorrow for Mrs Bossingham and yourself. He was a chum of mine since we joined up and it was on the 15th of December we attacked a certain hill and Jack and I advanced together. We reached the hill and dug in side by side but about 3 in the afternoon he went round the hill with a message and was hit in the back of the head by a piece of shell.

I saw him again at dusk and before he left for the dressing station but he didn't regain consciousness so it is a small consolation but a good one to know he didn't feel any pain.

Before I close I must tell you he died a brave soldier and everyone in A Company will miss him and especially the signal section which he belonged to as he was liked by everyone.
So please accept my heartfelt sympathy

I remain yours sincerely
Private SC Dring

Jack Bossingham in camp, probably soon after joining up.

Back row, second from the left.

Appendix 1

INDEX: ORDER OF BATTLE FOR 19 April 1917.

DESERT COLUMN: Formation and Support Troops

Australian and New Zealand Mounted Division

Imperial Mounted Division

EASTERN FORCE: Formation and Support Troops

52nd (Lowland) Division

53rd (Welsh) Division

54th (East Anglian) Division

74th (Yeomanry) Division

THE ORDER OF BATTLE FOR 19th April 1917

DESERT COLUMN
Major General (Lt-General) Sir PW CHETWODE. Bt. CB.DSO.

AUSTRALIAN AND NEW ZEALAND MOUNTED DIVISION Major General Sir HG CHAUVEL. KCMG. CB	IMPERIAL MOUNTED DIVISION Colonel (Major General) HW HODGSON CVO. CB

SUPPORT TROOPS

Royal Horse Artillery Leicester Battery Somerset Battery Inverness Battery Ayr Battery	**Royal Horse Artillery** 1/1 Nottinghamshire Battery 1/1 Berkshire Battery A and B Batteries Honorable Artillery Company
Field Ambulances 1st Light Horse 2nd Light Horse New Zealand Mounted 1/1st North Midland Mounted	**Field Ambulances** 3rd Light Horse 4th Light Horse 1/ 1st South Midland Mounted 1/ 2nd South Midland Mounted
Engineers 1st Australian Field Squadron	**Engineers** Imperial Mounted Division Field Squadron

ORDER OF BATTLE FOR 19 April 1917.

AUSTRALIAN and NEW ZEALAND MOUNTED DIVISION

1st Australian Light Horse Brigade
Lieutenant Colonel (Brigadier General) C F COX CB

1st Light Horse Regiment
Commanding Officer unknown

2nd Light Horse Regiment
Commanding Officer unknown

3rd Light Horse Regiment
Commanding Officer unknown

1st Australian Machine Gun Squadron

2nd Australian Light Horse Brigade
Colonel (Brigadier General) G de L RYRIE CMG

5th Light Horse Regiment
Lt Col LC WILSON

6th Light Horse Regiment
Lt Col WHITE

7th Light Horse Regiment
Lt Col GM Macarthur ONSLOW

2nd Australian Machine Gun Squadron

New Zealand Mounted Rifles Brigade
Colonel (Brigadier-General) EWC CHAYTOR CB

Auckland Mounted Rifles
Lieutenant Colonel CER MACKSEY

Canterbury Mounted Rifles
Lieutenant Colonel J FINDLAY

Wellington Mounted Rifles
Lieutenant Colonel W MELDRUM

New Zealand Machine Gun Squadron

22nd Mounted Brigade
Colonel (Brigadier-General) FAB FRYER

1/1 Lincolnshire Yeomanry
Commanding Officer unknown

1/1 Staffordshire Yeomanry
Commanding Officer unknown

1/1 East Riding Yeomanry
Major REYNARD

18th Machine Gun Squadron

ORDER OF BATTLE FOR 19 April 1917.

IMPERIAL MOUNTED DIVISION

3rd Australian Light Horse Brigade
Colonel (Brigadier General) JR ROYSTON CMG DSO

8th Light Horse Regiment
Lt Col LC MAYGAR VC

9th Light Horse Regiment
Lt Col WH SCOTT DSO

10th Light Horse Regiment
Major ACN OLDEN

3rd Australian Machine Gun Squadron

4th Australian Light Horse Brigade
Lieutenant Colonel (Brigadier General) JB MEREDITH DSO

4th Light Horse Regiment
Commanding Officer unknown

11th Light Horse Regiment
Commanding Officer unknown

12th Light Horse Regiment
Commanding Officer unknown

4th Australian Machine Gun Squadron

5th Mounted Brigade
General PD FITZGERALD

1/1 Warwick Yeomanry
Lieutenant-Colonel HA GRAY-CHEAPE

1/1 Gloucester Yeomanry
Major AJ PALMER

1/1 Worcester Yeomanry
Colonel HJ WILLIAMS

16th Machine Gun Squadron

6th Mounted Brigade
Lieutenant Colonel (Brigadier-General) TMS PITT

1/1 Buckinghamshire Yeomanry
Commanding Officer unknown

1/1 Berkshire Yeomanry
Commanding Officer unknown

1/1 Dorset Yeomanry
Commanding Officer unknown

17th Machine Gun Squadron

THE ORDER OF BATTLE FOR 19TH APRIL 1917

EASTERN FORCE-1
Major General (Lt-General) Sir CM DOBELL KCB.CMG.DSO.

Imperial Camel Brigade

1st [Australian & New Zealand] Battalion   Hong Kong & Singapore Camel Battery
2nd [Imperial] Battalion   1/1st Scottish Horse Field Ambulance
3rd [Australian & New Zealand] Battalion   Brigade Signals: Engineers:
Machine Gun Company

52nd Lowland DIVISION *Brevet Colonel* *WE SMITH*	53rd Welsh DIVISION *Major General* *AG DALLAS*	54th East Anglian DIVISION *Colonel* *SW HARE*	74th Yeomanry DIVISION *Brevet Lieut-Colonel* *ES GIRDWOOD*
155 BRIGADE	158 BRIGADE	161 BRIGADE	229 BRIGADE
156 BRIGADE	159 BRIGADE	162 BRIGADE	230 BRIGADE [joined 9/4/17]
157 BRIGADE	160 BRIGADE	163 BRIGADE	231 BRIGADE [joined 10/4/17]

THE ORDER OF BATTLE FOR 19TH APRIL 1917			
EASTERN FORCE-2 Major General (Lt-General) Sir CM DOBELL KCB.CMG.DSO.			
Support Troops			
C Squadron Glasgow Yeomanry	A Squadron Duke of Lancaster's Own Yeomanry	A Squadron 1/1st Hertfordshire Yeomanry	A Squadron 1/2nd County of London Yeomanry
261 Brigade RFA A/B/C Batteries 262 Brigade RFA A/B/C Batteries 263 Brigade RFA A/B Batteries	265 Brigade RFA A/B/C Batteries 266 Brigade RFA A/B/C Batteries 267 Brigade RFA A/B Batteries	270 Brigade RFA A/B/C Batteries 271 Brigade RFA A/B Batteries 272 Brigade RFA B/C Batteries	No Artillery
410th Field Company RE 412th Field Company RE 413th Field Company RE	436th Field Company RE 437th Field Company RE 439th Field Company RE	484th Field Company RE 486th Field Company RE 495th Field Company RE	5th Royal Anglesey Field Company RE 5th Royal Monmouth Field Company RE
1/1st Lowland Field Ambulance 1/2nd Lowland Field Ambulance 1/3rd Lowland Field Ambulance	1/1st Welsh Field Ambulance 1/2nd Welsh Field Ambulance 1/3rd Welsh Field Ambulance	2/1st East Anglian Field Ambulance 1/2nd East Anglian Field Ambulance 1/3rd East Anglian Field Ambulance	229th Brigade Field Ambulance 230th Brigade Field Ambulance 231st Brigade Field Ambulance

EASTERN FORCE - 3

Divisional Yeomanry

C Squadron Glasgow Yeomanry	A Squadron Duke of Lancaster's Own Yeomanry	A Squadron 1/1st Hertfordshire Yeomanry	A Squadron 1/2nd County of London Yeomanry

Divisional Artillery

261 Brigade RFA A/B/C Batteries	265 Brigade RFA A/B/C Batteries	270 Brigade RFA A/B/C Batteries	
262 Brigade RFA A/B/C Batteries	266 Brigade RFA A/B/C Batteries	271 Brigade RFA A/B Batteries	No Artillery
263 Brigade RFA A/B Batteries	267 Brigade RFA A/B Batteries	272 Brigade RFA B/C Batteries	

Divisional Engineers

410th Field Company RE 412th Field Company RE 413th Field Company RE	436th Field Company RE 437th Field Company RE 439th Field Company RE	484th Field Company RE 486th Field Company RE 495th Field Company RE	5th Royal Anglesey Field Company RE 5th Royal Monmouth Field Company RE

Divisional Medical Units

1/1st Lowland Field Ambulance 1/2nd Lowland Field Ambulance 1/3rd Lowland Field Ambulance	1/1st Welsh Field Ambulance 1/2nd Welsh Field Ambulance 1/3rd Welsh Field Ambulance	2/1st East Anglian Field Ambulance 1/2nd East Anglian Field Ambulance 1/3rd East Anglian Field Ambulance	229th Brigade Field Ambulance 230th Brigade Field Ambulance 231st Brigade Field Ambulance

ORDER OF BATTLE FOR 19 April 1917.
52nd (Lowland) DIVISION

155 Brigade
Lieutenant Colonel (Brigadier General) JB POLLOCK-M'CALL CMG

1/4th Royal Scots Fusiliers
Lieutenant Colonel H THOMPSON

1/5th Royal Scots Fusiliers
Major JB COOK

1/4th King's Own Scottish Borderers
Lieutenant Colonel JMB SANDERS

1/5th King's Own Scottish Borderers
Lieutenant Colonel SIMSON

155 Brigade Machine Gun Company

156 Brigade
Lieutenant Colonel AH LEGGETT

1/4th Royal Scots
Major JRO TAYLOR

1/7th Royal Scots
Lieutenant Colonel WC PEEBLES

1/7th Scottish Rifles
Lieutenant Colonel JG ROMANES

1/8th Scottish Rifles
Lieutenant Colonel JM FINDLAY

156 Brigade Machine Gun Company

157 Brigade
Colonel (Brigadier-General) CDH MOORE DSO

1/5th Highland Light Infantry
Colonel F MORRISON

1/6th Highland Light Infantry
Lieutenant Colonel J ANDERSON

1/7th Highland Light Infantry
Lieutenant Colonel JH GALBRAITH

1/5th Argyll & Sutherland Highlanders
Lieutenant Colonel BM LANNOWE

157 Brigade Machine Gun Company

ORDER OF BATTLE FOR 19 April 1917.

53rd (Welsh) DIVISION

158 Brigade
Major (Brigadier General) SF MOTT

1/5th Royal Welch Fusiliers
Lieutenant Colonel FH BORTHWICK

1/6th Royal Welch Fusiliers
Lieutenant Colonel F MILLS

1/7th Royal Welch Fusiliers
Lieutenant Colonel TH HARKER

1/1st Herefordshire Regiment
Lieutenant Colonel G DRAGE

158th Brigade Machine Gun Company

159 Brigade
Colonel (Brigadier General) JH Du B TRAVERS

1/4th Cheshire Regiment
Lieutenant Colonel GH SWINDELLS

1/7th Cheshire Regiment
Lieutenant Colonel HM LAWRENCE

1/4th Welsh Regiment
Lieutenant Colonel HJ KINSMAN

1/5th Welsh Regiment
Major JA PEMBERTON 29/3-20/4

159 Brigade Machine Gun Company

160 Brigade
Colonel (Brigadier-General) WJC BUTLER

1/4th Royal Sussex Regiment
Lieutenant-Colonel TM BRIDGES

2/4th Royal West Surrey Regiment
Lieutenant Colonel H St C WILKINS

2/4th Royal West Kent Regiment
Lieutenant-Colonel N MONEY wounded then Major AP HOHLER

2/10th Middlesex Regiment
Lieutenant Colonel VLN PEARSON

160 Brigade Machine Gun Company

ORDER OF BATTLE FOR 19 April 1917.

54th (East Anglian) DIVISION

161 Brigade
Lieutenant Colonel (Brigadier General) W MARRIOTT-DODDINGTON

1/4th Essex Regiment
Major GG EWER

1/5th Essex Regiment
Major WE WILSON

1/6th Essex Regiment
Colonel WJ BOWKER

1/7th Essex Regiment
Lieutenant Colonel LS DELAMERE

161 Brigade Machine Gun Company
Major JA WALKER

162 Brigade
Brevet Lieutenant Colonel (Brigadier General) A MUDGE

1/5th Bedfordshire Regiment
Lieutenant Colonel EW BRIGHTEN

1/4th Northamptonshire Regiment
Colonel JC BROWN

1/10th London Regiment
Commanding Officer unknown

1/11th London Regiment
Commanding Officer unknown

162 Brigade Machine Gun Company

163 Brigade
Major (Hon Colonel Brigadier-General) T WARD

1/4th Norfolk Regiment
Lieutenant-Colonel WA YOUDEN

1/5th Norfolk Regiment
Lieutenant Colonel BS GRISSELL

1/5th Suffolk Regiment
Lieutenant Colonel FA WOLLASTON

1/8th Hampshire Regiment
Major JFH MARSH

163 Brigade Machine Gun Company

ORDER OF BATTLE FOR 19 April 1917.

74th (Yeomanry) DIVISION

229 Brigade
Colonel (Brigadier General) R HOARE

16th Devon Regiment (Royal 1st & Royal North Devon Yeomanry's)
RA SANDERS

12th Somerset Light Infantry (West Somerset Yeomanry)
FNQ SHOULDHAM

14th Royal Highlanders (Fife & Forfar Yeomanry)
Sir J GILMOUR Bart M.P

12th Royal Scots Fusiliers (Ayr & Lanark Yeomanry's)
JD BOSWELL

4th Machine Gun Company

230 Brigade
Major (Brigadier General) AJ McNEILL DSO

10th East Kent Regiment (Royal East Kent & West Kent Yeomanry's)
Commanding Officer unknown

16th Sussex Regiment (Sussex Yeomanry)
Commanding Officer unknown

15th Suffolk Regiment (Suffolk Yeomanry)
Commanding Officer unknown

12th Norfolk Regiment (Norfolk Yeomanry)
Commanding Officer unknown

209th Machine Gun Company

231 Brigade
Major (Lieutenant Colonel) WJ BOWKER CMG DSO

10th Shropshire Light Infantry (Shropshire & Cheshire Yeomanry's)
Commanding Officer unknown

24th Welsh Regiment (Denbigh Yeomanry)
Commanding Officer unknown

24th Royal Welch Fusiliers (Pembroke & Glamorgan Yeomanry's)
Commanding Officer unknown

25th Royal Welsh Fusiliers (Montgomery Yeomanry & Welsh Horse)
Commanding Officer unknown

210th Machine Gun Company

Appendix 2
Casualty list criteria

AS WITH SO MANY OF the sources used during the research, the figures given for the casualties showed considerable variation. After many hours deliberation and consideration, the author came to the conclusion that a small variation between his own figures and any one of the many other sources was not significant, especially as the true figures were probably never available. The following criteria were developed and have been applied for the figures quoted.

KILLED; entry in the Gaza or Beersheba Cemetery Register or Jerusalem Memorial Register between the dates specified. Included are entries in Jerusalem Memorial, even if shown as Died of Wounds/Died elsewhere.

WOUNDED: lowest figures from diaries or other sources for wounded and killed and died of wounds to give TOTAL CASUALTIES. From this subtract KILLED from above then subtract missing figure from source to give final figure for WOUNDED. This figure is therefore the lowest figure possible.

DIED OF WOUNDS: entry in Gaza, Deir el Belah or Beersheba Cemetery Registers for dates specified. Other Died of Wounds in further cemeteries would have involved longer journeys and so the date and location of the wound cannot be determined, unless verified by diary entry, newspaper report etc. This figure has then been subtracted from the wounded total.

MISSING: Very difficult to determine as "missing" one day could turn up next day unwounded so should not be included as "wounded". However, missing have also been listed as "no trace" in reports and so end up on the Jerusalem Memorial. These conflicts led the author to the above criteria and it is to be stressed that although the discrepancy at the time between killed or wounded or missing would have been of enormous and crucial difference to the relatives of the man concerned, at the time of writing this account the question of small variations is somewhat academic. It is to be noted however, that no disrespect is intended nor should be inferred

Formula
1-Diary figures
0/16 Killed. 2/84 Wounded. 1/7 Died of Wounds. 2/15 Missing gives Total 5/122.
*This is the lowest total if more than one source.
2-Author's corroborated figures
0/18 Killed. 1/8 Died of Wounds gives Total 1/26
- Therefore 5/122 minus 1/26 becomes 4/96 wounded and missing.
- Then, subtracting 2/15 Missing gives a minimum total of 2/81 Wounded.

3-Final figures, as used
0/18 KILLED.1/8 DIED OF WOUNDS. 2/81 WOUNDED.
* Missing not shown for reason explained above.

Appendix 3
Casualty charts First Battle

158 BRIGADE CASUALTIES for 26/27 March 1917	
1/Herefordshire Regiment	6/Royal Welsh Fusiliers
Killed 5/34	Killed 2/17
Wounded 12/148	Wounded 11/131
DOW 0/2	DOW 0/4
5/Royal Welsh Fusiliers	7/Royal Welsh Fusiliers
Killed 3/56	Killed 8/92
Wounded 8/162	Wounded 7/164
DOW 0/1	DOW 1/1

159 BRIGADE CASUALTIES for 26/27 March 1917	
4/Cheshire Regiment	4/Welsh Regiment
Killed 0/8	Killed 2/54
Wounded 9/88	Wounded 10/125
DOW 0/6	DOW 1/3
7/Cheshire Regiment	5/Welsh Regiment
Killed 5/27	Killed 2/69
Wounded 5/94	Wounded 18/165
DOW 0/1	DOW 0/5

160 BRIGADE CASUALTIES for 26/27 March 1917	
4/Sussex Regiment	2/4 Royal West Kent Regiment
Killed 5/23	Killed Nil
Wounded 7/153	Wounded 0/6
DOW 1/2	DOW 0/1
2/4 Queens (Royal West Surrey) Regt	2/10 Middlesex Regiment
Killed 1/4	Killed 1/28
Wounded 7/81	Wounded 8/93
DOW 0/2	DOW 0/1

161 BRIGADE CASUALTIES for 26/27 March 1917	
4/Essex Regiment	6/Essex Regiment
Killed 8/171	Killed 7/80
Wounded 12/180	Wounded 11/193
DOW 1/20	DOW 0/4
5/Essex Regiment	7/Essex Regiment
Killed 8/106	Killed 4/48
Wounded 9/157	Wounded 5/100
DOW 1/19	DOW 0/2

162 BRIGADE CASUALTIES for 26/27 March 1917	
5/Bedfordshire Regiment	1/0 London Regiment
Killed Nil	Killed Nil
Wounded Nil	Wounded Nil
DOW Nil	DOW Nil
4/Northamptonshire Regiment	1/11 London Regiment
Killed Nil	Killed Nil
Wounded Nil	Wounded Nil
DOW Nil	DOW 0/2

163 BRIGADE CASUALTIES for 26/27 March 1917	
4/Norfolk Regiment	5/Suffolk Regiment
Killed 0/1	Killed 0/3
Wounded Nil	Wounded 1/23
DOW Nil	DOW Nil
5/Norfolk Regiment	8/Hampshire Regiment
Killed Nil	Killed Nil
Wounded Nil	Wounded Nil
DOW Nil	DOW Nil

VARIOUS CASUALTIES for 26/27 March 1917	
5/Light Horse Regiment	New Zealand Mounted Rifles Brigade
Killed 0/1	Killed 0/2
Wounded 2/10	Wounded 4/25
7/Light Horse Regiment	Killed 0/1

Appendix 4
Casualty charts Second Battle

161 BRIGADE CASUALTIES for 17-19 April 1917	
4/Essex Regiment	6/Essex Regiment
Killed 0/2	Killed Nil
Wounded 0/10	Wounded 0/11
DOW Nil	DOW Nil
5/Essex Regiment	7/Essex Regiment
Killed Nil	Killed 1/1
Wounded 0/2	Wounded 0/7
DOW Nil	DOW Nil

162 BRIGADE CASUALTIES for 17-19 April 1917	
4/Northamptonshire Regiment	1/10 London Regiment
Killed 8/130	Killed 1/44
Wounded 14/236	Wounded 7/134
DOW 0/2	DOW 0/3
5/Bedfordshire Regiment	1/11 London Regiment
Killed 0/10	Killed 3/105
Wounded 1/40	Wounded 10/255
DOW 1/0	DOW 0/6

163 BRIGADE CASUALTIES for 17-19 April 1917	
4/Norfolk Regiment	5/Suffolk Regiment
Killed 6*/149	Killed 0/4
Wounded 8/196	Wounded 5/78
DOW 0/10	DOW Nil
5/Norfolk Regiment	8/Hampshire Regiment
Killed 9*/198	Killed 8/179
Wounded 7/377	Wounded 5/165
DOW 0/13	DOW 0/11

* Plus, three officers killed on 19 April but unable to determine which battalion

IMPERIAL CAMEL CORPS BRIGADE CASUALTIES for 17-19 April 1917	
Killed 3/44	
Wounded unknown	

155 BRIGADE CASUALTIES for 17-19 April 1917	
4/Royal Scots Fusiliers	4/King's Own Scottish Borderers
Killed 2/58	Killed 6/34
Wounded 12/169	Wounded 8/133
DOW 3/8	DOW 0/3
5/Royal Scots Fusiliers	5/King's Own Scottish Borderers
Killed 4/26	Killed 10/77
Wounded 4/133	Wounded 7/196
DOW 0/3	DOW 2/9

156 BRIGADE CASUALTIES for 17-19 April 1917	
4/Royal Scots	7/Scottish Rifles
Killed 1/11	Killed Nil
Wounded 6/106	Wounded 0/11
DOW 0/6	DOW 1/0
7/Royal Scots	8/Scottish Rifles
Killed 0/14	Killed 1/11
Wounded 8/120	Wounded 9/144
DOW 0/6	DOW 0/5

157 BRIGADE CASUALTIES for 17-19 April 1917	
5/Highland Light Infantry	7/Highland Light Infantry
Killed 1/8	Killed 2/5
Wounded 1/41	Wounded 3/75
DOW Nil	DOW 3/2
6/Highland Light Infantry	5/Argyll & Sutherland Highlanders
Killed 0/4	Killed 0/3
Wounded 2/53	Wounded 0/33
DOW 0/1	DOW 1/2

158 BRIGADE CASUALTIES for 17-19 April 1917	
1/Herefordshire Regiment	6/Royal Welsh Fusiliers
Killed 0/7	Killed Nil
Wounded 2/16	Wounded Nil
DOW 0/3	DOW Nil
5/Royal Welsh Fusiliers	7/Royal Welsh Fusiliers
Killed Nil	Killed Nil
Wounded Nil	Wounded Nil
DOW Nil	DOW Nil

159 BRIGADE CASUALTIES for 17-19 April 1917	
4/Cheshire Regiment	4/Welsh Regiment
Killed Nil	Killed 1/5
Wounded 0/23	Wounded 1/27
DOW Nil	DOW 1/1
7/Cheshire Regiment	5/Welsh Regiment
Killed 0/6	Killed Nil
Wounded 0/15	Wounded 0/1
DOW Nil	DOW Nil

160 BRIGADE CASUALTIES for 17-19 April 1917	
4/Sussex Regiment	2/4 Royal West Kent Regiment
Killed 0/14	Killed 3/39
Wounded 1/49	Wounded 11/136
DOW 0/2	DOW 0/5
2/10 Middlesex Regiment	2/4 Queen's (Royal West Surrey) Regt
Killed 2/30	Killed Nil
Wounded 7/131	Wounded 1/26
DOW 0/6	DOW Nil

Machine Gun Corp CASUALTIES for 17-19 April 1917	
155 Brigade MG Company	158 Brigade MG Company
Killed 1/9	Killed 0/1
Wounded 4/19	Wounded Not recorded
DOW 1/0	DOW Nil
156 Brigade MG Company	159 Brigade MG Company
Killed Nil	Killed 0/1
Wounded 1/3	Wounded 0/6
DOW Nil	DOW Nil

NEW ZEALAND MOUNTED RIFLES CASUALTIES for 17-19 April 1917	
Auckland Mounted Rifles	Wellington Mounted Rifles
Killed 0/2	Killed 0/1
Wounded 1/16	Wounded 4/15
DOW Nil	DOW Nil
Canterbury Mounted Rifles	NZ MOUNTED RIFLES MG SQUADRON
Killed 0/3	Killed 0/1
Wounded 0/28	Wounded 1/16
DOW Nil	DOW Nil

1 LIGHT HORSE BRIGADE CASUALTIES for 17-19 April 1917	
1/Light Horse Regiment	3/Light Horse Regiment
Killed 0/1	Killed 0/1
Wounded 0/2	Wounded 0/8
DOW Nil	DOW Nil
2/Light Horse Regiment	1/Australian MG Squadron
Killed 0/2	Killed Nil
Wounded 0/5	Wounded 1/7
DOW Nil	DOW Nil

2nd LIGHT HORSE BRIGADE CASUALTIES for 17-19 April 1917	
No casualties recorded for 5/LHR, 6/LHR or 7/LHR	

3rd LIGHT HORSE BRIGADE CASUALTIES for 17-19 April 1917	
8/Light Horse Regiment	10/Light Horse Regiment
Killed 0/10	Killed 0/8
Wounded 6/61	Wounded 10/122
DOW Nil	DOW Nil
9/Light Horse Regiment	3 LH Brigade MG Squadron
Killed 1/15	Killed 0/1
Wounded 5/61	Wounded 4/-
DOW Nil	DOW Nil

4th LIGHT HORSE BRIGADE CASUALTIES for 17-19 April 1917	
4/Light Horse Regiment	12/Light Horse Regiment
Killed Nil	Killed 0/5
Wounded Nil	Wounded *
DOW Nil	DOW Nil
11/Light Horse Regiment	4th LH Brigade MG Squadron
Killed 0/11	Killed 0/1
Wounded *	Wounded Nil
DOW Nil	DOW Nil

* Wounded total for brigade given as 15/103; unable to define further.

5th MOUNTED BRIGADE CASUALTIES for 17-19 April 1917	
1/1 Warwickshire Yeomanry	1/1 Worcestershire Yeomanry
Killed 0/9	Killed 1/3
Wounded 3/13	Wounded 2/17
DOW Nil	DOW Nil
1/1 Gloucestershire Yeomanry	
Killed 0/2	
Wounded 0/12	
DOW Nil	

6th MOUNTED BRIGADE CASUALTIES for 17-19 April 1917	
Buckinghamshire Yeomanry	Dorsetshire Yeomanry
Killed 0/6	Killed Nil
Wounded 0/18	Wounded 0/5
DOW Nil	DOW Nil
Berkshire Yeomanry	
Killed 1/3	
Wounded not recorded	
DOW Nil	

22nd MOUNTED BRIGADE CASUALTIES for 17-19 April 1917	
Lincolnshire Yeomanry	East Riding Yeomanry
Killed Nil	Killed 0/1
Wounded Nil	Wounded Nil
DOW Nil	DOW Nil
Staffordshire Yeomanry	
Killed 0/2	
Wounded Nil	
DOW Nil	

Appendix 5
Gallantry Awards
London Gazette citations by permission of Guildhall Library, City of London.

First or Second Battles of Gaza

DISTINGUISHED SERVICE ORDER

Major George Guy EWER
1/7th Essex Regiment
For Conspicuous Gallantry and Devotion to Duty
He displayed great ability and resource under fire, organising the ammunition and water supply of his brigade and supervising the collection of wounded and the dispatch of prisoners. He performed valuable services, and the success of the operations was largely due to his efforts.
LG 16 August 1917

Major Thomas Henry PARRY
1/5th Royal Welch Fusiliers
For Conspicuous Gallantry and Devotion to Duty
He showed great courage and skill whilst leading his company in an attack, and it was largely owing to his example that the attack made such good progress. Although twice wounded, he continued to command until put out of action by a third.
For the 26 March 1917.
LG 16 August 1917.

Captain Robert Jebb FEW
2/4th Queen's (Royal West Surrey) Regiment
For Conspicuous Gallantry and Devotion to Duty
He displayed fine judgement and great coolness in assisting to organise the withdrawal of an advanced section of our line under heavy shell-fire.
LG 16 August 1917.

Captain Arthur Llewellyn Baldwin GREEN
1/1st Herefordshire Regiment.
For Conspicuous Gallantry and Devotion to Duty.
He led his men with great dash and determination in an attack, and although wounded, refused to leave them until he received a further severe wound which fractured his thigh.
LG 16 August 1917.
For the 19 April 1917 as he is shown as leading a patrol and being seriously wounded on this date.

Captain Arthur Preston HOBLER
2/10th Middlesex Regiment
For Conspicuous Gallantry and Devotion to Duty
After all company commanding officers had become casualties, he displayed the greatest courage and ability in collecting and reorganising detachments of other units during our attack, in organising the advance and sending excellent reports to headquarters.
LG 16 August 1917.

Captain Frederick Henry LINTON
1/4th Welsh Regiment.
For Conspicuous Gallantry and Devotion to Duty
During an attack he showed great courage and initiative in being one of the first to enter the enemy's lines, disarm prisoners and establish communications. He displayed the greatest gallantry and good leadership throughout.
LG 16 August 1917.

Captain Frank MILLS
1/6th Royal Welch Fusiliers
For Conspicuous Gallantry and Devotion to Duty
He showed the greatest coolness and skill when in charge of the firing line of his battalion during an attack, directing operations and sending back accurate messages under heavy fire. The success of the assault was due to his fine example.
LG 16 August 1917.
Awarded for the 26 March, as he was with 229 Brigade on the 19 APRIL

Captain William Eric WILSON
1/5th Essex Regiment
For Conspicuous Gallantry and Devotion to Duty
After leading his company with great gallantry in an assault, he took command of his battalion, his senior officers having become casualties, and carried out his duties with great ability, defeating a strong hostile counter-attack.
LG 16 August 1917.

Captain Edward William WALKER
1/7 Royal Welch Fusiliers
For Conspicuous Gallantry and Devotion to Duty
He led his company forward and, assisted by an officer and a few men of another unit, captured an important point and held out against sharp counter-attacks until the remainder of the enemy position was won. He personally captured a machine-gun and a large number of prisoners.
LG 16 August 1917.
For the 26 March 1917.

Second Lieutenant Lionel Hadwen Fletcher BEACH
2/4th Queen's (Royal West Surrey) Regiment
For Conspicuous Gallantry and Devotion to Duty
He led his company forward to cover the withdrawal of advanced troops, remaining under heavy rifle-fire and shell-fire for two hours, until severely wounded during the action.
For the 26 March 1917.
LG 16 August 1917.

Second Lieutenant George HUDGELL
Yeomanry attached 1/5th Welsh Regiment
For Conspicuous Gallantry and Devotion to Duty
After his commanding officer and second-in-command were wounded, he assumed command, and although severely wounded himself, and kept his men going. He set a splendid example of courage and endurance, and although in considerable pain, remained in command until he was sent away.
For the 26 March 1917.
LG 16 August 1917.

Second Lieutenant George Elliss NELSON
1/7th Cheshire Regiment.
For Conspicuous Gallantry and Devotion to Duty
At a critical moment, when our advance was held up, he collected sufficient men to move forward and strengthen the line. By his fine example and disregard of danger under heavy fire he eventually led this line, which was composed of several different units, into the enemy's position.
LG 16 August 1917.

Second Lieutenant Edward Millard Grubb WRAY
1/5th Essex Regiment
For Conspicuous Gallantry and Devotion to Duty
Although in the second wave of the attack, noticing that his company commander had become a casualty, he at once went forward and took command, leading the attack which cleared the trenches of the enemy. Having vigorously supervised the consolidation, he volunteered to return and report the situation to his Commanding Officer. Finding on his way his company commander, who was unable to move, he brought him in under cover despite a heavy fire. Later, he volunteered to get in touch with the battalion on the flank, and succeeded in establishing communication with it. His conduct throughout was exceptional and by his utter disregard of danger and by his cheerfulness he did much to encourage his company.
LG 24 August 1917

First Battle of Gaza
MILITARY CROSS

Captain Guy Sefton CONSTABLE
1/4th Royal Sussex Regiment
For Conspicuous Gallantry and Devotion to Duty.
When our advance was held up by the enemy's fire he took an advance position with a small party, and held out for the remainder of the day within a few yards of the enemy's trench under heavy fire, and after being himself wounded. His initiative and gallantry were most marked.
LG 16 August 1917

Lieutenant Francis Guy BARKER
1/1st Herefordshire Regiment
For Conspicuous Gallantry and Devotion to Duty.
Although badly wounded in the leg he continued to lead his company until the following day, successfully resisting a hostile counter-attack. He set a fine example of courage and endurance.
LG 16 August 1917.

Lieutenant Charles MOSS
1/7th Cheshire Regiment
For Conspicuous Gallantry and Devotion to Duty.
He led his company with exceptional gallantry to the objective, which he reached in an hour, although continuously under fire, over a distance of five-thousand yards. He continued to lead his company against the enemy's support trenches, inflicting many casualties and materially assisting the success of the operation by his personal example of disregard of danger.
LG 16 August 1917.

Second Lieutenant Parcell Rees BOWEN
Welsh Regiment attached 159th Brigade Machine Gun Company
For Conspicuous Gallantry and Devotion to Duty.
He displayed great gallantry and skill in handling his guns under very trying conditions, and behaving with great resource and initiative in outflanking a house used as divisional headquarters and compelling the inmates to surrender.
LG 16 August 1917.

Second Lieutenant William Percy DODD
1/5 Royal Welch Fusiliers
For Conspicuous Gallantry and Devotion to Duty.
He led his platoon with the greatest coolness and daring, inspiring all ranks with the utmost confidence by his fine leadership. He was wounded whilst leading his men forward in the final assault which captured the position.
LG 16 August 1917.

Second Lieutenant William Archibald FOY
1/4th Royal Sussex Regiment
For Conspicuous Gallantry and Devotion to Duty.
He performed excellent work in directing the Lewis guns of his own and other companies, moving from gun to gun continually under heavy fire until wounded. He then made his way to another gun and gave his orders for its better employment before his wound was dressed.
LG 16 August 1917.

T/Second Lieutenant Arthur Wilfred GRAHAM
1/4th Cheshire Regiment
For Conspicuous Gallantry and Devotion to Duty.
When his battalion's objective was under heavy artillery fire, he collected a large number of men and led them to the final assault. He was the first into the enemy's position, inspiring great confidence in his men by his fine example of courage and fearlessness under fire and under difficult conditions.
LG 16 August 1917.

Second Lieutenant George LATHAM
1/7 Royal Welch Fusiliers
For Conspicuous Gallantry and Devotion to Duty.
After taking part in the final assault of the enemy's position, he pushed forward with the remainder of his platoon and men of other units, under heavy machine-gun and rifle fire, and cleared and consolidated a position of great tactical value. With the help of another officer he captured a number of enemy staff and prisoners, showing exceptional capabilities and great gallantry throughout.
LG 16 August 1917.

Second Lieutenant Charles Hilton SPENCE
Cheshire Regiment attached 159th Brigade Machine Gun Company
For Conspicuous Gallantry and Devotion to Duty.
While covering the advance of his battalion he rendered very valuable service by bringing his guns into action on the flanks. He brought them up at great personal risk. He then went forward with the assault, and by his prompt action located and knocked out an enemy field-gun
LG 16 August 1917.

First or Second Battles of Gaza
MILITARY CROSS

Captain John COOK
RAMC attached Royal Field Artillery
For Conspicuous Gallantry and Devotion to Duty.
He went out under heavy shell-fire, attending the wounded, and carrying them to cover, and setting a fine example of fearlessness and devotion.
LG 16 August 1917.

Captain Hubert Edward JOHN
1/4 Welsh Regiment
For Conspicuous Gallantry and Devotion to Duty.
In order to inspire confidence in his men he moved forward to the firing line, and by his presence materially improved their morale at a critical moment. He was severely wounded during the operations.
LG 16 August

Captain Frederick William MILLER
2/10 Middlesex Regiment
For Conspicuous Gallantry and Devotion to Duty.
On several occasions during an attack he went forward to the firing line to report on the situation. He set a splendid example of courage and determination throughout two days of fighting and rendered most valuable assistance.
LG 16 August 1917.

Captain John Fox RUSSELL
RAMC attached 1/6 Royal Welch Fusiliers
For Conspicuous Gallantry and Devotion to Duty.
He showed the greatest courage and skill in collecting wounded men of all regiments, and in dressing them, under continuous shell and rifle fire.
LG 16 August 1917.

Lieutenant John Alexander GOODMAN
1/4 Welsh Regiment
For Conspicuous Gallantry and Devotion to Duty.
He handled his platoon with great courage and contempt of danger under very heavy fire at close range, displaying fine leadership and setting a splendid example.
LG 16 August 1917.

Lieutenant Jack Chalmers PESKETT
1/4 Royal Sussex Regiment
For Conspicuous Gallantry and Devotion to Duty.
He led his platoon with coolness and courage, afterwards successfully withdrawing them from a difficult position and finding his way, with all the men under his command to another part of the firing line.
LG 16 August 1917.

CF 4th Class Reverend Henry Samuel Frank WILLIAM BA
Army Chaplains Department attached 2/10 Middlesex Regiment
For Conspicuous Gallantry and Devotion to Duty.
He displayed magnificent courage and devotion in collecting wounded from the open, under heavy shell fire, helping the medical officer at the regimental aid post, and remaining out all night searching for wounded. He showed complete disregard for his own personal safety, and rejoined his battalion in an exhausted condition.
LG 16 August 1917

T/Captain Lawrence Lancaster SATOW
RAMC attached Royal Welch Fusiliers
For Conspicuous Gallantry and Devotion to Duty.
He established a dressing station within effective range of the enemy's position, where he attended to the wounded throughout the day and the following night under fire the whole time. It was entirely owing to his disregard of danger and his devotion to duty that many of the wounded were collected and evacuated.
LG 16 August 1917.

Lieutenant Arthur Gerald Phillips WILLS
RAMC attached Cheshire Regiment
For Conspicuous Gallantry and Devotion to Duty.
He remained at his aid post under heavy shell fire for eighteen hours without rest, by his gallantry and fine example encouraging his bearers to work continuously until the last case was safely evacuated.
LG 16 August 1917.

T/Lieutenant Robert Beattie MARTIN
RAMC attached 1/7 Royal Welch Fusiliers
For Conspicuous Gallantry and Devotion to Duty.
He showed the greatest gallantry in attending to the wounded under very heavy fire at a moment when the enemy had turned machine-guns on them. He displayed the utmost fearlessness and skill in getting most of them away into a place of safety.
LG 16 August 1917.

Second Lieutenant John Seddon BARTON
Royal Field Artillery
For Conspicuous Gallantry and Devotion to Duty.
Whilst acting as Forward Observation Officer he behaved with the greatest gallantry and coolness, and maintained communication with his battery at a critical time.
LG 16 August 1917.

Second Lieutenant Howel Arnold EVANS
1/5 Welsh Regiment
For Conspicuous Gallantry and Devotion to Duty.
He showed great pluck and determination during an attack on and after the capture of a strong enemy position, being exposed to heavy fire throughout. His ability was most marked.
LG 16 August 1917

Second Lieutenant John Cuthbert DOWNIE
2/10 Middlesex Regiment
For Conspicuous Gallantry and Devotion to Duty.
He led his company to the assault at the point of the bayonet, was the first to reach the captured position and by his personal example was responsible for the capture of number of prisoners. He afterwards reorganised his company, showing great initiative and ability under heavy shell and rifle fire.
LG 16 August 1917.

Second Lieutenant Noel GILBERT
Royal Welch Fusiliers
For Conspicuous Gallantry and Devotion to Duty.
He showed the utmost disregard of personal danger in maintaining communication with the firing line during the attack, continually carrying urgent messages himself, which were of the greatest importance. He did valuable service reorganising the men and in carrying in wounded under heavy fire.
LG 16 August 1917.

Second Lieutenant Archibald Henry LEE
1/5 Welsh Regiment
For Conspicuous Gallantry and Devotion to Duty.
He went back and collected reinforcements under heavy machine-gun and rifle fire at close range, regardless of his own safety. He then organised and successfully led the final assault from his part of the line.
LG 16 August 1917

Second Lieutenant John Morgan RICHARDS
1/7 Royal Welch Fusiliers.
For Conspicuous Gallantry and Devotion to Duty.
When his Captain and other company officers had become casualties he took command, and it was due to his splendid example that he carried his men forward under very heavy fire to the final successful assault.
LG 16 August 1917.

Second Lieutenant George SHEPHERD
2/10 Middlesex Regiment
For Conspicuous Gallantry and Devotion to Duty.
When the left flank of his battalion was exposed, he pushed forward with three men and covered it for half-an-hour without assistance, under a cross-fire from machine-guns, setting a very fine example to his company.
LG 16 August 1917.

Second Lieutenant Ernest Stanley RUSSELL
1/1 Herefordshire Regiment
For Conspicuous Gallantry and Devotion to Duty.
He led his men with great skill during an attack, afterwards displaying great coolness and courage in resisting a hostile counter-attack.
LG 16 August 1917.

Second Lieutenant Douglas Barker WATSON
2/10 Middlesex Regiment
For Conspicuous Gallantry and Devotion to Duty.
When acting Adjutant, he performed most valuable services to his headquarters, crossing a ridge three times in daylight through heavy machine-gun and rifle fire, to obtain exact information as to the situations and dispositions of his battalion. He successfully accomplished his task under very difficult circumstances.
LG 16 August 1917.

Second Battle of Gaza
MILITARY CROSS

Captain Stuart Keppel REID
1/4 Royal Sussex Regiment
For Conspicuous Gallantry and Devotion to Duty.
He led his company with great judgement and coolness under heavy fire. By his skilful use of his Lewis gun he prevented a counter-attack on his exposed flank, having appreciated the danger at the right moment.
LG 16 August 1917

Lieutenant Robert Stanley COBB
2/4 Royal West Kent Regiment
For Conspicuous Gallantry and Devotion to Duty.
By his able handling of a few men and some Lewis guns, he enabled the troops on his right to get within assaulting distance on the enemy's position. He also showed exceptional courage and initiative in filling up gaps as they occurred, finally taking command of his battalion when all the senior officers were out of action.
LG 16 August 1917.

Lieutenant Cecil Lawrence DUNKERLEY
2/4 Royal West Kent Regiment
For Conspicuous Gallantry and Devotion to Duty.
After all the gun crews of a tank had become casualties, he ascertained how to work the gun, and kept up fire during the withdrawal of the tank, thus preventing further counter-attacks on the part of the enemy.
LG 16 August 1917.

Lieutenant Charles Eric FINDLAY
1/8 Scottish Rifles
For Conspicuous Gallantry and Devotion to Duty.
He displayed the greatest courage in leading his company and holding ground which he had won. When ordered to withdraw he did so in perfect order, under heavy hostile machine-gun and rifle fire at close range. He himself brought in one wounded man and set a splendid example throughout.
LG 16 August 1917

Lieutenant Henry Eric Gibb SUTHERLAND
1/4 Royal Scots Fusiliers
For Conspicuous Gallantry and Devotion to Duty.
When in command of an advanced detachment he held his ground for many hours under intense fire until forced to retire through both flanks being attacked. He conducted the retirement with the greatest steadiness, bringing back some of his wounded, and afterwards returned and brought in more of them.
LG 16 August 1917

Second Lieutenant Alexander William PHILLIP
Highland Light Infantry
For Conspicuous Gallantry and Devotion to Duty.
With great skill and fearlessness, he led a patrol under very heavy fire to a hostile redoubt in order to locate the enemy front trench. Although severely wounded he brought back valuable information.
LG 16 August 1917.

Second Lieutenant Alexander Robert MacEWAN
1/5 Highland Light Infantry
For Conspicuous Gallantry and Devotion to Duty.
He led a patrol with great skill and success to the top of a ridge in order to locate the enemy's trenches. His task was exceptionally difficult as the front edge of the ridge was held by the enemy, and his patrol had to climb a steep escarpment under heavy shell and machine-gun fire in order to get to the top of the ridge.
LG 16 August 1917

Second Lieutenant William SMELLIE
1/5 Royal Scots Fusiliers
For Conspicuous Gallantry and Devotion to Duty.
He displayed the greatest courage and disregard of danger when commanding his platoon in an assault. Having lost all his men except three in the attack, he reorganised and again rushed the position under heavy machine-gun fire, and, despite his losses he maintained an important position throughout the day, the loss of which would have caused a serious gap in our line. He showed a magnificent example throughout.
LG 16 August 1917

Second Lieutenant Sydney Charles ROBERTS
1/5 King's Own Scottish Borderers.
For Conspicuous Gallantry and Devotion to Duty.
After the capture of a hostile redoubt by his battalion he greatly distinguished himself by leading a charge and repulsing a strong counter-attack, afterwards setting a fine example to his men by his coolness and determination under intense fire of every description.
LG 16 August 1917

Second Lieutenant Claude HODGSON
2/4 Royal West Kent Regiment
For Conspicuous Gallantry and Devotion to Duty.
On the 19th April he showed great coolness and initiative after the capture of Samson's Ridge. He collected all the men round him and pushed forward down the slope taking up a line in the low ground, the fire from which suppressed the enemy's counter-attack. At dusk he withdrew to the main line and showed extraordinary courage and skill in consolidating the ridge and ground to the west of it. He also carried wounded men to cover under enemy fire and in fact the successful consolidation of the left was almost entirely due to him
LG 16 August 1917

First Battle of Gaza
DISTINGUISHED CONDUCT MEDAL

300798/789 Private George Albert Edward LAW
1/7 Essex Regiment
For Conspicuous Gallantry and Devotion to Duty in showing unremitting attention to the wounded under heavy artillery fire, when acting as stretcher-bearer.
LG 16 August 1917.

1855/477061 Corporal Thomas Charles MAIN
RAMC attached 1/5 Essex Regiment
For Conspicuous Gallantry and Devotion to Duty.
He dressed the wounded under heavy fire and continued to work during the whole of the night and the following day, giving the greatest assistance to the medical officer.
LG 16 August 1917.

250146 Sergeant (A/CQMS) Hubert REED
1/5 Essex Regiment
For Conspicuous Gallantry and Devotion to Duty.
He displayed great coolness and initiative in assisting to reorganise the line, also making many journeys under heavy fire to recover wounded and remove them to the dressing station.
LG 16 August 1917.

275173 CSM Frederick John ROLPH
1/6 Essex Regiment
For Conspicuous Gallantry and Devotion to Duty.
He showed great fearlessness and sound judgement in selecting positions for his men when under fire, and behaved very finely throughout.
LG 16 August 1917.

250106 Sergeant (A/CSM) William COOPER
1/5 Essex Regiment
For Conspicuous Gallantry and Devotion to Duty.
He reorganised and took command of his company when all its officers and the company sergeant-major had been put out of action.
LG 16 August 1917.

250259 CQMS (A/CSM) John Ernest Victor COOTE
1/5 Essex Regiment
For Conspicuous Gallantry and Devotion to Duty in repeatedly going into the vicinity of the enemy's position and bringing back wounded.
LG 16 August 1917.

300435 CSM Harold Frederick DOYLE
1/7 Essex Regiment
For Conspicuous Gallantry and Devotion to Duty.
After a portion of the enemy's trench had been occupied, he showed great coolness and initiative in rallying his men and leading the attack, which entirely cleared the enemy from the remainder of the trench. He was subsequently wounded.
LG 16 August 1917.

275258 Corporal Alonzo Frederick FIDDES
1/6 Essex Regiment
For Conspicuous Gallantry and Devotion to Duty.
He showed great skill and determination handling his Lewis gun and putting two machine-guns out of action.
LG 16 August 1917.

235104 CQMS C VAUGHAN
1/1 Herefordshire Regiment
For Conspicuous Gallantry and Devotion to Duty.
At a moment when his battalion was in front of the rest of the Brigade and consequently in danger of becoming under their fire, he walked calmly across the fire-swept zone of about four-hundred yards and informed the firing line of the position of his battalion. He had previously shown the greatest skill and courage in leading his company to the attack.
LG 16 August 1917.

234987 L/Corporal G JAMES
1/1 Herefordshire Regiment
For Conspicuous Gallantry and Devotion to Duty.
He worked continually under fire as stretcher-bearer, displaying great gallantry and skill in collecting the wounded and giving valuable assistance to his medical officer.
LG 16 August 1917

290019 Sergeant GH HIBBOTT BAR TO DCM
1/7 Royal Welch Fusiliers
For Conspicuous Gallantry and Devotion to Duty when in charge of regimental stretcher-bearers, in carrying back from an advanced position with absolute disregard for his personal safety. The following day he showed exceptional gallantry in removing from exposed positions after the enemy had turned machine-guns on them.
LG 16 August 1917.

291238 Private J DIXON
1/4 Cheshire Regiment
For Conspicuous Gallantry and Devotion to Duty.
When in charge of ammunition and water convoys, he repeatedly took then up to the firing-line under heavy fire. On another occasion he averted a stampede under sudden and unexpected artillery fire, and his coolness and ready presence of mind on all occasions inspired those under him with the greatest confidence.
LG 16 August 1917

240028 CSM J JONES
1/5 Welsh Regiment
For Conspicuous Gallantry and Devotion to Duty.
He displayed a magnificent example leading his men to the final assault under heavy fire, afterwards leading a party to cleat enemy dugouts.
LG 16 August 1917.

240007 CQMS SH McGREGOR
1/5 Welsh Regiment
For Conspicuous Gallantry and Devotion to Duty.
He repeatedly brought up ammunition to the advanced firing-line under heavy fire, afterwards taking charge of a platoon which had lost its officer, and leading it to the final assault with great gallantry.
LG 16 August 1917.

First or Second Battles of Gaza
DISTINGUISHED CONDUCT MEDAL

240011 CSM JW JENKINS
1/5 Royal Welch Fusiliers
For Conspicuous Gallantry and Devotion to Duty in carrying up ammunition to the firing-line continuously all day, under very heavy fire. On many occasions on his way back from the firing-line he carried wounded men, showing absolute disregard of his personal safety and setting a splendid example to all ranks.
LG 16 August 1917.

29216 Sergeant R FLATMAN
2/10 Middlesex Regiment
For Conspicuous Gallantry and Devotion to Duty.
At a moment when ammunition was urgently required at a captured position he unhesitatingly led a carrying party across a fire-swept zone and, although wounded, completed the work successfully and distributed the ammunition. He set a splendid example to all those with him.
LG 16 August 1917

292111 Sergeant G HORNE
2/10 Middlesex Regiment
For Conspicuous Gallantry and Devotion to Duty.
When all his officers had been killed or wounded, he rallied the men and held an advanced position until reinforced. He set a splendid example of initiative and determination to his company, who were badly shaken by shell-fire.
LG 16 August 1917

292187 L/Sergeant E NATHAN
2/10 Middlesex Regiment
For Conspicuous Gallantry and Devotion to Duty.
On two occasions he organised parties and brought in wounded from the open under heavy fire. He also carried water and ammunition to the front trenches, setting a most magnificent example to the whole battalion by his untiring efforts to assist in anything that was required.
LG 16 August 1917.

Second Battle of Gaza
DISTINGUISHED CONDUCT MEDAL

200004 Sergeant Thomas Cornelius BRIODY
1/4 Northamptonshire Regiment
For Conspicuous Gallantry and Devotion to Duty.
Although wounded in two places, he continued to lead his platoon with great gallantry until wounded for a third time in the head.
LG 16 August 1917.

200044 CSM Harry HARDY
1/4 Northamptonshire Regiment
For Conspicuous Gallantry and Devotion to Duty.
Although twice wounded he did valuable work in rallying the men, collecting stragglers and forming a strong firing line at a moment when all his officers had become casualties.
LG 16 August 1917.

240224 Corporal T J WALKER
1/5 Norfolk Regiment.
For Conspicuous Gallantry and Devotion to Duty.
He took his part of the firing line and directed the fire with great coolness after all the other NCO's in his company had fallen. When compelled by heavy losses to retire, he did so in good order, forming a new firing line in another position.
LG 16 August 1917.

330388 Sergeant J W PEARSON
1/8 Hampshire Regiment
For Conspicuous Gallantry and Devotion to Duty.
He displayed the utmost fearlessness in fighting his way into an enemy redoubt and capturing twenty of the enemy single-handedly. He successfully conducted them to the rear and then returned to the firing line.
LG 16 August 1917.

240522 Private J BELL
1/4 Royal Scots Fusiliers
For Conspicuous Gallantry and Devotion to Duty.
At a critical moment during a hostile counter-attack he showed great coolness and resource in personally bringing his Lewis Gun into action when the team had become disorganised. Throughout the whole day his conduct was magnificent.
LG 16 August 1917.

201607 Private J KIRKPATRICK
1/4 King's Own Scottish Borderers.
For Conspicuous Gallantry and Devotion to Duty.
When he saw that no officers or NCOs were left, he rallied all the men he could, and led them in a charge on an enemy redoubt, which he captured. He also volunteered three times to carry messages from the redoubt to the advancing troops at great personal risk.
LG 16 August 1917.

240579 CSM R TOWNSEND
1/5 King's Own Scottish Borderers.
For Conspicuous Gallantry and Devotion to Duty in rallying his men after they had been repulsed from an enemy redoubt, and leading them with great determination again to the attack.
LG 16 August 1917

"Took command of B Company at Gaza when all the officers were either killed or wounded. He died of wounds received at Mughar. He was the son of Sergeant C Townsend (Bandmaster)"

War History of the 1/5 KOSB by Captain GF Scott Elliot page 320

327/320000. Sergeant A MESSER
Royal Army Medical Corps attached
For Conspicuous Gallantry and Devotion to Duty.
When in charge of stretcher parties, he displayed exceptional fearlessness and energy in rescuing wounded from positions of extreme danger. This entailed four hours work over extremely difficult country under constant fire. He was completely exhausted at the finish.
LG 16 August 1917.

200353 Corporal P BRYANT
1/4 Royal Sussex Regiment
For Conspicuous Gallantry and Devotion to Duty.
After his platoon commander had been killed, he took command of the platoon and led them to the assault with great skill and courage.
LG 16 August 1917.

First Battle of Gaza
MILITARY MEDAL

275167 L/Sergeant Sidney Arthur BOND
1/6 Essex Regiment

200514 Private Spencer DENNY
1/4 Essex Regiment

250508 Private Ellis Allen George JORDAN
1/5 Essex Regiment

300314 L/Corporal Stanley Ridgeley LEITCH
1/7 Essex Regiment

300826 Corporal Walter Henry LLOYD
1/7 Essex Regiment

201136 Corporal John Henry NYE
1/4 Essex Regiment
"Among other gallant incidents was that of Sergeant Nye, of B Company, 4th Essex, who later fell at the Third Battle of Gaza. He led his section in the rush at Green Hill and came up against a huge Turk, unarmed, who still showed signs of fight. Dropping his rifle, Nye fought it out with his fists and overcame his adversary."

Essex Units in the War; Volume Five. J W Burrows. Page 157.

200070 Sergeant James PAGE
1/4 Essex Regiment

200644 Private Albert PEACOCK
1/4 Essex Regiment

200579 Private William PURKIS
1/4 Essex Regiment

275117 Corporal Albert Henry Frederick
1/6 Essex Regiment

251337 Sergeant Edward WHITE
1/5 Essex Regiment

241057 Private Harry James UNITT
1/5 Welsh Regiment

200268 Private Elvet THOMAS
1/4 Welsh Regiment

200329 Private Vernon Lloyd WILKINS
1/4 Welsh Regiment
Details in The South Wales Press newspaper 20 June 1917

241600 Private Watkin GOULD
1/5 Welsh Regiment

200073 Private Thomas James JONES
1/4 Welsh Regiment
Details in The Welshman newspaper 29 June 1917

241086 Private William LLOYD
1/5 Welsh Regiment

201034 Private Stephen REES
1/4 Welsh Regiment
Details in The South Wales Press newspaper 20 June 1917

200140 Sergeant Ernest Frank GRINSTEAD
1/4 Royal Sussex Regiment

200627 Private Alfred Charles Thomas RICHARDSON
1/4 Royal Sussex Regiment

200784 L/Corporal Archibald Edmond TESTER
1/4 Royal Sussex Regiment

3560/206592 L/Sergeant Walter Albert FROST
2/4 Queens (Royal West Surrey) Regiment
"For Conspicuous Bravery and Coolness in attending to and collecting the wounded on the 26/27 March 1917".

(2/4 Queens (Royal West Surrey) Regiment War Diary May 1917.

3556/201207 Private Samuel FULTON
1/4 Cheshire Regiment
"For doing brilliant work as company runner under fire during the fighting of the [19/3] at Gaza, he was very quick in carrying messages and in particular carried back the message which secured the artillery fire which resulted in the capture of the position".

159 Brigade War Diary.

3420/201123 Private William Noble HIGHAM
1/4 Cheshire Regiment
"For volunteering to bring up ammunition for the machine-guns and continued to do this throughout the afternoon the whole time under heavy fire and under no cover he also assisted in bringing in several wounded lying in the open".

159 Brigade War Diary.

2413/200610 Private Walter HOLYOAKE
1/4 Cheshire Regiment
"For locating with the Barr and Stroud Rangefinder a line of trenches, under heavy rifle fire, he came back to two successive lines giving them ranges and positions, enabling covering fire to be opened".

159 Brigade War Diary.

1552/200235 L/Corporal William URINOWSKI
1/4 Cheshire Regiment

"For very gallantly leading his section during the GAZA operation of 26 March during the attack on the position, when he collected a few men and cleared a ridge of the enemy snipers. He also surrounded a house in the enemy's position and took twenty-six prisoners. The following day this NCO, though slightly wounded by shrapnel, continued to perform his duties".

159 Brigade War Diary.

200699 Private Frederick WEBB
Suffolk Regiment attached 1/7 Cheshire Regiment

"Immediately following the capture of the CITADEL work, volunteers were called for to carry back a message to Brigade HQ to convey this information, telephone and visual communication having failed. Private Webb and another man came forward. As Webb was not exactly sure of Brigade HQ position he was not given the message. About 20 minutes later volunteers to carry a second message conveying the same information were called for and Webb again came forward and was allowed to be bearer of the message. His action was the most commendable for not only was the CITADEL still being shelled by our heavy artillery but an enemy trench which enfiladed the last 300 yards of the approach to the point where Private Webb had to leave cover was still in the enemy's hands and lying towards the direction to Brigade HQ. In the course of his journey Private Webb was twice wounded before handing over the message to another man to carry on".

159 Brigade War Diary.

290170 L/Corporal James WRIGHT
1/7 Cheshire Regiment

"This young NCO was in charge of a Lewis Gun during the advance against the GAZA eastern works on the 26 March. Seeing the line he was with in a state of uncertainty he ran forward in company with Private Broadhurst and Private Hulley and established his gun where he could cover a further advance. This he did while at the same time he caught a party of about forty Turks in close order who were retiring in front of the then advancing 161st Infantry Brigade on his left flank. His example was most noticeable and his coolness and energy under fire worthy of great praise".

159 Brigade War Diary.

290620 Private Frank BROADHURST
1/7Cheshire Regiment

"This man was part of the Lewis Gun crew under L/Corporal Wright and he behaved with great gallantry accompanying his leader to an advanced position under heavy fire and by his coolness and courage materially assisted in the effective fire created by this gun at a very critical period in the advance against the enemy's works at Ali el Muntar on 26 March 1917".

159 Brigade War Diary.

132/200026 L/Sergeant William George INCE
1/4 Cheshire Regiment
"For conspicuous gallantry and devotion to duty during the GAZA operation, he rendered invaluable assistance to the Medical Officer during the heavy influx of wounded to the Regimental Aid Post on 26 March and on the night of 26/27 when forty-two severely wounded cases which the field ambulance could not collect were left in the Medical Officer's hands. On news being received of the retirement of the battalion and on the advance of Turkish reinforcements in large numbers the Regimental Aid Post became exposed to heavy shell-fire and was therefore untenable with the only eight stretcher-bearers available it became a difficult problem to evacuate the wounded. Sergeant Ince rendered very great assistance in evacuating the wounded, the forty-two cases were moved a distance of three-and-a-half miles under shell-fire and deposited with the field Ambulance. Sergeant Ince although almost exhausted by his action, continued his duties with the battalion".

159 Brigade War Diary.

452134 L/Corporal D MOSES
Royal Engineers attached 53 DIVISION
"He was in charge of the telephone detachment (Brigade Signal Section) which accompanied the 1/4 Cheshire Regiment and 1/5 Welsh Regiment into action at GAZA on the 26 March 1917 and laid two and a half miles of wire under heavy shell and rifle fire. He showed coolness under fire and initiative in the performance of his duties."

159 Brigade War Diary May 1917.

49347 Corporal Frederick Arthur PARKER
161 Brigade Machine Gun Company

49382 Private Claude Roland WARREN
161 Brigade Machine Gun Company

First or Second Battles of Gaza
MILITARY MEDAL

235849 L/Corporal William Henry WHEELER.
1/1 Herefordshire Regiment

235852 Private Christopher BRAIN
1/1 Herefordshire Regiment

235967 Sergeant Sydney Herbert FARMER
1/1 Herefordshire Regiment

240528 Private Hedley CREWE
1/5 Royal Welch Fusiliers

265370 Private William DAVIES
1/6 Royal Welch Fusiliers

240086 Private Edward GRIFFITHS
1/5 Royal Welch Fusiliers

265458 Private John HUGHES
1/6 Royal Welch Fusiliers

265293 Corporal Robert Samuel JONES
1/6 Royal Welch Fusiliers

290189 Private George Harold LLOYD
1/7 Royal Welch Fusiliers

265342 Sergeant Richie Richards PARRY
1/6 Royal Welch Fusiliers

290046 Private Harry PUGH
1/7 Royal Welch Fusiliers

290122 Private William John RICHARDS
1/7 Royal Welch Fusiliers

240492 Private Edwin Stephen Joseph ROBERTS
1/5 Royal Welch Fusiliers

240285 Sergeant Gwilym ROBERTS
1/5 Royal Welch Fusiliers

240730 Private Samuel Henry ROGERS
1/5 Royal Welch Fusiliers

265266 L/Corporal Alfred WILKINSON
1/6 Royal Welch Fusiliers

265507 Private John WILLIAMS
1/6 Royal Welch Fusiliers

3053/206513 L/Corporal William Ernest RANSOM
2/4 Queen's (Royal West Surrey) Regiment
"For Conspicuous Bravery in taking ammunition to the firing line and for securing under heavy fire an abandoned machine gun".
                    2/4 Queen's (Royal West Surrey) Regiment War Diary May 1917.

293346 Private William BLOOMFIELD
2/10 Middlesex Regiment

293661 Private Frederick CLIFFORD
2/10 Middlesex Regiment

293381 Sergeant Frederick Hawkins LENYGON
2/10 Middlesex Regiment

292141 Private Percival Edwin NORRIS
2/10 Middlesex Regiment

290801 Private John Patrick PURVIS
2/10 Middlesex Regiment

291979 Private John Richard RAYMENT
2/10 Middlesex Regiment

291839 Private Cyril RICH
2/10 Middlesex Regiment

4556/202140 Private Herbert Fisher CAPON

3228/201346 Private John Leslie MOSS

3298/201396 Private Horace Walter ROFFEY
2/4 Queen's (Royal West Surrey) Regiment
"For taking their Lewis Gun into a gap in the firing line and silencing an enemy machine gun thus enabling the line to be made good".
                    2/4 Queen's (Royal West Surrey) Regiment War Diary May 1917

149 Private F BELLAMY
RAMC attached 53 DIVISION

2201/366238 L/Corporal Richard John WILLIAMS
RAMC attached Royal Welch Fusiliers

452034 Sapper Thomas Sidney BEVAN
Royal Engineers attached 53 DIVISION

56486 Private William BRACE
159 Brigade Machine Gun Company

49493 L/Corporal John William BRIGHT
160 Brigade Machine Gun Company

56556 Sergeant Louis CALDWELL
159 Brigade Machine Gun Company

49459 Sergeant Harry Ernest WILDING
160 Brigade Machine Gun Company

735382 Gunner Joseph FARMSTONE
Royal Field Artillery attached 53 DIVISION

740028 Fitter Staff Sergeant William Vazie SIMONS
Royal Field Artillery attached 53 DIVISION

452300 Sapper Richard David PUGH
Royal Engineers attached 53 DIVISION

19671 Private C HART
52nd DIVISION Army Cyclist Company

318096 Private J HARVEY
Royal Army Medical Corps attached 52 DIVISION.

Second Battle of Gaza
MILITARY MEDAL

6039/202592 Private Henry John BROWN
2/4 Royal West Kent Regiment
"On the 19 April he showed great bravery in taking up ammunition from the dump to his Lewis Gun after two had been killed carrying it 600 yards under heavy fire".

2/4 Royal West Kent War Diary May 1917

6046/202599 Sergeant George Alfred CHERRISON
2/4 Royal West Kent Regiment
"On April 19th he showed great coolness and presence of mind in leading his men to the attack on SAMSON RIDGE and reorganising after the assault under heavy fire".

2/4 Royal West Kent War Diary May 1917

6049/202602 L/Corporal William Henry George DAWSON
2/4 Royal West Kent Regiment
"On April 19th he showed great bravery and coolness in signalling with a flag from SAMSON RIDGE when all wires had been cut. This he did for two hours and his conduct was highly courageous being under heavy fire all the time".

2/4 Royal West Kent War Diary May 1917

4058/201386 Private Alfred George HUNT
2/4 Royal West Kent Regiment
"On 19th April he carried messages throughout the day under heavy fire. On one occasion he succeeded in getting into communication with a company after two other runners and signallers had been wounded in the attempt."

2/4 Royal West Kent War Diary May 1917

4768/203546 Private David TODD
2/4 Royal West Kent Regiment
"On the 19th April he took charge of a section of the line in the absence of an officer, leading them forward and displaying great coolness and courage under heavy fire. He also organised a party in the new trench position".

2/4 Royal West Kent War Diary May 1917

2482/200879 Private Donald Stewart WATSON
2/4 Royal West Kent Regiment
"On April 19th he went 50 yards in front of the firing line and sniped the enemy when leaving a communication trench. On several occasions he took messages under heavy rifle and machine-gunfire. He took a wounded officer behind the line under heavy fire and then returned to his place in the firing-line".

2/4 Royal West Kent War Diary May 1917

201217 Private William James GRANGE
1/4 Essex Regiment.

201184 Private Arthur LUDDINGTON
1/4 Essex Regiment.

275079 Corporal Gilbert Wilson PHILLIMORE
1/6 Essex Regiment.

200673 Private John WALKER
1/4 Royal Sussex Regiment

201407 Private William JONES
1/4 Northamptonshire Regiment
"Has shown great devotion to duty and since the action on 19th April has been in charge of patrols and snipers, on two occasions has stayed out 24 hours observing and sniping, accounting for four of the enemy, and bringing back valuable information".

1/4 Northamptonshire Regiment War Diary May 1917

200504 Private Charles Henry NORTON
1/4 Northamptonshire Regiment
"In the action on the 19th April throughout the day did splendid work by twice taking messages under fire and returning to the firing-line. Showed great coolness, pluck and determination".

1/4 Northamptonshire Regiment War Diary May 1917

200177 L/Corporal Albert WATTS
1/4 Northamptonshire Regiment
"In the action on 19th April he was in charge of advanced stretcher bearer squad and went forward with the battalion. Through heavy shell fire he did marvellous work bringing in wounded and throughout the day and night of the 19th/20th did invaluable work".

1/4 Northamptonshire Regiment War Diary May 1917

203453 Private Leroy WEST
1/4 Northamptonshire Regiment
"Since the action of the 19th April has done excellent work as a patrol and sniper, he has on two occasions stayed out 24 hours observing and sniping".

1/4 Northamptonshire Regiment War Diary May 1917

451471 Rifleman GS BROUGHTON
1/11 London Regiment

453120 Rifleman W DOE/DOVE
1/11 London Regiment

Sergeant RW HEARD
1/11 London Regiment

475178 Corporal LH PAGET
Royal Army Medical Corps attached 1/4 Norfolk Regiment

200058 Corporal F RICKWOOD
1/4 Norfolk Regiment

241214 Private J BLACKSTOCK
1/4 Royal Scots Fusiliers

201165 Private J CUNNINGHAM
1/4 Royal Scots Fusiliers

200111 Private A DAVIDSON
1/4 Royal Scots Fusiliers

240402 Private D McCLURE
1/7 Royal Scots Fusiliers

240962 Private H KERR
1/7 Royal Scots Fusiliers

240653 Private I FARRELL
1/4 King's Own Scottish Borderers.

200804 Private AH RULE
1/4 King's Own Scottish Borderers

200444 Private T STENHOUSE
1/4 King's Own Scottish Borderers

200741 Private W SELF
1/4 Norfolk Regiment

266273 Private IF ANDERSON
1/7 Scottish Rifles

291104 Private P SLAVEN
1/7 Scottish Rifles

330237 Rifleman EW PARSONS (Officer's Servant)
1/8 Hampshire Regiment
"When his officer was wounded on 19.4.17 he proceeded to bandage him although exposed to heavy machine-gun fire. During the operation the officer was struck in three more places but Parsons continued his work and successfully got the officer back to the Dressing Station."

1/8 Hampshire Regiment War Diary May 1917.

Rifleman Parsons later recalled the action of the day.

"At 7.30 in the morning we went over the top, the ground was almost as smooth as a football pitch and we didn't stand a hope in hell. We got three parts of the way over to our objective when my officer, a Lt Butler, went down; he had been hit in the side. As I knelt beside him dressing his would a piece of shrapnel hit my helmet taking the peak completely off of it. Bullets were flying all around us. As I got Lt Butler to his feet and started to help him back to our lines he was hit again, this time in the foot. I continued to drag him back and eventually reached the safety of our own lines. I later travelled with him as his batman to Kantara and then on to Cairo where he was to go into hospital and I was to rejoin the battalion. He fully recovered and returned to his home in Australia".

Lt Butler wrote to Mrs Parsons after the award had been made:

"I want to congratulate you and your husband on the distinction that has fallen on you all by your son winning the Military Medal for his conduct on the 19th April and for his particular good service ever since he joined the Regiment. I know how proud you will be of him and he fully deserves it. You will see now that the high opinion I have always had of him is shared by his commanding office. Your son was with me when he was told by the adjutant of his being awarded the Military Medal and his first thought was of the pleasure it would give his mother. He is fit and cheerful as ever, always ready for anything especially to help someone else."

Rifleman Parsons own comments on the battle were summed up by him as "I thought that Gallipoli was bad but this was three times worse. I'm very lucky to be alive and never thought that I would get out in one piece." (He was later to be wounded in the Third Battle of Gaza)

Isle of Wight Rifles D J Quigley page 19

330587 Rifleman AV SALMON (Signaller)
1/8 Hampshire Regiment
"Rifleman Salmon was on telephone duty from 0700 on the 19.4.17 until he could be relieved at 15.30. During the whole of this period he was constantly exposed to heavy shelling and machine-gun fire over an advance of 2000 yards in open country. Although the men carrying the reel of wire were twice replaced as they became casualties, the instrument and reel struck and the wire cut by bullets, Rifleman Salmon remained at his post in a most exposed position and maintained communication throughout with Brigade".

1/8 Hampshire Regiment War Diary May 1917.

49861 Private C LEONARD
162 Brigade Machine Gun Company
"For devotion to duty in remaining out with and successfully bringing in his section officer when wounded in April last before GAZA".

162 Brigade Machine Gun Company War Diary December 1917

Appendix 6
Bibliography

Main sources used are shown in bold type

History of the 53rd Welsh Division (T.F)
Major Dudley Ward

Yarn of a Yeoman
S F Hatton

History of the 1/5th Suffolk Regiment
Captain A Fair and Captain E D Wolton

Essex Regiment: Essex Territorial Infantry Brigade
John William Burrows

With the 1/5th Essex in the East
Lieutenant-Colonel T Gibbons

History of the 1/5th Battalion Bedfordshire and Hertfordshire Regiment
Captain F A M Webster

The 52nd (Lowland) Division 1914-1918
Lieutenant Colonel R R Thompson

The War History of the 1/5th King's Own Scottish Borderers
G F Scott-Elliot

The 74th (Yeomanry) Division in Syria and France
Major C H Dudley Ward

History of the 60th Division (2/2 London Division)
Colonel PH Dalbiac

The Story of Two Campaigns
Official War History of the Auckland Mounted Rifles 1914-1919
Sergeant C G Nicol

The Yeomanry Cavalry of Worcestershire 1914-1922
By 'C'

Official History of the War. Egypt and Palestine. Two Volumes
His Majesty's Stationery Office

A Yarn of War-Palestine and France 1917-1919
E R Boyd

Historical Records of the Montgomeryshire Yeomanry

Northampton and the Great War
W H Holloway

The Great War 1914-1919. William Graham & Co Glasgow

Tonbridge School and the Great War

For Remembrance. Soldier Poets who have fallen in the War
A St J Adcock

Kelly's Handbook 1916
Kelly's Directories Ltd

University of Edinburgh Roll of Honour 1914-1919

The 16th Sussex Yeomanry

With the 8th Scottish Rifles 1914-1919
Colonel J M Findlay

The 1/5th Highland Light Infantry 1914-1918
Compiled by Officers of the Battalion

The Cavalry Journal No 100 and 101
The Royal United Service Institution

The War Record of the Northern Assurance Co Ltd 1914-1918

The New Zealanders in Sinai and Palestine
Lieutenant Colonel C G Powles

The Palestine Campaigns
Wavell

Dulwich College War Record 1914-1919
J J Kelher

With Allenby's Crusaders
John Moore

Isle of Wight Rifles
D J Quigley

While every effort has been made to obtain permission from copyright holders for quotations from books, this has not always been successful due to the publications being almost a hundred years old in many cases. The original publishers of some have been through several changes of ownership and, once again, the final owners have been impossible to trace. Any omissions are entirely the responsibility of the author, who would be grateful to hear from such publishers or individuals, in order to acknowledge them in future editions.

Appendix 7
Appeals for information

THE AUTHOR IS INDEBTED TO the Editors of the following newspapers and journals which published appeals for information during the initial stages of research for this book in 1984. They are listed in the order in which the author wrote to them and this does not imply any preference.

Aberdare Leader, Alyn & Deeside Observer, Ampthill News, Army Medical Services Magazine, Ascot News, Beccles & Bungay Journal, Brentwood Gazette, Bury Free Press, Cambridge Evening News, Alcester Chronicle, Alton Gazette, Beds & Bucks Observer, Berkhamstead Gazette, Biddulph Chronicle, Chester Chronicle, Dalton News, Channel Islands Informer, Chatham Rochester & Gillingham News, Chelmsford Weekly News, Chester Observer, Diss Express, Dunstable Gazette, East Anglian Daily Times, East Fife Mail, Newcastle Evening Chronicle, Edinburgh Evening News, Hereford Evening News, Evening Echo (Basildon & Southend), Eastbourne Herald, Doncaster Free Press, Cambridgeshire Times, Cardigan & Tivyside Advertiser, Bridgnorth Journal, Congleton Chronicle, Halstead Gazette, Harborough Mail, Guardian Weekly, Gloucester Journal, Grantham Journal, Great Yarmouth Mercury, Barnet Press Group, Essex and Hertfordshire Countryside, Herts Advertiser, Herne Bay Gazette, Exmouth & East Devon Journal, Guernsey Weekly Press, Lincoln, Rutland & Stamford Mercury, The Legion, Kettering & Corby Post, Lowestoft Journal & Mercury, Inverness Courier, Northampton Mercury & Herald, Daventry Weekly Express, Chippenham News, Pembroke County & West Wales Gazette, Pensioners Voice, Dorset Mail, Oxford Journal, Northampton & Bedford Life, St Dunstan's Review, St Albans Review, Salisbury Journal, Salisbury Times, Ross Gazette, New Zealand News UK, Tenby Observer, Warminster Journal, Barry & District News, Birkenhead News, Wirral News, Border Telegraph, Banstead Herald, Barking & Dagenham Post, Bebington News, Croydon Advertiser, Bognor Regis Observer, Chichester Observer & Midhurst/Petworth Observer, Beverley Guardian, Borehamwood & Elstree Post, Basingstoke Weekend Gazette, Buxton Advertiser, Burton Daily Mail, Burnley Express, Dawlish Gazette, Denbighshire Free Press, Mid Devon Times, Diehards Newsletter, Haileyburian, Harrovian, Kidderminster Shuttle, Lancashire Evening Post, Lancashire Guardian, Largs & Millport Weekly, Lea Valley Mercury, Lincolnshire Echo, Loughborough Echo, Melton Mowbray Times, Milton Keynes Mirror, Newport & Market Drayton Advertiser, Reading Chronicle, Scarborough Mercury, Tonbridgian, Torbay News, Walthamstow Guardian, Warwick Advertiser, Westmorland Gazette, Wrexham Leader, Whitby Gazette, Whitehaven News, Worcester & Hereford Adnews.

Appendix 8
Appreciation

THE AUTHOR WOULD LIKE TO express his overwhelming gratitude to the following people who took the time and trouble to reply to his appeals for information. In many cases irreplaceable documents, photographs and letters were sent on trust and in many other cases the thanks came from the respondents for the recognition which the author was trying to give to the formerly unsung men and women of the Palestine Campaign. The author visited several of the veterans and their families and was met with warmth and respect on every occasion. Much of the information has been incorporated into the account, with more detailed accounts being added as cameos, without which the initial aim of the book to record the battles from the perspective of the men and women who were there would have been impossible to achieve.

Rory Moore [Imperial Camel Corps Old Comrades Association], Professor Peter Liddle [Sunderland Polytechnic, later Keeper of the Liddle Collection, Leeds University], Keeper & Staff of the Public Records Office [Kew Gardens], Staff of the Imperial War Museum, London. Staff of the Commonwealth War Graves Commission.

Fred Frostick, North Walsham, Norfolk [Norfolk Regiment], Mr G Rudland, Cromer, Norfolk [Norfolk Regiment], Stanley Ward, West Worthing, Sussex, James Westgate, Bungay, Suffolk [Norfolk Regiment], Mrs Palmer, North Walsham, Norfolk, Mr FJ Walkey, Thetford, Norfolk,

Bob Mansell, Mountain Ash, Mid-Glamorgan [father 5/Welsh Regiment], Mr Oldknow, Lancing, Sussex [re Gunner Oldknow Tank Corps], Mr F Hughes, Worthing, Sussex Mr G Berry, Bury St Edmunds, Suffolk.

Mrs Lily Miller, Chelmsford, Essex [re William May Miller, Essex Regiment], Mr Jackson, Cuffley, Hertfordshire [re Gunner Joe Guthrie MM].

Alf Hawkins, Barnet, Hertfordshire [5/Welsh Regiment], Mrs V James, Waterbeach. Mr F Stowe, Flitwick, Bedfordshire. George Myatt, Sandbach, Cheshire [Cheshire Regiment],

Mr E D Wolton, Ipswich [Captain 5/Suffolk Regiment], Mr R J Beaumont, Norwich [Norfolk Yeomanry], Mr R Scillitoe, Colchester, Essex [Bodyguard to General Allenby].

Jack Whitehurst, Congleton, Cheshire [nephew of John Hatton], Sam Jones, Chester [father in 5/RWF], Mrs A Scott, Rochester, Kent, Mr Parker, Halstead, Essex [MM with 5/Essex], Mr S J Ranson, Long Melford, Suffolk [5/Suffolk Regiment], Charles Syder, Norwich, Mr W Feasey, Bournemouth, Hampshire [2/4 Hampshire Regt], Miss C Campion, Cleethorpes, Lincolnshire. Mrs P Smith, Chester [Daughter of Captain Nelson DSO Cheshire Regt], Mrs F Cook, Laindon, Essex.

Mrs H Warren, Much Wenlock, Shropshire [Father MM with Duke of Lancaster's Own Yeomanry] Mr T Batchelor, Bridgnorth, Shropshire [5/Norfolk Regt], George Simms, Fareham, Sussex [Sussex Yeomanry].

Mr T W H Musson, Grantham, Lincolnshire [Lincolnshire Yeomanry], Mr T Owers, Romford, Essex [Brother of Comyns Owers, Essex Regt].

Mr S Gaskin, Harpenden, Hertfordshire [5/Norfolk Regt].

Mr H Carter, New Milton, Hampshire [11/London Regt]. George Atkins, Northampton [Stretcher bearer 4/Northamptonshire Regt], Mr C Attewill, Glastonbury, Somerset [4/Essex Regt].

Mr S Tucker, Dorchester, Dorset [Dorset Yeomanry]. Major A Kingsbury, Virginia Water, Surrey [5/Royal Welch Fusiliers], Frank Seeley, Market Rasen, Lincolnshire [Lincolnshire Yeomanry], Mrs B Grabham, Melksham [Father with 4/Wiltshire Regt].

Mrs Atter, Rothwell. Miss N J Meager, Cowes, Isle of Wight. Mr Morris le Fleming, Knebworth, Hertfordshire. Mrs A Blowes, Lowestoft. Captain TP King, Acton [London Irish Regiment], Mrs D Langley, New South Wales [Father with Camel Corps], Mr C S Williams, Ilford, Essex [271 Brigade RFA].

Mr R S Price, Rhyader, Wales [Father with Hereford Regt], Mr G Caudwell, Burton on Trent, Staffordshire [Staffordshire Yeomanry], Mr J Moore, Dagenham [brother killed with 5/Norfolk Regt], Mr Harold Goodwin, Worcester [Worcester Yeomanry], Mrs M Johnstone, Largs [father Major with Royal Scots Fusiliers], Dr K A Mercer, Carnforth, Lancashire [Father with Warwickshire Yeomanry at Huj],

Mrs H Stalker, Galashiels [daughter of Captain Cochrane, KOSB], Mr Darby, Nazeing. Mr R Parker, Gainsborough, Lincolnshire [father with 4/Welsh], Mrs E Coles, Teddington [father with 2/10 Middlesex Regt], Mr McNaught, West Kilbride. Mr S Burtenshaw, Great Yarmouth [Sergeant 5/Norfolk Regt], Mr F G Cook, Hinckley [father killed with 4/Northampton Regt], Mrs Scott, Loughborough [VAD in Egypt], Mr E White, Bourne End, Buckinghamshire [163 Brigade MGC], Mr H Bayley, Woodhall Spa, Lincolnshire [father with North Staffordshire Yeomanry & Northampton Regt], Mrs Owens, Sanderstead, Surrey [VAD at Cairo, husband at Gaza].

William Marshall, Chichester [Artillery at Third Gaza], Mrs M Wright, Market Rasen, Lincolnshire [father with 4/Welsh], Miss Evans, Chichester [daughter of Lieutenant Evans 5/Essex Regt], Mrs Dawson, Ramsgate, Mrs M Svasand, Norway.

Miss P Bossingham, Lincoln [brother killed with 5/Suffolk Regt], Mr G Blunt, Chichester [father with 3/County London Yeomanry], Mr B L Ratcliffe, Menton, France [ADC General Palin], Miss D Keeling, Seaview, Isle of Wight [father with Norfolk Regt], Mrs C Day, Bury St Edmunds, Suffolk [father Military Cross with Buckinghamshire Yeomanry], Mr E Abrams, Walton-on-the-Naze, Essex [Essex Regiment], Mrs Common, Crail, Fife [father with 4/KOSB].

Mrs Hains, Lincoln [father John Leonard Bird Suffolk Regiment], Brigadier-General J M Mc Neill, Shepton Mallet, Somerset [father Brigadier General of 230 Brigade],

Miss Quilter, Maldon, Essex [brother killed with Essex Regiment]

Mrs Hilary Warren, Much Wenlock, Shropshire [daughter of Corporal Arthur Jarvis, Duke of Lancaster's Own Yeomanry] Major Vivian Bailey, Stamford, Lincolnshire. Mr Frank Stowe, Flitwick, Bedfordshire. Commander PHB Taylor OBE RN, Diss, Norfolk [nephew of Major Harold Meadows Taylor MC, Norfolk Regiment]

Mr H Mann, Croydon, Surrey. Mr Arthur Henry Noakes, Reading, Berkshire [Royal East Kent Yeomanry]. Mr William Jenkins, Loughton, Essex [West Somerset Yeomanry] Mrs Dawson, Caerlon, Gwent. Mrs Whiteside, Chatham, Kent [wife of Private Whiteside RAMC-died 1933]. Frank Hollis, Luanda, Angola [London Regiment] George Cook, Brighton, Sussex [London Regiment], Mr V Jackson, Heysham, Lancashire. Mrs P Ellis, Chelmsford, Essex. Mr RW Ruffell, Allhallows, Kent [2/4 Queens] Mrs AK Atter [daughter of Sgt WH Earl, 4/Northamptonshire Regiment] Mr G Gwyther [nephew of Driver GV Gwyther RFA died of wounds 4 November 1917]. Mr Perkins, Bury St Edmunds, Suffolk [Royal Bucks Hussars]

Mr RR McKerlie, Selkirk, Scotland [5/Kings Own Scottish Borderers] Mr John Ingram, Kettering, Northamptonshire [nephew of Private Charlie Ingram 4/Northamptonshire Regiment] Mr J Sandy, Boncath, Dyfed [son-in-law to Mr AE Bullock MC 2/10 Middlesex Regiment] Mr PL Evans, Chichester, Sussex. Mr W Shore, Cowes, Isle-of-Wight [1/11 London Regiment] Mr F Hughes, Worthing, Sussex.

Mrs C Palmer, North Walsham, Norfolk [daughter of George Bindley 4/Norfolk Regiment] Mr G Gilham, Bishop's Stortford, Hertfordshire. Mrs B Maple, Tiverton, Devon. Mr D Hudson, Faversham, Kent [MGC] Mr CH Perkins, Newmarket, Suffolk [Royal Bucks Hussars] Mr Joseph Mayne, Burton-upon-Trent, Staffordshire [Staffordshire Yeomanry] Mrs Godfrey, Leicester [husband in Staffordshire Yeomanry] Mr Alfred Hickling, Guelph, Ontario, Canada [1/8 Hampshire Regiment] Mr C Mills, Cleckheaton, West Yorkshire [Royal Field Artillery].

Mrs Jowers, Waltham Cross, Hertfordshire. Mr Glyn Owen Corwen, Clywd [father with 7/Royal Welch Fusiliers] Mrs M Simmonds, Pembroke Dock, Dyfed [father with 4/Welsh Regiment] Mrs DM Wise, Rayleigh, Essex [father Gunner A Callow, Berkshire Royal Horse Artillery] Mr George Boyd, Birkenhead, Cheshire [Cheshire Yeomanry] Mr Bill Shrosbree, Bury St Edmunds, Suffolk [brother George 1/10 London Regiment]

Permission for quotations in the text:

Page 144/145 from History of the 1/5th Bedfordshire Regiment
Copyright © Frederick Warne & Co 1930
Reproduced by permission of Frederick Warne & Co

Extracts from War Grave and Cemetery Registers by permission of Commonwealth War Graves Commission.

Extract from Official History of Australia in the War of 1914-1918
Reproduced by permission of the Australian War Memorial.

Extracts from Official History of the War: Egypt & Palestine
Her Majesty's Stationery Office
Out of copyright, but with appreciation

Imperial War Museum for permission to reproduce photographs and extracts from documents; acknowledged in the text.

Public Records Office for extracts from War Diaries reproduced by permission

Extracts from The London Gazette reproduced by kind permission of Guildhall Library, City of London.

Appendix 9
Conventions and Abbreviations

Lewis Gun

machine-gun but Machine Gun Corps

division but 54 Division

brigade but 158 Brigade

2nd Australian Light Horse Brigade; then 2/LH Brigade

4th Light Horse Regiment; then 4/LHR

1/5th Essex Regiment; then 5/Essex

A Battery, 271 Brigade, Royal Field Artillery; then A/271, RFA

Brigadier-General over Brigadier General.

CAPTAIN CHESTER for first mention; then Captain Chester.

2nd Lieutenant over 2/Lieutenant or 2/Lt

wadi but Wadi el Saba

Tel over Tell

Wadi el Saba over Wadi es Saba

Qamle over Gamli and Qamli.

Wadi Ghuzze over Wadi Ghuzzi

Tawal Abu Jerwal over Towal abu Jerwal

2/75 killed means 2 Officers and 75 other ranks killed. These figures have been kept separate in line with the reporting of casualties at the time and help to convey some scale of loss in the command structure. From printed sources, there is generally more detailed information about an officer casualty than a man from the ranks. The author does not wish to imply any greater significance in the way in which these figures are recorded.

The photograph above is of Captain H K Chester and was the inspiration for the original research and eventual writing of this book.

© Martin J Glen 2018

www.ingramcontent.com/pod-product-compliance
Lightning Source LLC
Chambersburg PA
CBHW080909230426
43665CB00018B/2549